"Through part memoir, part th[...] tion and action, Sharon Ellis [...] one of hope, healing, and possibility. She shows how honoring [...] of one's life, the gift of deep friendships, and love of family can pave the way for restoration to self, to others, and to God."

—Joanne Lindstrom, Associate Professor of Ministry, McCormick Theological Seminary

"Ellis Davis reflects upon the sexual and domestic violence she experienced as a child, teen, and adult, all from men she should have had every reason to trust. She unflinchingly describes the cataclysmic impact these evils have had upon her overall well-being and boldly challenges community leaders, both spiritual and secular, to adopt appropriate collaborative and strategic responses. I strongly recommend this tome."

—Al Miles, Lead Chaplain, The Queen's Medical Center, Honolulu

"Sharon Ellis Davis uses autobiography to educate her audience about the truth and trauma of sexual and domestic violence. Hers is a painful and powerful journey shared by too many women of faith. It is a remarkable story of a remarkable woman's strength and courage. She battles not only the abusive men in her life but also the church and herself. Reader, be aware: the truth will make you flinch before it sets you free."

—Marie Fortune, Founder, FaithTrust Institute

"A raw and lucidly vulnerable memoir of Ellis Davis's journey of healing from the trauma of multiple experiences of sexual violence. She bravely draws back the curtains of silence, inviting us to look closely at the all-too-familiar world of sexual abuse. . . . A compelling read for victims, victim advocates, and pastoral-care practitioners seeking or needing an autobiographical account of healing in the journey toward freedom and wholeness. Ellis Davis bares her soul."

—Mitzi J. Smith, Professor of New Testament, Columbia Theological Seminary

"*The Trauma of Sexual and Domestic Violence* is a soul-stirring account of Sharon Ellis Davis's personal experience. . . . Ellis Davis's penchant for truth telling, compassion for victims and survivors of domestic abuse, and masterful storytelling inspire hope, inject humor, and bestow agency on readers who are preparing or ready to be agents of change."

—JoAnne Marie Terrell, Associate Professor of Theology, Ethics & the Arts, Chicago Theological Seminary

"Addressing domestic violence through new lens is needed now more than ever before. This jewel Sharon Ellis Davis has penned not only is a gift to the field of pastoral care in our current times but, because of its reflective narratives, also serves victims of domestic violence with compassion and sensitivity. I highly recommend this personal, pastoral, and professional work for its vulnerability, transparency, and timeliness to an issue that continues to hide in the margins of the fabric of our society."

—Danielle J. Buhuro, Executive Director, Sankofa CPE Center

"This book is a history of truth by an inner child that grew up too soon. Reading the history of a grown survivor is like reliving the pain all over again with her, at the same time knowing that God is ever-present at all times. I couldn't put the book down. I just wanted to shout, 'You go, girlfriend.' Strength comes from within, and strength is 'her.' I can't wait for the next book of truths."

—Patricia Ann Davenport, Executive Director, Our House

"A usable masterpiece. Many times, scholars from the academy write books that are helpful only for those who work in the academy. . . . Not so with Ellis Davis. She knows both sides of the street and writes in a way that those in the academy, those in the church, those in the counseling suites, and those who are trying to find a way out of the morass created by this trauma can be reached. I recommend her book highly."

—Jeremiah A. Wright Jr., Pastor Emeritus, Trinity United Church of Christ

October 19, 2022

To Jen,
Thank you for the work of mindfulness to bring about healing and wholeness. We all must do our part. Blessings to you.
Shan

The Trauma of Sexual and Domestic Violence

Shaun Ellis Davis

Healing!

The Trauma of Sexual and Domestic Violence

Navigating My Way through Individuals,
Religion, Policing, and the Courts

Sharon Ellis Davis

CASCADE *Books* • Eugene, Oregon

THE TRAUMA OF SEXUAL AND DOMESTIC VIOLENCE
Navigating My Way Through Individuals, Religion, Policing, and the Courts

Copyright © 2022 Sharon Ellis Davis. All rights reserved. Except for brief quotations in critical publications or reviews, no part of this book may be reproduced in any manner without prior written permission from the publisher. Write: Permissions, Wipf and Stock Publishers, 199 W. 8th Ave., Suite 3, Eugene, OR 97401.

Cascade Books
An Imprint of Wipf and Stock Publishers
199 W. 8th Ave., Suite 3
Eugene, OR 97401

www.wipfandstock.com

PAPERBACK ISBN: 978-1-6667-1541-5
HARDCOVER ISBN: 978-1-6667-1542-2
EBOOK ISBN: 978-1-6667-1543-9

Cataloguing-in-Publication data:

Names: Ellis Davis, Sharon, author.
Title: The trauma of sexual and domestic violence : navigating my way through individuals, religion, policing, and the courts / Sharon Ellis Davis.
Description: Eugene, OR : Cascade Books, 2022 | Includes bibliographical references and index.
Identifiers: ISBN 978-1-6667-1541-5 (paperback) | ISBN 978-1-6667-1542-2 (hardcover) | ISBN 978-1-6667-1543-9 (ebook)
Subjects: LCSH: Sexual abuse victims. | Survivors. | Christianity. | Religious aspects. | Domestic violence.
Classification: BV4596.A25 .E45 2022 (print) | BV4596.A25 .E45 (ebook)

All rights reserved. No part of this book may be reproduced or transmitted in any form or by any electronic or mechanical means, including information storage and retrieval systems, without permission in writing from the publisher, except by reviewers, who may quote brief passages in a review.

Except for my immediate family, friends, and significant clergy, who gave permission to use their names and actual context, the other names are fictitious even where the events are factual.

Dedication

This book is dedicated to the memory of my mother,
Annelle Ellis Hawkins, who in many ways was the first survivor I knew; to women survivors of sexual trauma and domestic violence who lived through it only to discover there was more trauma to come; and in memory of women murdered by their partners or whose trauma and weariness lead to their suicide.
May the words contained within give women power to continue to tell our stories of survival, thriving, and becoming more than a conqueror so that victims of sexual trauma and domestic violence will know there is hope.

Contents

Preface xi

Acknowledgments xvii

Introduction xxi

Chapter 1. Childhood Sexual Violence 1
  Reflection: Trauma and Impact of Childhood Abuse 16
  Discussion 20
  Poem: Stolen, Not Lost 21

Chapter 2. The Escape Plan 22
  Reflection: Trauma-Informed Pastoral Care Practices 38
  Discussion 42
  Activity: Referral List 42

Chapter 3. Sin, Shame, Guilt, and Dirty Stains 43
  Reflection: Providing Theological Clarity 53
  Discussion 57
  Activity: Scripture as Resource or Roadblock 57

Chapter 4. I Made It to Hell 58
  Reflection: Forgiveness and Domestic Violence 71
  Discussion 74
  Activity: Commit to Act 76

Chapter 5. Prepare for War in Times of Peace 77
  Reflection: Navigating Systems and Institutions of Power 95
  Discussion 102
  Activity: Build Coalitions, Gain Understanding 102

Chapter 6. Contradictions in Church and Circumstances 103

　Reflection: Exploring Black Liberation, Womanist, and Feminist Theological and Biblical Scholarship as Tools of Navigation 113

　Discussion 119

　Activity: Collaborate to Eliminate 120

Chapter 7. Me, My Mind, My Body and My Home—All Depressed 121

　Reflection: How Do We Navigate Self Care in Mind, Body, and Spirit in Times of Trauma, Crisis, and #BlackLivesMatter? 139

　Discussion 141

　Activity: Self-Care 142

Chapter 8. Concluding Thoughts: Reflections and Lessons—Blessings, Trauma, and Resilience 143

　Reflection: I Continue to Learn and Grow 158

　　On My Relationship with the Church of My Formative Years 158

　　On My Relationship with the Church Currently 160

　　On My Escape-Plan Husband Number 1, Buck 160

　　On My Abusive Husband Number 2, Greg 161

　　On My I-Married-Him-for-Protection Husband Number 3, Joel 161

　　On the Importance of Friendship 162

　　On My Thoughts about My Father 164

　　On My Current Husband, Rev. Dr. Edward Smith Davis 166

　　On My Relationship with Myself 168

Afterword 171

Bibliograhpy 179

Preface

ON SEPTEMBER 23, 2020, 195 days after Breonna Taylor, a Black woman, was shot and murdered in her own home by police officers, Kentucky Attorney General Daniel Cameron announced that none of the officers involved would be charged with any crime related to her murder. After midnight, those officers entered Breonna Taylor's home while she and her boyfriend were sleeping, executed a *no-knock warrant* without wearing required body cameras and without a supervisor present. Newsfeeds report that once police were inside the home, Breonna and her boyfriend were startled; he fired a shot and then called 911 for police assistance. The officers returned fire, killing Breonna. The anger of injustice, the horror of the moment, and the protest continued with emphasis on, and the articulation of, the now all-too-familiar chant, *"Black lives matter."* This is the ethos within which this book is written and the finality with which this particular paragraph is forged.

Co-creators of the Black Lives Matter (BLM) mantra and movement—Alicia Garza, Patrisse Cullors, and Opal Tometi—spearheaded what has now evolved into a global protest against racism, systemic oppression, and police killing. One of the rhetorical strategies of this movement includes naming Black men and women the police have killed. Some of those named are Rayshard Brooks, twenty-seven; Daniel Prude, forty-one; George Floyd, forty-six; Breonna Taylor, twenty-six; Atatianna Jefferson, twenty-eight; Aura Rosser, forty; Stephon Clark, twenty-two; Botham Jean, twenty-six; Philando Castille, thirty-two; Alton Sterling, thirty-seven; Michelle Cusseaux, fifty; Freddie Gray, twenty-five; Janisha Fonville, twenty; Eric Garner, forty-three; Akai Gurley, twenty-eight; Gabriella Nevarez, twenty-two; Tamir Rice, twelve; Michael Brown, eighteen; and Tanisha Anderson, thirty-seven. Missing from this list is Elijah McClain.

Elijah McClain died after police in Aurora, Colorado, responded to a citizen's call to police of a suspicious person walking through the neighborhood. While Elijah was walking home from a convenience store listening to music in his headphones, the police detained him, applied a carotid hold until Elijah began to vomit, falsely reported he attempted to reach for their guns, and disabled their body cameras. Adding to this list of Black people killed while in police custody are Sandra Bland, who mysteriously died in a Waller County, Texas, jail while detained after a non-moving violation; and Jacob Blake of Kenosha, Wisconsin, who was shot in the back seven times by officers while three of his sons witnessed this attempted murder from the backseat of his SUV. These names represent not only current issues of racism, but the historical roots beginning with enslavement, Jim Crow laws, the Civil Rights era, and times in which Black bodies were killed by White supremacists and police who were present to protect White bodies from Black bodies they regarded as less than human and viewed as dangerous savages.

Black bodies continue to be dehumanized, abused, and killed with impunity through a system many consider to be deeply rooted in structural racism and White supremacy. An all-too-common phrase repeated on social media states, "The system is not broken, it was built that way." As with movements in the past, the Black Lives Matter movement arose to create a counter-narrative that loudly proclaims Black Lives Matter. However, the cry within Black communities has mainly focused on killing Black male bodies with minimal mention of the Black women also killed by the police. While compiling this list, I was surprised by the number of Black women who have been killed, yet not surprised by the frequency with which Black women's and Black transwomen's names are omitted. The omission is incredibly disheartening in the silence of Black men who cry for justice for the intentional killing of Black men since the period of enslavement. I speak more to this in my previous book, titled *Battered African American Women: A Study of Gender Entrapment*. The ignoring, shunning, and muting of names of Black women killed by police compelled Black women to counter by speaking with a clear, definitive, and loud roar, "Say her name!" This is the roar that kept Breonna's name in the spotlight and that garnered protest, helped men and women to stay focused on her name and remain vigilant, waiting for the very moment on September 23, 2020, when the fate of the officers was announced. According to the law, the officers acted legally.

The Kentucky Attorney General who conducted the press conference to announce the findings on the police shooting of Breonna did so with no regard for a human being killed in her own home. He did it with little regard to the trauma she and her boyfriend endured at that moment, disoriented from sleeping and not knowing who broke into their home. He made his proclamation without mentioning that the legally armed boyfriend was arrested and charged, although shooting first only to protect Breonna and himself from intruders. And the Attorney General proclaimed the officers' innocence without noting that two policy requirements for executing a no-knock warrant were ignored—there was no supervisor on the scene, and the officers were not wearing body cameras. Instead, one officer was charged with *wanton endangerment* since a shot passed through the glass doors in Breonna's home towards the home of a White neighbor, thereby endangering the White neighbor. There was no acknowledgment that over twenty shots were fired into Breonna's home wantonly endangering a Black woman who had not done anything illegal. The State's Attorney had more of a matter-of-fact persona that spoke loudly and clearly—the police were justified.

This horrifying and traumatic moment resulted in many women wondering about the significance of Black women's lives and the worth of a murdered Black woman, as Breonna's family was awarded a $12 million settlement. At the same time, only one officer was charged and released on a $15,000 bond for a stray bullet hitting her White neighbor's wall. This insult, along with the 195-day delayed decision to not charge the officers with her death, sparked the social media community of Black women to ask two fundamental questions amid protest, unrest, anger, and grief: "Is twelve million dollars the value of a Black woman's life?" and "Do Black women's lives really matter?"

The latter question—"Do Black women's lives really matter?"—has been asked down through the years in some form or fashion. It was asked during the Women's Suffrage Movement by Sojourner Truth and others, Black Feminist, Womanist, and ordinary Black women who have specifically experienced sexual and interpersonal violence at the hands of White slave masters and their families and at the hands of men, both Black and White. It was asked during times when Black women experienced sexual violence by their pastors. Black women's bodies have always been under the control of individuals and institutions within patriarchal systems of power, engaging in both micro and macro misogynistic behaviors.

Dr. Martin Luther King Jr.'s protest tactics were through nonviolent resistance. I listened to a YouTube interview of Dr. King being interviewed by CBS anchor, Mike Wallace, where he was asked about his solid stance and commitment to nonviolence. Dr. King insisted "that nonviolence is the most potent weapon available to oppressed people in their struggle for freedom and justice. I feel that violence will only create more social problems than they will solve. That in a real sense it is impracticable for the Negro to even think of mounting a violent revolution in the United States."[1] When the host informed Dr. King that there were others who disagreed, Dr. King acknowledged this and again reiterated that he would never turn away from non-violent resistance, asserting that "the cry of Black Power is, at the bottom, a reaction to White Power to make the kind of changes necessary to make justice a reality for the Negro. I think we have to see that a riot is the language of the unheard."[2]

I am compelled to ask: What is the language of Black women and girls who, as victims/survivors of sexual and interpersonal violence, are silenced on multiple levels, and who have not been properly included with the voices of the oppressed? What is the language of these same Black women who stand side-by-side with those whose oppression is dramatized daily while their own voices are silenced unless it involves Black male advocacy and sacrifice? This book speaks of at least two ways the unheard can be heard. First, by Black women taking responsibility for caring for ourselves and by participating in activities that celebrate and increase our wellness. Second, by telling our stories and encouraging others to tell their stories in ways that confront injustices on every level of our collective being.

One way I have committed to celebrate and increase my wellness came from my participation with an organization called GirlTrek. In the past couple of months, I have been engaged with two twenty-one-day, five-days-a-week walks with GirlTrek called Black History Boot Camp. GirlTrek, a health movement for women and girls, was founded by two women, Morgan Dixon and Vanessa Garrison. The Black History Boot Camp was designed to promote health, but it is also a meditative walk celebrating, during the first twenty-one days, the foremothers who blazed the trail for African American women. Each day of walking contains a

---

1. Martin Luther King, quoted in Wallace, "MLK: A Riot Is the Language of the Unheard."
2. Wallace, "MLK: A Riot Is the Language of the Unheard."

Black history story and a playlist of music representing each foremother and her work.[3] Over 300,000 women participate in this march daily.

Both the lessons learned during the protest and the stories of our foremothers reminded me that Black people have always been people of resiliency. We have always made ways out of no way, as well as worked toward and inspired change—often amid our suffering. These stories inspired me deeply to remember that my story is not simply about the pain but also the progress, the survival, and the resiliency birthed inside of me, which has allowed me not to be a victim but a victor. This book encourages this healing and resiliency for Black women survivors who have suffered more traumatization than even they realize.

And finally, this book encourages women's healing through storytelling. It encourages women never to allow their story to be told by anyone determined to oppress, harm, or silence their voices. As women victims/survivors, we must change the conversation and not allow individuals, communities, or institutions to steer us into telling a story that does not represent our experiences and the truths we know to be truths yet have been fearful of telling. And we do that by owning our stories, encouraging others to tell their stories, and controlling the narrative.

> *"Until the lion [lioness] learns how to write,*
> *every story will glorify the hunter."*
> —J. NOZIPO MARAIRE, ZIMBABWEAN WOMAN DOCTOR

---

3. See the website: www.GirlTrek.org.

Acknowledgments

Life is a journey and not a destination. Writing this book was the most difficult fifteen-year journey I have ever undertaken. Gaining the courage, confidence, wisdom, and permission to put this story in writing three years ago took an entire village of friends, teachers, encouragers, students, advocates, allies, and male and female colleagues, who continue in this work alongside me and others. With fear and trembling, I began this project. Although this list is not exhaustive, I want to acknowledge those who played a significant role in my life and academic and writing journey.

I thank my mother, the late Annelle Ellis Hawkins, who loved me furiously. Her wisdom still lives within me today, twelve years after her death in November 2009. She was my first teacher, psychologist, and theologian. I owe a great deal to both of my parents for bringing me into the world. My father, the late Rev. Samuel Lee Ellis, was not the sum total of any transgressions his life journey included. Despite his limitations, or in addition to them, he played a positive role in my development. This reality will always be a place of contradiction in my mind as I continue working through trauma.

To my husband, Rev. Dr. Edward Smith Davis, thank you for providing me space to work, offering advice, perspectives, and wisdom, and for your contributions to my book. Thank you for loving me even amid my triggers, which convinced me that I could find safety in you. To my blended family, Ozell Hickman, Cameron Davis, Sharell Holmes, Bianca Davis, Ashley Davis, and her twin, the late Andrew Davis, thank you for all your love and unfailing support. My siblings, Gloria Howell, Peggy Dennis, and Linda Wilburn, will always be a treasure in my life. As the baby in the family, I recognize I might have brought some distress and grief. I am grateful for your love and support and for allowing me to serve as your pastor later in life. I listened to your advice, although you will swear I did not. Your gifts to me growing up and now were and are invaluable.

I acknowledge my best friends, Retired Police Officer Rhonda Doyle-Turnbough, Rev. Delores Johnson, MDiv, and Rev. Marsha Thomas, MDiv, who serve as my confidants, wisdom bearers, sister-girls, and more for and over thirty-five years, respectively. Thank you for contributing your wisdom toward the production of this book. I appreciate my two other friends, Rev. Brenda Burney, MDiv, and Rev. Nanette Banks, MDiv. I consider both to be very good friends, though Nannette, in fun, has warned me that I might fall to a second-tier best friend for mentioning her by name here; I can't resist, given her support and kindness. Brenda, thanks for your friendship and wisdom. Nannette, thanks for your friendship and especially for the advice you offered me after reviewing my original manuscript.

I am grateful to my friend Sharon Stolz for the many times we shared private messages, feelings, and content for this book. During this past year of writing, she held me in her heart, especially during the aftermath of the killing of Black men by police. She is a friend, advocate, and trusted ally. And thanks to my friend Serene Bridgett Hollingsworth, not simply for your friendship but also for your willingness to be vulnerable and authentic in our serious times of intense dialogue. Thanks for your contribution to my book. Sister-friend Sheryll Flo-Rue Bray, thank you for your friendship and all the support you continually offer. Rev. Danielle Buhuro, DMin and PhD candidate, as well as my daughter in the ministry, thank you for your support and constant encouragement for me to be faithful and inclusive on the journey. You are the gift that keeps on giving.

I want to profoundly thank and acknowledge those who edited my manuscript and supported and coached me. Dr. Rachel Panton, PhD, of Women Writing Wellness, who served as my mentor/editor/coach; and Elder Tracy Thompson, DMin, pastor, advocate, and former student, I asked to read the manuscript and volunteered her editing skills. I am grateful for Rev. Dr. Raedorah C. Stewart of iWrite.Solutions LLC—my book developer, style editor, and submission coach through the publisher's process—thank you for offering your skills and using your gifts for such holy purposes.

To my former students of Chicago Theological Seminary, McCormick Theological Seminary in Chicago, and United Theological Seminary in Dayton, Ohio, thanks for allowing me to enter your spaces. Know that you taught me well, which was one of my requirements—that I learn from you! Whoever I am today I greatly attribute to your willingness to share and to allow me to grow through your wisdom and candid evaluations. Finally, I want to acknowledge the professors who mentored me, offered great insight and advice, believed in me when I did not believe in myself, and who were sources of encouragement during my journey. Thank you, Professors Susan Thistlethwaite, JoAnne Marie Terrell, Laurel Schneider, Lee H. Butler Jr., Julia Speller, Stephanie M. Crumpton, David Daniels, Lois Gehr Livezey, and Homer Ashby. You all are the best of the best. Professor Linda Thomas, I will never forget your words to me in 2000 as I was preparing to study for my doctor of philosophy degree, "Be teachable." Know that I always will. And Professor Kathy Lyndes, thank you for being a part of our writing and reading group, along with Professor Laurel Schneider, as together we wrote and evaluated each other's dissertations and Laurel's book-in-progress. Without this group, I am confident I would still be trying to figure it out. And Kathy, thank you and Louis for feeding me after my first battle with cancer. I offer a special thanks of gratitude to my Pastor, Rev. Dr. Jeremiah A. Wright Jr., who nurtured my gifts into the ordained ministry and birthed my love for justice and liberation.

Finally, thank you, God and God's Son, Jesus, for carrying me through.

Please note: except for my immediate family and friends and significant clergy, who permitted me to use their names and actual context, all names are fictional.

Introduction

Race, class, and gender/gender identity are three critical areas that Black women who experience sexual and domestic violence have had to navigate when seeking safety, protection, and justice. Of these three roadblocks, issues of race have had prominence and priority within Black communities, and for valid reasons. The Black community (men, women, and youth) have historically rallied together in protest and action to make demands for justice, change, equal rights, and transformation of institutions and systems that have consituted the ethos of racism. Men, women, and children/youth have been arrested, dragged, beaten, seriously wounded, and killed together. Yet, during the historic campaigs for justice, the remaining seeds of unrest and injustices—class and gender/gender identity, which also impact Black women in general, and women and children impacted by sexual and domestic violence specifically—were not historically part of the rhythms of the walk and talk of protests, thus rendering Black women invisible. And being rendered invisible has consequences. I will offer two examples of how Black women can be rendered invisible.

In early September 2020, I was speaking to the owner of a potential publishing company. I will call him Peter. Peter and I were having a conversation regarding my experience of domestic violence. He is a self-identified White male who is eighty-eight years old and a scholar of theology and ethics himself. We exchanged pleasantries regarding our shared vocation as theologians. What occurred next caught me by surprise. The conversations we had were mutually interesting, which kept our talk going on for a few more minutes. I shared some of my story with Peter as a survivor of domestic violence. After I finished, he was silent for a few moments. Then he began speaking slowly and reflectively, admitting that he knew by talking with me that I had a middle-class status as a Black woman, and then expressed with shock, "I never really thought of Black women as victims." With his speech slowing down again, he continued, "I guess that means I was thinking it was . . . [long pause] . . . only White women then," as if to indicate that he had just that moment realized the impact of what he was saying. I was caught off guard with his statement but allowed him to continue with his comments and questions because I was now more interested in the remainder of his thoughts than in confronting and clarifying that moment. We ended up talking a bit longer. I was grateful for the entire conversation, which I would like to speak more about one day. However, I never stopped pondering those words: *I never thought of Black women as victims.* For me, this was the epitome and embodiment of Black women's invisibility.

The other instance occurred during my employment as a police officer. Many Black officers, both men and women, routinely joined the Black organizations led by male police officers committed to justice and antiracism work within the Department. These leaders offered advice and mentoring to young officers new on the job, such as when they advised women officers not to become undercover officers in the area of prostitution. The officers believed that Black women were being targeted and used specifically for these purposes. The group was loud and vocal and committed to keeping the Department accountable to the community and to Blacks within the Department. They worked tirelessly toward this end and were often punished by Department leadership who would assign them to guard vacant buildings and not offer opportunities for leadership and promotion within the Department.

One of those leadership opportunities required passing promotional exams. However, Black officers lagged behind White officers, predominantly White male officers, who successfully passed exams with scores high enough to be promoted. Consequently, after keeping up enough noise regarding this issue, the Black male leadership of the league was invited into negotiations. After months of negotiation, the Black officers were excited when they realized a decision had been reached. However, to the chagrin, dismay, and disappointment of Black women officers, the negotiations did not turn out well for them in particular.

The final decision agreed upon by all was that Black male officers would be placed on a separate list, and a relatively large percentage of them would be promoted from that list. However, Black women were placed on the promotion list labeled "women officers" and promoted at a lower percentage than those on the Black male list. Once again, the women were not only rendered invisible, but they were also literally removed from being Black to being a woman, and one not deserving of the rights offered to Black men. In both of these examples, it became clear how Black women were erased and rendered invisible from within the Black community and from within White sectors of society.

Even today, it continues to take Black women standing together to have the name of women killed by police included in the lists of victims. Thus, the Black Lives Matter mantra needed a refrain, *Say Her Name*. Invisibility has a function. Invisibility is the failure to see another as fully human and deserving of justice. Invisibility in this case is synonymous with seeing individuals as non-persons. For non-persons, justice is elusive. Invisibility functions as a barrier for those who are victimized and treated unfairly to being acknowledged as victims. Therefore no movement toward justice is necessary. And when Black women are rendered invisible, the consequences can be devastating. Women are then viewed as dispensable, not worthy of protection, blamed for their victimization, taken advantage of, and not taken seriously. This includes LGBQT+ persons who often have even higher rates of violence and murders within their communities. Consequently, amid racism, sexism, homophobia, misogynistic and patriarchal attitudes and behaviors, many Black women have declared that they have never felt safe, even in their own homes and within Black institutions. These facts and more motivated and called me to write this book—*The Trauma of Sexual and Domestic Violence*.

Years before Kimberlé Crenshaw coined the term "intersectionality" (1989), I had begun repeating the words "making the connection" in reflection on my journey through sexual and domestic violence. I have spoken of making the connection in small groups both formally and informally. Long before I knew of work on intersectionality, I sincerely believed I was a lone wolf attempting to speak about a topic no one else had considered.

My *connection* statement was derived mainly from my personal experience with domestic violence and how I had to navigate through individuals/communities, the church, the police/court systems, and my abusive household. Later this experience of mine was given historical confirmation through an encounter with slave narratives, such as the book written by Linda Brent, *Incidents in the Life of a Slave Girl*. My own story of my police officer husband's physical and sexual violence nearly mimicked Brent's description of the physical and sexual violence perpetrated by her slave master and his wife

Throughout her book, Brent spoke of terroristic violence by her owners while being blamed by her enslaved husband for her victimization. While reading Brent's and similar narratives of enslaved women, a light bulb went off in my head. Perhaps if batterers' groups could get Black men to see how their tactics often mimic what was done to enslaved women, I thought, they would make that connection to this horrific moment in history and ultimately begin the necessary work toward healing. Yet, statistics show that sexual and domestic violence against women and children remains prevalent, and when it comes to Black women, much of this violence occurs in our own homes.

According to the National Coalition Against Domestic Violence:

- On average, nearly twenty people per minute are physically abused by an intimate partner in the United States. For one year, this equates to more than 10 million women and men.
- One in seven women and one in twenty-five men have been injured by an intimate partner.
- On a typical day, there are more than 20,000 phone calls placed to domestic violence hotlines nationwide.
- Only 34 percent of people who are injured by intimate partners receive medical care for their injuries.
- Domestic victimization is correlated with a higher rate of depression and suicidal behavior.

Further, in terms of Sexual Violence,

- One in five women and one in seventy-one men in the United States have been raped in their lifetime.
- Almost half of the females, 46.7 percent of males, and 44.9 percent of victims of rape in the United States were raped by an acquaintance. Of these, 45.4 percent of female rape victims and 29 percent of male rape victims were raped by an intimate partner.

When it comes to homicides, a study of intimate-partner homicides found that 20 percent of victims were not the intimate partners themselves, but family members, friends, neighbors, persons who intervened, law enforcement responders, or bystanders.[4]

---

4. See the National Coalition Against Domestic Violence (NCADV) website: www.NCADV.org.

These statistics demonstrate how domestic violence is not simply a personal issue between partners, but something that impacts the entire community, including children. The NCADV reports that not only are one in five children exposed to domestic violence; 90 percent of them are eyewitnesses to the violence. The NCADV report covers the economic impact as well as the mind, body, spirit connections, reporting that victims of sexual and domestic violence are vulnerable to HIV/AIDS and other sexually transmitted diseases as a result of forced intercourse, and the violence can contribute to physical responses such as heart disease and high blood pressure, PTSD, and various types of addictions, such as alcohol and drug addiction. NCADV's "Fact Sheets" point to the connection between domestic violence and systemic racism and racist structures perpetrated against both Black men and women (links to all "Fact Sheets" can be found on the website). As it relates to Black females, it is important to note that 51.3 percent of homicides are a result of domestic violence.

The Center for Disease Control (CDC) developed a division named the National Intimate Partner and Sexual Violence Survey (NISVS), which utilizes a national telephone-surveying method to measure the impact of intimate partner violence (IPV) over the past year. It also measures the impact of IPV and sexual violence (SV) over the life span. This organization, realizing that little is known within the LGBQT community about issues of violence, decided to take on that task. Its findings prove that the impact within these communities are even higher than in heterosexual relationships. The NISVS states, among other facts, that:

- Approximately one in eight lesbian women (13 percent), nearly half of bisexual women (46 percent), and one in six heterosexual women (17 percent) have been raped in their lifetime. This translates to an estimated 214,000 lesbian women, 1.5 million bisexual women, and 19 million heterosexual women. They also report that bisexual persons experience their first completion rape between the ages of eleven and twenty-four.

- And, four in ten gay men (40 percent), nearly half of bisexual men (47 percent), and one in five heterosexual men (21 percent) have experienced SV other than rape in their lifetime. This translates into nearly 1.1 million gay men, 903,000 bisexual men, and 21.6 million heterosexual men.[5]

5. See the Center for Disease Control (CDC) website: www.cdc.gov/violence prevention/nisvs/.

Finally, as it relates to childhood abuse, the CDC violence prevention section also speaks to issues of child abuse that include physical, sexual, and emotional abuse and neglect. The CDC-Kaiser Adverse Childhood Experience (ACE) study speaks about the impact of abuse on children: its impact can extend across the life span into future violence, victimization, and perpetration. Two-thirds of the adults in their study had experienced at least one ACE, and one in five experienced three ACEs, and this lasting impact can have negative health and well-being outcomes.

These are just a few of the alarming statistics related to violence against women and children, not to mention the alarming statistics regarding the murders of transwomen, especially Black transwoman. These statistics represent a moral imperative toward addressing this pandemic. And it is time to ask male Black-led liberation movement leaders, pastors, and scholars to include the stories of sexual and domestic violence against Black women as part of their narrative in helping to define and militate against the oppression of Black women from within and without. This book asserts through storytelling that keeping hope alive alone is not the solution. For many Black women survivors of violence, the hope for intervention, protection, and accountability has faded. Their cries have gone unheard. James Weldon Johnson, in his writing of "Lift Every Voice and Sing," now considered the Black National Anthem, states it best when he writes of the experience of injustices "felt in the days when hope unborn had died."[6] Hope alone is not enough.

The Trauma of Sexual and Domestic Violence is a form of experiential education. This experiential education privileges personal narratives as a starting point for biblical, ethical, theological, psychological, and sociological inquiry, especially as the inquiry relate to the impact of trauma on women survivors of sexual and domestic violence. The book brings awareness to ways victims/survivors have had to navigate their way around institutions such as the criminal-justice system and the church to seek safety and justice in the midst of consistent blaming, shaming, and being judged. Finally, *The Trauma of Sexual and Domestic Violence* is about victims/survivors understanding their resiliency, strength, and

---

6. "Lift Every Voice and Sing," often called "The Black National Anthem," was written as a poem by NAACP leader James Weldon Johnson (1871–1938) and then set to music by his brother John Rosamond Johnson (1873–1954) in 1899. It was first performed in public in the Johnsons' hometown of Jacksonville, Florida, as part of a celebration of Lincoln's Birthday on February 12, 1900, by a choir of five-hundred schoolchildren at the segregated Stanton School, where James Weldon Johnson was principal. See Johnson, "Lift Every Voice and Sing."

power to assert their visibility and to show up unapologetically in the continuing and seemingly unending quest toward justice-making, healing, hope, and wholeness.

Each chapter has three sections. The first section involves telling my personal story of sexual and domestic violence and its impact, which in many ways represents our collective stories of survival in the midst of seeking safety, care, and justice. The second section is designed to reflect on some of the main issues within the chapter to help the reader understand trauma and the ways trauma affects our whole lives. And the final section offers opportunities for discussion, whether in academic spaces, study groups, or among individuals. Critical thinking and being comfortable with being uncomfortable are required. I desire the discussion to ultimately center the individual voices, thoughts, stories, and perspectives, as I believe we learn better in community.

Finally, I pray the results will move us all toward a greater understanding of ourselves as collectively belonging to the circle of life, committing ourselves as individuals to moving toward transformation and justice-making as a pathway toward individual and collective healing, forgiveness, and reconciliation with ourselves and others. We may not all be guilty, but we are all responsible.

Chapter 1

Childhood Sexual Violence

A FEW YEARS AGO, I was contacted by The Institute for Youth Ministry, an organization associated with Princeton Theological Seminary to write an article for *Engage,* a digital space to speak about everyday happenings in the life of ordinary people. *Engage* discussed various topics from social media where important questions would arise regarding what should be the Christian response to issues presented. The Institute's goal was to invite participants to write short articles on suggested topics presented to them. The articles were then posted on the Institute's website. Youth participants were encouraged to read the articles and add their responses to the original article. The ultimate goal was to create opportunities for dialogue within a larger group framework. The articles posted along with the responses would be available for others to download and use as a resource to jump-start meaningful discussions among youth groups pertaining to the issue(s) presented. In this particular series, seven of us from a variety of vocations and practices had been approached to write an article on the topic, "Pastor or Predator? Sexual Misconduct in Youth Ministry."

The premise surrounding this upcoming series was to engage the topic of clergy sexual abuse that had been in the public eye for over twenty years and mainly in association with the Catholic Church. Yet very little attention had been given to clergy sexual abuse in general as a complex human problem that transcends race, class, gender, and denomination. I agreed to participate in the project. We were given free rein to shape the article as we desired. Our charge was to write an article that would elicit questions from the readers that could ultimately be discussed by various groups of people and would focus mainly on our Christian response to these issues. Although I agreed to write the article, as I was comfortable speaking about the topic informally, as a seminary professor providing training to faith communities, inside I was fearful and slightly anxious. I became resistant to writing this article, yet I persisted, pushed those feelings aside, and prioritized writing. It might be helpful to say this now: my behavior of pushing feelings aside and engaging in busyness is a lifelong pattern, a common behavior of victims/survivors of sexual violence. However, after writing the article, I realized I was writing in preparation for exposing my sexual violations within my family of origin.

I began writing this article reflecting on how some pastors have historically been complicit in what today is known as engaging in theological malpractice-behaviors that empower and excuse male perpetrators while shaming and blaming victims/survivors of sexual and domestic violence. This has especially impacted African American women, women from marginalized demographics, and LGBTQ+ persons of color who previously relied on and trusted the church to be a source of care, comfort, and intervention. Now many of these same people have been hurt by this same institution and are rejecting and/or pondering whether the Black church in particular, and the church in general, is a safe place for Black women. These reflections reminded me of my own experiences within the Black church.

I am a product of the Black church and very proudly hail it as the place that taught me about Jesus. While this is true, however, I have done very little to call the church out on its duplicity, culpability, hypocrisy, and complicity for the various ways that pastors within my Black church tradition have played into the sexual victimization of vulnerable children, youth, and women. For me, these experiences were about more than the duplicity, culpability, hypocrisy, and complicity of the Black church. It was also about the same thing being demonstrated in the home of a pastor who caused harm within my family structure. I titled the article "Holders of Secrets of Clergy Sexual Abuse." Those who ministered to youth were reminded that they might become the holders of secrets of those to whom they ministered, but whose clergy sexual abuse had followed them into adulthood, along with the accompanying wounds of holding that secret for many years. Within this context, I discussed what it meant and required of them as holders of these secrets.

After reading and reflecting on this now published article, I realized the vulnerability of adults who were sexually abused as children.

They still hold these secrets and are possibly looking for someone they can trust to hear their story. I am one of those adults. Who could I trust with my secret? Who would provide a safe space and provide the kind of spiritual care I needed? I was a holder of a secret that I trusted very few people to hold and even fewer to hold deeply. This resulted in pain and trauma that only worsened over time. Finally, I recognized that I had become the unnamed aggregate of countless women who as children and youth were sexually violated by clergymen. For me, that clergyman was my father. Whenever I spoke publicly on issues of clergy sexual abuse, I told *my* story, bit by bit, of sexual abuse at the hands of my late father, Rev. Samuel Lee Ellis. The gravity of the resulting trauma was so great that even as a woman, I could not dare name this devastation that took place in my young life.

Early in my adult years, I briefly had this conversation with my sister, Linda. We spoke about the abuse, but I was not able to articulate this to anyone else. It would be several years before I dared speak about the abuse again, and that was, in varying moments, to my three best friends, Rhonda, Delores, and Marsha. My three best friends were the ones I talked to the most about the abuse, and I faced very different responses.

Rhonda, who I refer to as my positive-thinking friend, was very affirming. She always tended to put a positive spin on any issue in life. So, when the conversation would come up, she would always encourage my ability to move forward and found ways to honor my father in the process. I was not ready to go deeper into the conversation, so positivity was good enough for me. I learned when I needed a positive frame for difficult issues, Rhonda was the one to call.

Delores, who I refer to as my sister-twin (we shared the same birth sign), was always ready to *go in* with me whenever I wanted to vent about any anger or feeling I would experience toward my father. So, speaking to her about sexually abusive behavior became my outlet when I wanted to curse—whether talking about this subject specifically or about sexual abuse generally. With Delores, I had someone who was, like myself, able to just tell it like it is, say it bluntly, all while cursing about it.

Marsha, however, is my critical questioning friend. If I came to her with an issue, I had to be prepared to answer the deep questions she intended for me to expound upon. Although she brought this unique gift to the table, I was most times unwilling to go as deep with the conversation as she desired. Changing the subject was a way to focus on something else. Nevertheless, Marsha became that person, when I wanted to go deeper into my thoughts, with whom I spoke the most.

The unique gift of all three of my best friends is that we, regardless of the topic and how painful the topic might be, would always find time for laughter. My friends, with their different personalities and approaches to communication, were a gift. I could still bring up a subject and engage the topic anyway I desired. I just had to know who was best to call at the moment.

The walls I had erected to protect myself were very much fortified by then, and I was unwilling to break them down out of fear of what I might feel or discover about myself. Years after my father's death in 1984, I revealed the abuse to my pastor, Rev. Dr. Jeremiah Jr. When I finally revealed the sexual violation to my pastor, I recognized from my initial encounter that I was very angry. Pastor Wright and my father had been close, and I wanted to tell him so that he would be just as angry at my father as I was in that particular moment. At that moment, I simply wanted someone to choose me over my father. My pastor did not fulfill my desire. He simply listened pastorally and offered comforting words. However, the anger and rage I wanted him to feel at my father just did not happen.

A few years before my mother's death in 2009, I finally told her about Daddy. At this particular moment, I was only brave enough to allude to being sexually abused, but not brave enough to have *that* conversation. I believe my mother picked up on my reticence. She affirmed and believed me and was sad abuse had happened. Our conversation was short and typical of my behavior pattern. I moved to another subject. My job all those years, as a child, was to protect my mother from any harm. This desire continued into adulthood, so protecting her from the pain of my father's actions was my number-one priority. And, before I married my current husband, Edward Davis, I did share my story with him. This was just about it for who I spoke to about my childhood sexual abuse.

I never forced the conversation. I never trusted anyone to fully understand or to offer me what I needed. At least, this was the narrative when the actual reason for my limited engagement centered around my unwillingness to be vulnerable and place my care in anyone's hands but my own. So, even with these revelations, I continued to suffer in silence. And this, unbeknownst to me, impacted my emotional growth and development during all the stages of my life. Yet, I fearfully held tight onto the real story throughout my adulthood and as a professional public speaker.

It was many years later when I understood how my childhood experiences were impacting my life. It was a gradual realization. And by this time I was not certain if I was even ready to talk about it professionally in my teaching, advocacy work, or through the written word. The fear and trepidation that kept me silent was also connected to fear of what others might feel about me telling this story, especially my siblings and extended family. How these revelations of my father being my violator would impact my relationship with my family and would damage my father's legacy, reputation, and status was always front and center in my mind even though he was no longer alive.

Sharing one's personal story of suffering and trials is seen as generally unnecessary. Often, the storyteller is accused of attempting to bring damage to particular family members by offering false accusations, revealing family secrets, or saying things to others that could equate to lessening someone's value. These things are fearlessly protected in my family's history. To reveal anything negative has previously been met with fierce defense that threatens/silences other family members from sharing their truth. Indeed, persons can expect hostility, denial, and attempts to discredit others' truth. Having been socialized with the same family loyalty mandate, I shared similar feelings also until I recognized the harm this particular violation has caused me down through the years to mind, body, and spirit. Telling my truth is not an attempt to hurt. Rather, it is an attempt to heal. It was healing for me, healing within our family structure, and healing within our wider society.

Sexual violence within family structures and the Black church structure is real and not specifically limited to my nuclear family. Infidelity is real within family structures and within our Black church structures. And many times, if we face our truth, many have been the violator both at home and within our Black church structures. At other times, we have been the victims of both. How can we truly be free when people are suffering in silence, all for the sake of protecting others even to our detriment? Where in our lives has denial brought us freedom?

I now see telling my story as a necessary component in continuing my journey of freeing and healing. That journey began in my family of origin and admitted the good as well as the dysfunctional and painful. This truth-telling is my way of coming to terms with the totality of my experiences without romanticizing or justifying the pain. Healing begins with truth-telling. This requires, for me, breaking this unwritten code of silence, making space for healing, and making space for others to tell their story if they choose. I am now empowered to speak up for this little girl who felt unheard, afraid, angry, vulnerable, and conflicted in my feelings.

My name is Sharon Ellis Davis and I am a victim/survivor of childhood sexual abuse.

I am aware of two things as I share my story. First, I am the holder of the truth of my childhood's sexually abusive relationship and other physical violations committed by my father. At the same time, I am the holder of multiple other truths regarding my father, which is not my story to tell. My story is complicated simply because my life was filled with both joy and pain, happiness and sorrow, tears and laughter, and quite a bit of anger and rage misdirected at others. My father was more than a perpetrator—he was a victim and a survivor himself. He was a preacher and teacher who both helped and hurt others, and I have struggled most of my life trying to make sense of my feelings for him and of our relationship as father and daughter. Second, although I remain fearful, I am well aware at this stage of my life that healing and freedom occur when the truth is told. Paraphrasing a biblical text, I know the truth will make me and others free. And freedom is what I seek.

Our family was of modest means. We managed well, although I remember hearing arguments about money mostly at Christmastime. My earliest memory of Daddy being a pastor was during our time living on the north side of Chicago, Illinois. Originally, he was, along with his siblings, a member of a Pentecostal church founded and pastored by my paternal grandfather. However, my most vivid memories were during the time my father served as the founding pastor of a Pentecostal church located on the north side of Chicago, where we resided until I was fifteen years old.

Daddy's church was considered *a storefront church*. My mother was a beautician, and her business was situated directly at the rear of the church. Our family structure consisted of my father, Samuel, and my mother, Annelle, who birthed three children, Peggy, Linda, and me. My oldest sister, Gloria, is my father's and his first wife's (Roslyn's) child. I learned later in life that my father and Roslyn had another son, Samuel. He died at a very young age after falling out of the window. I did not meet Gloria, as I remember, until I was in eighth grade. Therefore, I always refer to Peggy as my oldest sister, simply by habit.

My parents and we three siblings lived upstairs from the church. Most of the addresses where we lived had this same arrangement. Growing up in this environment found us, as children, spending several days a week in church, attending Sunday school, morning service, and night service. Then there was Bible class, choir rehearsals, church meetings, attending other denominational church events, etc. Our storefront church was small and, as children and youth, we were always required to attend. Some of our neighborhood friends would stand outside of the church mocking us by clapping their hands and imitating movements we made in church, all meant to teasingly get under our skin as they did not have the same church requirements as we did.

On some level, I truly resented being in church that much. Yet, on another larger level, the church was our life. Our social community with other youth was through church relationships. Our flirting with boys, having so-called boyfriends, or seeing boys we liked was through the church. The women and men who became colleagues and friends of my parents produced some of my closest friends who felt like family. Later as an adult, people would ask me if I truly liked going to church. After some thought, I would answer yes. The church was all we knew! Our family life and the church seemed to be profoundly integrated.

Daddy's disappointments and relationships in the church deeply influenced our family life for both good and bad. Daddy had what my mother named mood swings. The swings seemed to range from being joyful to being angry with many other swings in-between. One of those negative swings occurred around our secular records being on top of his church music. Our denomination was conservative and preached being in the world but not of the world. This was interpreted to mean we could not do much of anything that was fun, that we limited the types of clothes we could wear (no shorts, pants, etc.), and, as for dancing, forget it! However, one of the joyful things about my father was that he allowed us to dance and engage in other activities considered "worldly."

Except on one particular night, his mood swing went negative. He came home and happened to notice our 45 RPM records intermixed with his church music. He began breaking every one of them. We cried that day. Fortunately, Mother compensated by providing, without Daddy's knowledge, the money to repurchase the records.

Daddy treated Mother like a queen, I believed. He would say wonderful things to her and about her, and I assumed he loved her. Yet, there were far too many times when I would see Mama crying silently. Not wanting to see my mother cry marked the beginning of feeling I needed to protect her from being hurt even at the cost of not telling her about the sexual abuse. Through the years, Mother would attribute most of Daddy's pathologies, which included his tendencies toward painful and physically damaging bouts when we were whipped by him without mercy, to his upbringing and his relationship with his father. She explained how Daddy and the other siblings experienced abuse by his family. She said that the younger siblings had a healthier and more loving father relationship. They were the ones who were more successful in life than Daddy because they did not receive this type of treatment.

These stories were told to my mother and came directly from Daddy telling his truth to her. Mother always considered his background and the resulting mood swings as something she needed to heal and explain to us so that we would understand him better. This is the attitude she always had, and she passed that on to us, as she desired that we consider his behavior as not his fault but the fault of his pain and upbringing. She knew about his extra-marital affair(s). She was acquainted with one member of our congregation who was having an affair with Daddy. Daddy always confessed his affairs and offered reasons to my mother for having them.

My mother bore this even though I knew of and felt her pain. I tell this part of my mother's story only because of how it connects to my understanding of Daddy's incestuous behavior toward me. The progression of this story is Mother's to tell, and she is deceased. Yet, Mother and I had healthy conversations about Daddy's mood swings, and she tried all she could to shield all of us from his wrath and the physical results of these swings. Except for exhausting me with the excuses Mother made for Daddy's behavior, we did have honest conversations. I never added his sexually abusive behavior to the list of issues we spoke about. I referred to it as *night-time visits* because it always occurred after everyone was in bed for the night and assumed asleep.

Actually, and for the life of me, I do not understand how this was able to occur. We lived a modest life, and I remember mostly sleeping in the same bedroom as my sisters. Most significantly, I have no memory of sleeping in my own room. Did one of my siblings witness this abuse? It is all a mystery to me. Yet, these night visits occurred from when I was nine until I went to high school. Although the sexual abuse did not involve sexual intercourse, as many understand incest to be, it did involve sexual contact and inappropriate touching. For two and perhaps three times a week for five or more years, my body was inappropriately touched, fondled, and manipulated for Daddy to receive sexual pleasure. I refuse to offer any more descriptions because it is not my intent to give any unnecessary information. But it is an attempt to say that this should *never* have been my experience of a parent who was supposed to love, support, and protect me. Rather, my father became my predator, my abuser, and my tormentor.

In retrospect, I recognize that my experiences of being sexually abused by my father as a child, of being taken advantage of sexually by another clergy who crossed boundaries with me, and the impact of the sexual and domestic violence I experienced over my life compel me to write this particular story. This story of childhood sexual abuse is foundational to my truth-telling. Nothing disturbs my sensibilities in this stage of my life but the sexual violence and abusive behavior of my father. I am free now to tell my stories and make sense of them, advocate on behalf of survivors, and seek justice for others who have been violated. And now I can tell them without tears or re-traumatization.

In just the past ten years or so, whenever I would share my stories of both sexual violations and physical abuse by my father, it would bring tears and emotional lows that I found strange to experience. I had not put this abuse to rest. I thought I was healed and had come to terms with the whole of my life story. And that feeling, for the most part, is true. I believe I have done much to heal and am proud of the woman I am today. However, I realize now that when it comes to my father, I have avoided, denied, and refused to deeply engage this subject, thus slowing my healing in this area. Making this connection between who I am now, for better or worse, and my relationship with my dad must take center stage at this point in my life if I am to complete the healing, continue to be free, and to live my best life.

After suffering this kind of sexual and physical violation as a child, how do you explain having sexual feelings in these experiences while at the same time hating every moment of the interaction? As an adult, how do you determine what makes for a healthy sexual experience when all that you know is keeping secrets, hiding, and denying sexual feelings, believing that sex is only appropriate in the nighttime initiated by a male, and enjoyment of sex is for your mate alone? How do you reconcile feeling as if your body is never yours, and that others are entitled to touch your body at will? How do you navigate your unworthiness following any of these experiences? This is the harm Daddy's sexual and physical abuse left me to negotiate my way through. The abuse perpetrated by my father gets to the root of all of this. It required that I make these connections.

My father died in December of 1984, just shy of his sixtieth birthday. Many years after my father died, I had another conversation with my mother about my father's abuse of me. This time, it was not as superficial as before. That conversation occurred in 2008 after my second bout with colon cancer. I would spend every other weekend with my mother when I took chemotherapy. She insisted on taking care of me from Friday until Monday when the nurse would arrive to disconnect me from the chemotherapy fanny pack I wore the entire weekend after receiving chemo all day. We had the opportunity to talk about many things, and one conversation was around Daddy's abusive behavior. In the second conversation with her, I asked my mother two questions: Would she have left my father if she had known about the sexual abuse, and what did she think about me writing about this abuse? Without any hesitation, she answered yes and, "Baby, do anything you believe you need to do. And if writing about it helps, please feel free to do so. I don't mind you doing this at all." I remember those affirming words to this date.

Both of my mother's responses brought me both relief and release from holding sexual abuse inside of me. At that time, it also lessened the desire for me to write about this experience. What I experienced was the freedom to not *have* to write out of anger of feeling unheard and unaffirmed. My mother affirmed and supported any decision I would make. Although I realized that 2008 was not the time to write this book, I knew that one day I would. This decision gave me time to discern my underlying feelings regarding my mother and other issues still impacting my behavior.

There were at least three lingering feelings of hurt that continued to leave me bound and without a voice to express the pain. One lingering feeling was my inability to understand why my mother could not intuitively sense what was going on in my life and protect me. The second lingering feeling is from the many years during and after the abuse of being afraid for any of my friends to come by the house, fearing they would be touched or treated inappropriately by my father. And the third lingering feeling, even until this day, was confusion around how love and violence existed simultaneously.

One more thing to note regarding my girlfriends: my need to protect them from being victims of what I was experiencing was paramount. I felt I needed to prevent any more injury, so keeping them out of the presence of my father was my overarching goal. In this, my childhood friendship process was stifled and hampered by the ghost of possibilities. I never felt easy with my female friends being in the same space, even with my presence, with Daddy. However, as it relates to the love and abuse actions and behaviors of my father, I was left with even more confusion and pain.

As her daughter, and according to my young way of thinking, my mother should have known that I was being abused. After all, I constantly wanted to go with her when she left the house. I begged her to let me leave with her. Could she not have sensed that something was wrong? Could she not have asked me why I was trying to leave with her? As much as I loved my mother, I held feelings of resentment towards her most of her life. This resentment hampered me from expressing my love more fully toward my mother as I had desired. I was stuck in this feeling until 2007, while she helped to care for me during my recovery from the chemotherapy phase with my second bout of colon cancer.

Where I never confronted my mother about her inactions, the time we spent intimately together enabled me to release any consternation I had thinking she failed to protect me. The truth is that she did not know, and my attempt at trying to understand why she did not know was hurting my inner child. My quest for understanding was not to fault my mother for not knowing what I was experiencing. I do not blame her for my abuse. I do not blame myself for the abuse. I blame my father for his choice to harm my mind, body, and spirit.

Daddy's tendencies regarding corporal punishment were severe. In his mood-swinging behaviors, I was whipped for offenses Daddy made up, and I was whipped for things that were real offenses against what I knew to be the rules of the house. Regardless, the beatings were the same: they occurred at the moment of the offense, I was always partially nude, and they were very painful and caused physical damage. The whippings generally involved having me remove the top half of my shirt. Many of the beatings took place with Daddy's thick black belt he always had visible on his bedroom door. He used it on my back to inflict painful welts. After such a whipping, my mother and I cried as she nursed my wounds with salve.

As an adult, these whippings reminded me of the flagellation/whippings done to enslaved Black people as punishment for not submitting to their master's wishes. As I grew older, learning the stories of enslaved Blacks and seeing these similarities re-surfaced the trauma I experienced from childhood and made it as real as it was during my childhood. I view Mother's actions of nursing my wounds and repeating words such as "*I keep telling you all to do the things your father says for you to be*" as synonymous with acts perpetrated on slaves (and beyond) to control their bodies, disempower, dehumanize, and create fear toward total submission to their captors. These feelings, fears, and scars continued into my adult years. As an adult, I began to connect these whippings to the sexual violence. In many ways, they felt the same.

One of those offenses continues to grieve my spirit. We were at our family's home church that my grandfather founded. I cannot remember how old I was, but I was younger than twelve years old, and I am not certain why this incident happened because it took place so quickly. Daddy and others were trying to lift his wheelchair-bound mother up the few stairs into the church sanctuary. As they were lifting the wheelchair and going up the stairs, I was behind them preparing to enter the sanctuary when all of a sudden Daddy kicked me out of his way. This caused me to fall down the stairs and back into the narthex. Although I was not physically injured, I was emotionally wounded and the depth of that pain has never gone away. I felt ashamed that the same Daddy that crept into my room at night to get his sexual needs met would at the same time want to injure me to that extent. I was hurt on the emotional level, shamed, and felt as if I meant nothing to my father.

One level of confusion was my thinking about how someone could violate me with these physical whippings and in the next moments have me sit on his lap, hug him, and demand that I tell him I love him. Sitting on Daddy's lap felt like sexual abuse occurring again, and it was a part of my pain and his pleasure in demanding me to tell him I loved him. I complied. Consequently, the physical, emotional and sexual abuse experienced as a child and their connection to love continued to have a negative impact on my relationship choices even as I knew the difference intellectually. Equating violence and sexual abuse with love language, and claiming love is one of the consequences of the sexual trauma, shaped how I understood relationships as an adult.

Another consequence was never being able to understand my love for my father and what that would look or feel like. How do I negotiate the past trauma with the other joys, laughter, and good times I experienced in my family? Who was my father? Eventually, I began using social media, specifically Facebook, to learn from others who my Daddy was outside of being my abuser or the other pathologies I knew existed—this and to discover if the narrative I created about his whole personhood contained an authentic and accurate depiction of his life.

December 10, 2018, the anniversary of Daddy's passing, was no exception. I took to social media with this proclamation I posted on Facebook:

> I would not let this day go by without taking the time out to remember my father, who passed away on this date, December 10th, 1984. His death was an untimely death from blood clots following surgery. He was just eight days shy of his 60th birthday. Before he died, he served as the Associate Pastor for Sick Visitation for Trinity United Church of Christ under the Leadership of Rev. Dr. Jeremiah A. Wright Jr. He also served as the Founding Pastor on the near north side of Chicago for many years during much of my siblings' and my childhood through teenage years. However, one story many of you do not know has to do with my father's passing and my connection to this story. I received a call from my mother that he had taken a turn for the worse and that I should go to Michael Reese Hospital right away. The hospital was near my job location. I was working within the crime laboratory of the Police Department which was located very near to the hospital. Also, this day was special because I was one day shy of celebrating the anniversary of my 6th year as a Police Officer. I left immediately for the hospital and was the first person to arrive. Based on my experience as well as my mother telling me that the hospital staff informed her Daddy had "taken a turn for the worse," I quietly assumed he had already passed. After arriving at the hospital and evading the hospital staff who I knew would want me to gather in the small room where they would break the news to the family of his passing, I located Daddy's hospital room and quietly entered and shut the door. I stood by him just looking at him and reflecting. My emotions were all over the place. I finally left to join my family in the waiting room but was happy I got to spend those moments alone with Daddy. I had so much I wanted to say. A year later, I was enrolled in seminary and moving toward ordained ministry. My mother always said afterward, and for years until her death, in 2009, she believes Daddy's spirit entered me in some fashion and that this call, which I still can't explain in detail how or why it happened, was a result of our encounter in the room. Thirty years later I am still "one of them today"! Blessings Daddy, I love you! Continue to rest from your labor to reward.
>
> From your namesake, SLE (Sharon Lorraine Ellis)
> In memory, SLE (Samuel Lee Ellis)

As usual, after each year's post, Facebook responses swiftly arrived, filled with compliments and fond memories of Daddy from family members, church members, and those who knew him in other capacities. The following are a couple of statements paraphrased as examples of the compliments he received. Nancy reflected:

> I remember that day like it was yesterday. Rev. Ellis looked so very peaceful . . . I remember being in the room and everyone standing around him. They were singing and praying. What an awesome man of God he was. He had sat by my side after eye surgeries and prayed for me. I believe your mom was correct. You have been blessed with his servant's spirit!

Tanya recalled:

> He was quite a man of God, with a big heart, and great sense of humor! He and my mom were a pair when they got together! [lol]

Pearl remembered:

> How well do I remember. He always called me Sister Dancing . . . When he would see me, he would say here she comes. So profound could teach the Word.

Belinda rejoined:

> He will always hold a special place in my heart because it was in his sermon, "Try Tens," that I joined the church. Continue to rest peacefully, servant of God.

These responses, along with the many other remarks posted to Facebook, were a joy to read. First, they helped me to understand the significant contributions Daddy made in ministry and life. Second, they enabled me to hear from others about how they appreciated my father's ministry, his helpful ways, his deep theological stances, as well as his ability to preach and teach. They understood, appreciated, and respected my father, the gifts he brought to ministry, and the myriad ways he cared for others. Finally, and most importantly, these statements also helped me to crystalize my previous comments describing how the relationship was complicated. These stories allowed me to speak about how sexual abuse by him did not define the totality of our relationship as a family or him as an individual. I know Daddy was more than the person who sexually and physically abused me and more than the physically abusive one. This does not excuse his treatment of me or anyone else he had wronged. I am just saying that our relationship was complicated.

I am most grateful because I know at some point his life changed for the better. I no longer feel the need to post these memories anymore on the anniversary of my father's death. I decided to just let his life speak for itself and to allow his soul to rest in peace as I learn to be peaceful. I have learned more about my father in death than I knew or appreciated in his life. For me, that is joy. I thank those who through the years gifted me with their words. The words have become a part of my healing process.

I pray that these positive words will never be taken back because of Daddy's behavior toward me as well as others. What I do wish is that in Daddy's death and through the lens of my experience, we learn that life is more complicated than the words we use, the labels we give others, and the understandable disdain we feel toward our abusers, as well as the abuse of others. I make no apologies for my father's behavior toward me. I make no excuses for abusers of any sort. This behavior is wrong and there should be consequences. I do not know if Daddy had mental illness or not. I do not know the real cause or his need to do this to me. I can only describe him as I experienced him. But I have no name, other than the technical terms we have used over the years, for what and how we were as a family. This is mainly why I will always say it was a complicated and conflicted relationship. Yet this complicated and conflicted relationship added greatly to who I am today, and the feelings I experienced, as a result, are fluid. I feel a range of emotions. I mentioned at the end of my Facebook post about loving my father. I hold multiple truths within my body; multiple truths about Daddy; and they were each, at the time I experienced them, true.

Those who know of my experience have asked if I hate my father. As I have reflected over the years, sometimes the answer is "yes" and other times the answer is "no." Today, as I think about this question, it connects to what might be my ultimate pain of never really having a father. I was a product of a two-parent household without the benefit of normalcy or a paternal role model. Rather, it was pathological. In that reflection, the victims/survivors respond to the question again: Did I hate my father? While I didn't *hate* him, I just did not know how to love him while desiring to be fully loved by my father. The sexual abuse abruptly stopped somewhere between eighth grade and the beginning of high school.

This book cannot come close to telling you how this relationship with my father traumatized me way before I knew what trauma was. The trauma I experienced made me believe the abuse (sexual and physical) was always present. I eventually escaped what I had always believed to be an unsafe environment called home. Growing up, there were only three options for leaving home at eighteen: going away to college, joining the military, or getting married. The first two were not an option for me. I chose to set myself free through marriage. In December 1970, just before my eighteenth birthday, I got engaged. Five months later, I was married. I had fought my way to freedom. I did not begin to understand how difficult freedom would be. Even after his death, Daddy was still present. For many years, I experienced him coming out of the television set wearing his infamous striped pajamas and holding his thick black belt. I have had nightmares experiencing him in my bed, and me fighting to break free of him or forcing myself to wake up. To this day on some mornings, I hear him calling my name loud enough to wake me up. He would say one word, "Sharon." I believe I responded to this trauma the best I was able and with what power I had for the first eighteen years of my life. Yet, the harm had been done, and the struggle and consequences were real.

Reflection: Trauma and Impact of Childhood Abuse

Trauma is a natural response to life events, and there are natural body and mind reactions to the trauma. Our body/mind connection can cause us to respond in various ways. For example, we can run away from it. This is called *flight*. We can act out against it. This is called *fight*. Or we can do nothing about it. This is called *freeze*. These actions occur whenever someone feels threatened by potential emotional or physical harm. This is the case for many victims/survivors of sexual and domestic violence. In my life experiences of childhood sexual abuse, my response was always to *freeze* as I believed I had no other alternative. As an adult victim, however, I chose to take *flight*, as I demonstrated in leaving my parents' home, getting married, and in my multiple divorces. Yet, as an adult survivor, I was determined to not experience abuse of any kind again from anyone. My reactions were to *fight*. This knowledge helped to explain my responses within abusive and threatening situations, but it did not help in the guilt and shame I experienced from believing I could have made better choices.

Of course, as a child, these were not questions I could intellectually ask. Yet, my body acted it out as a child and as an adult through negative sexual behaviors, allowing others to take advantage of my body, allowing my body to be both sexually and physically violated, and making unhealthy relationship choices throughout my life. It was in the bedroom of my childhood where the embodiment of sexual and physical abuse took shape.

The answer was also located in my childhood home bedroom. Once upon a time, there was a place called home where I grew up with a story no one knew. It was in the bedroom of my childhood where I lost my belief in men and their ability to care for me. It was in the bedroom of my childhood where I lost my respect for sexual encounters. It was in the bedroom of my childhood where I learned my body could be used by any man if it could be used by my father. It was in the bedroom of my childhood where I learned I was not in control of my body or my sexuality. It was in the bedroom of my childhood where I learned to be still and not notice, believe, or feel what was going on. It was in the bedroom where I learned I was not worthy of any man's love. It was in the bedroom of my childhood where I learned I was not worthy of being a priority or worthy of respect and love. It was in the bedroom of my childhood where I learned my job was to be still, compliant, silent, and submissive. It was in the bedroom of my childhood where I learned the meaning of objectification. And it was in the bedroom of my childhood where I learned I could be harmed by others, and they could feel free to act with impunity. It all began in my family of origin's home, in my bedroom, where I had already learned subconsciously and received in mind, body, and spirit who I would become as an adult survivor of childhood abuse and its impact. I needed to get to the root of the matter for the sake of moving toward wholeness and wellness.

The CDC-Kaiser study offers a list of what experiences can be classified as adverse childhood experiences (ACEs):[1]

- experiencing violence, abuse, or neglect
- witnessing violence in the home or community
- having a family member attempt or die by suicide

Also included are aspects of the child's environment that can undermine their sense of safety, stability, and bonding, such as growing up in a household with:

1. "Adverse Childhood Experiences."

- substance use problems
- mental health problems
- instability due to parental separation or household members being in jail or prison

This list is not exhaustive of the examples of ACEs, and it is noted that these experiences can be prevented.[2] Please note the examples above are not meant to be a complete list of adverse experiences as there are many other traumatic experiences that could impact health and well-being.

CDC-Kaiser's "Adverse Childhood Experience" study details the impact of abuse on children across their life span. Two-thirds had experienced at least one ACE and one in five experienced three. These can have a lasting impact on their long-term health and well-being. And, in addition "can have a tremendous impact on future violence, victimization, and perpetration, and lifelong health and opportunity."[3]

The book *The Courage to Heal* by Ellen Bass and Laura Davis speaks specifically to adult women survivors of childhood sexual abuse. Some effects on women survivors mentioned are "a lack of trust, intimacy, and sexuality."[4] The authors are aware of two important factors. First, adult survivors, like me, may not know whether or not they were victims of childhood sexual assault. Second, they are aware survivors may have difficulty admitting they were abused. On the issue of determining if you are a victim of sexual abuse, the authors offer a series of indicators. When you were a young child or teenager were you:

- fondled, kissed, or held for an adult's sexual gratification?
- forced to perform oral sex?
- raped or otherwise penetrated?
- made to watch sexual acts?
- subjected to excessive talk about sex?
- fondled or hurt genitally while being bathed?
- subjected to unnecessary medical treatments that satisfied an adult's sexual needs?
- shown sexual movies or other pornography?

2. "Adverse Childhood Experiences."
3. "Adverse Childhood Experiences."
4. Bass and Davis, *The Courage to Heal*, xvi.

- Forced to take part in ritualized abuse in which you were physically, psychologically, or sexually tortured?[5]

The second issue of acknowledging that you were sexually abused resonates with me. My father was also a pastor. When I began writing I had difficulty naming my father as the one who sexually abused me. In my initial writing of chapter 1, I mentioned my father as committing clergy abuse as I had learned about boundary training through my work at FaithTrust Institute (Seattle, WA). When a friend and colleague read that section of my paper, she called me and challenged me on how I described my father. I then realized that naming the abuse as a clergy boundary violation, which I had experienced in my lifetime, was easier than admitting to myself and the world that my father both physically and sexually abused me. I had to return to the chapter to actually name the abuse and the perpetrator.

I am grateful to Bass and Davis for empowering me to name the elephant in the room and the accompanying shame felt by adult victims/survivors of childhood sexual abuse. They reassure us, "It is not easy to acknowledge that you were abused. But that acknowledgment is the first step in healing."[6]

Healing is possible even if, in the end, it feels differently than what you imagine healing to feel like. It happens when we learn to engage in self care and when we learn that self care is not the same as being selfish. It happens when we become advocates for change within our communities and speak out against sexual and interpersonal violence. It happens when we challenge institutions and individuals who engage in racist, sexist, misogynistic, patriarchal, homophobic, and patriarchal behaviors, recognizing that all of these issues are interconnected. It happens when we formally and informally continue to study and learn more about these issues and challenge ourselves to become change agents and difference makers. It happens when we challenge religious institutions that have historically been oppressive to women as well as to LGBQT+ persons, and are otherwise disconnected toward issues that adversely affect women. And it happens when we decide to take full responsibility to do the work that brings about healing and wholeness in ourselves and the world.

---

5. Bass and Davis, *The Courage to Heal*, xxv.
6. Bass and Davis, *The Courage to Heal*, xxv.

Discussion

Marie Fortune, founder and senior analysist of FaithTrust Institute (Seattle, WA), formally known as the Center for the Prevention of Sexual and Domestic Violence, and author of *Sexual Violence: The Sin Revisited*, addresses how many church people describe the moral implication of their violence. She observes:

> Another common interpretation of the wrong of rape or sexual abuse articulated by survivors of childhood sexual abuse or abuse by clergy . . . is of having lost something as a way of describing the consequences of the betrayal of trusting the experience. In this they are reaching for a moral norm by which to establish the wrongness of their experience. Of course, the flaw here is that this language of "loss" completely avoids agency or responsibility on the perpetrator. The passive voice of loss ultimately reflects on the survivor and her or his carelessness in "losing" something valuable. This is a reasonable effort again within a patriarchal context in which support for placing responsibility for an offense (betrayal of trust and violation of boundaries) on the person with the power (parents, teachers,waslergy, etc.) is unlikely.[7]

Here Fortune clearly states that women or men who are sexually abused have experienced a theft because "something is being taken away."[8] It is not about losing something. It is about something being stolen, thus the poem below is titled, "Stolen, Not Lost":

- Based on Fortune's theological and ethical dialogue above, coupled with the poem below, how do you situate sexual violence in general during a time when women are blamed and shamed for their own victimization?

- How does Fortune's theological assumptions impact your thinking about adult survivors of sexual abuse?

---

7. Fortune, *Sexual Violence*, 70–71.
8. Fortune, *Sexual Violence*, 70–71.

Poem: "Stolen, Not Lost"[9]

I learned a valuable lesson today about responsibility. I now know where to leave the shame and blame. I am beginning to discover the truth—many of my precious gifts were stolen, not lost! You stole my unquestioned belief in my Heavenly Father's love; you stole the preciousness of solitude in God's presence. You stole the joy of coming together to share the Eucharist.

You stole my reverence for the deep meaning of a church family. You stole my ability to be quiet and hear God's voice. You stole my belief in the phrase, "God answers prayers." You stole the joy I felt in calling myself, "Christian." You stole my ability to find comfort in going to confession. You stole my innocence and twisted my trust in mankind. You stole my hope for a better tomorrow and instilled doubt.

You stole my love of life and wanting to live. You stole my belief in the basic goodness of people. You stole a significant part of my childhood and adolescence. You stole my desire to become a loving adult woman. You stole my right to easily risk council without suspicion. You stole the inner peace I experienced entering God's house.

You stole my many treasures, and guilt is yours. Someday, you will answer to God for your many thefts. Someday, justice will be based on the evilness of your actions. Today, I leave the responsibility at your feet, where it belongs.

Today, I was given a profound gift and hope for tomorrow. I was helped to see your behavior in the truest light. I choose not to be forever damaged by your multiple thefts. I choose to fight to regain my stolen gifts, as that is my right.

I will grieve those stolen gifts that will always be blemished. I will strive to be wiser and not cynical because of your thefts. I will go forward strengthened in faith as I know the truth—"So many of my precious treasures were stolen, not lost!"[10]

---

9. Reprinted with permission by the owner, FaithTrust Institute. Composed by Marian Lovelace (1993), a survivor of childhood abuse by multiple Catholic priests. She illustrates the difference between something you lost and something that has been taken away from you.

10. Fortune, *Sexual Violence*, 70–71.

Chapter 2

The Escape Plan

HAVING AN ESCAPE PLAN called *marriage* turned out to be not at all what I expected. At eighteen years old, I had no idea of how being in love was supposed to feel or how to express and act out those feelings in a relationship. In fact, the only conversation I remember having about love was with my mother. It was not really a conversation. Rather, it was something my mother often cited when the word *love* came up in our family conversation. Mamma would look at us and say in her comedic voice, "You know what love is? Love is something shaped like a lizard, you hold it tight around the neck and squeeze it by the gizzard." When my mother said these words, it caused all of us to laugh no matter how many times she said it. This definition is always my go-to today, not because it made sense to me, but because it made me laugh, and I wanted others to laugh also. I am still unaware if this phrase has any real meaning. Perhaps it was some "ancient Chinese secret"[1]—spoken tongue-in-cheek.

Yet, I knew nothing at all about love except to proclaim that we were in love, announcing our engagement as I showed off my ring to my parents during the Christmas holidays of 1969. This was five months before my eighteenth birthday. What I did have access to during my pre-teen years until I turned eighteen years of age were my coveted love/romance stories from a popular magazine of my day, *True Confessions*, family-themed sitcoms, and music of the 60s and 70s. These became my primary models for how to approach relationships alongside internalized childhood experiences of sexual and physical violence.

---

1. This was a 1970s commercial tagline used by Calgon Water Softener laundry detergent.

True Confessions was nothing like the medium-to-hardcore pornographic magazines that exist today. However, although it was on display and could be purchased by anyone, it was a hot item for us teens and not allowed in our household. Consequently, the reading headquarters was in my bed at night with the cover over my head to shield the flashlight beam. I used to read the tantalizing romance stories contained therein. The magazine consisted of love and lust stories that always involved descriptions of some type of sexualized act. Reading the magazines offered me, at the least, an opportunity to think about how lovemaking happens and what romance could feel like. The stories of love and romance, coupled with the description of sex acts, made me long to experience these feelings in relationship with boys and later with adult men.

I could see myself enjoying sex and romance. It provided a fantasy world that could one day be a reality. However, it was by the television sitcoms of the late 60s and 70s that I was ultimately influenced, especially as it related to love and marriage. The messages of these sitcoms shaped my understanding of what marriage should be and is where I developed my ideal and model for loving married relationships and eventually having children.

Television sitcoms of the late 60s and some of the 70s, such as *Father Knows Best, The Lucy Show, The Brady Bunch, My Three Sons,* and *The Partridge Family,* became my standard of how a picture-perfect marriage should look and feel. These sitcoms gave me a collective ideal of how love and marriage worked. Some of the ideals I conceptualized from sitcoms were:

- Love meant happiness was natural and came easy.
- Marriage was a happily-ever-after guarantee.
- If there were arguments, they would be resolved quickly.
- Communication was *the* key to a happy marriage.
- Marriage equaled fidelity.
- Family vacations and time spent together as a family was understood and desired.
- Home included a white picket fence, 2.5 children, and a dog.
- Every family had a station wagon and took vacations together regularly.

My favorite of the sitcoms was *The Brady Bunch*. Its catchy tune and theme song remains in my memory bank and influenced me the most. This sitcom's theme song left an impression on me as a young adult, and even today it conjures up pseudo-romantic feelings and a desire to return to these ideals. The lyrics are:

> *Here's the story of a lovely lady who was bringing up three very lovely girls.*
> *All of them had hair of gold like their mother, the youngest one in curls.*
> *It's the story of a man named Brady who was busy with three boys of his own.*
> *They were four men living all together, yet they were all alone.*
> *Till the one day when the lady met this fellow.*
> *And they knew that it was much more than a hunch,*
> *that this group must somehow form a family.*
> *That's the way we all became the Brady bunch.*
> *The Brady bunch, the Brady bunch.*
> *That's the way we became the Brady bunch.*

It is obvious today that so many of my generation think of the Brady Bunch as the ideal family model. Or at least it was the ideal TV model for family life. We loved to sing the song. We loved this family as if they were our own family. The Brady Bunch is iconic, so much so that they have recently renovated their sitcom home, and the family, in this process, has been invited to several television late-night shows. Moreover, some of those who loved them, as I did, may experience them as a model for their relationships. Having grown up in such a confusing, sexually and physically violent household filled with infidelity, this family more than others became my model. This was not an intentional process. It was a subconscious process and, unbeknownst to me, this sitcom had shaped my entire life and relationship expectations, shaped my worldview, and shaped my concept of love, relationships, and especially of marriage.

Although I was in a supposedly ideal household consisting of mother, father, and siblings, the sitcoms signified what I desired in the perfect family. And perhaps that is the clue. The sitcoms represented what I desired. I desired to know what real love was and what constituted family love. The sitcoms represented this for me. Consequently, I defaulted to the sitcom examples where life was simple and troubles don't last forever. My default notions consisted of a home where children were protected and loved, families stuck together, home was safe, and vacations together were part of the norm.

This was my goal as I entered into a marriage that was doomed to fail from the beginning because of the standards I brought into this commitment. I was mesmerized watching the show, and every single scene added to my romantic and idealistic definition of how life ought to be. Again, expectations continued long into my adult life and, even now, continue to creep into my fantasy of what marriage should be like, although I know better.

Music was and continues to be vital in my life. Just as in my childhood, there seemed to be a song for every feeling that existed. No matter what you think, feel, need, experience, and hope for, music is always there to help shape that narrative into desired expectations. Of course, the romance records were my go-to as I thought more about relationships. Although I heard the break-up songs, the make-up songs, and the horrible relationship songs, the romance music stuck in my heart, mind, and soul. These contained the melody of my longings. All three of these mediums—*True Confessions* magazines, sitcoms, and romantic lyrics—became in many ways the image that I continued to search for in life and in my dreams.

These were my realities of marriage. This is the attitude I took that evening when we broke the news to my parents that we were engaged while simultaneously waving my ring finger around, showing it off to the rest of the family. No, I did not know what love was, but I learned how things would work out through sitcoms, and that was enough for me. These ideals were even powerful enough for me to deny internally the real reason I was getting engaged and married—to escape the pain and sadness that continuously shadowed my home life—even though there were plenty of good times to remember and draw upon.

My fiancée, Buck, was one year older than me. I am not certain how, when, or if Buck fell in love with me, nor I with him. It is possible that we were never in love with one another. I literally have no memory of our dating process. I do remember that he and my sister's former husband, Nod, were first cousins and our families knew each other through their marriage. But we did not know Buck in the same way. As families, we spent holidays together at my parents' house, played cards, and often as youth we visited each other's church. Although the relationship is different now, we all remain connected in various ways. I remember Nod had a brother that I really thought was handsome, or as we would say in our youth, he was really cute. I remember wanting to date him, but he had a girlfriend, and they seemed to be inseparable. However, when Buck came on the scene was not clear to me. Buck's presence made the family connection wider. It was a natural connection because everyone on his side was already family friends. We were both young, so does it really matter how or when we fell in love? Perhaps Buck also had a story that motivated him to get married young. Perhaps fate called us together to escape whatever we each needed to escape.

Of course, after I/we announced our engagement, my parents gave us the talk about the ins and outs of marriage and our being so young, seventeen and eighteen, respectively. We listened and convincingly stated we were ready. I went full speed ahead into my new life. Our marriage took place in August of 1970, approximately five months after my high school graduation. Today, I wonder why my parents were not more aggressive in insisting we *not* marry, especially because we were young. Perhaps one part of the equation was that Daddy might have had residual guilt from his sexually violent behavior toward me, or perhaps he simply wanted to see me happy. My mother, who was at least aware of the physical impact of Daddy's disciplinary tactics, mood swings, etc., in some way might have been glad to see me making my exit. I really believe this to be her truth, because right after my marriage to my current husband in 2003, she said to me, "I can finally have peace and rest knowing that you have someone in your life who loves you and can make you happy, feel safe, and care for you. I am confident now that I can finally rest knowing this. He is a good man, and I love him, too."

Yes, I believe that is where she was then, and in 2003 she was finally convinced. Or, perhaps they both understood I was stubborn and, as a newly grown woman, they knew I would make my own choices. Or perhaps they simply believed me and decided to let well enough alone and plan for the wedding. Life will always hold more questions than answers. Nevertheless, it was August 1970, and I had finally found freedom, safety, and independence. Love or no love, I was ready to give marriage my all.

As I reflect on my television role models of the past, I sincerely believed I could do my part to make a happy marriage. Buck and I had our first child, Ozell; we separated not long after he was born. There were some significant events that occurred within our marriage that facilitated our early separation and eventual divorce. Two events involved my sincere but failed efforts to be the perfect wife. Another factor revolved around infidelity, which led me on a downward spiral mentally, spiritually, and physically.

As I write about these events, they seem to be so trivial that it embarrasses me to even speak about them in this space. Yet, the connections to my future actions require these stories to be told. As a *good wife*, I made certain I cooked for my husband daily. Isn't that what a wife is supposed to do? Being a *good wife* was the ideal, versus simply a woman who runs the street, hangs out in taverns, has multiple sex partners, and was what I heard men refer to "as easy." I wanted to be that *good wife*, and all my actions in this short-lived marriage sought that ideal.

My husband worked in the afternoons and did not get off of work until 11:00 p.m. Although 11:00 p.m. was late for thinking about dinner, my quest to be the *good wife* drove my determination to care for him in this way. My goal was to ensure that when my husband came home from work, he would see me looking my best when I greeted him, and to have my version of a well-cooked meal with elaborate table settings (tablecloths, real silverware, salt, and pepper shakers, etc.). This would say to him, "I'm doing something special just for you." The very first time I implemented this plan left a lasting impression. My husband came home from work. I greeted him with a kiss and fully dressed as if I had never been to bed. We sat down at the table together to eat. I was feeling pretty proud of myself for the wifely efforts I had made. My husband picked up his fork, got some spaghetti, ate it, spit it out, and announced to me that the spaghetti was nasty. I was devastated. I silently cried. I could not believe that this would be his only reaction to all my efforts.

Certainly, that is not how that would have happened on my sitcoms. In that reality, I would be appreciated and gently led into how I could cook this dish better. Or perhaps he would eat the spaghetti and make the sacrifice to tolerate it for my well-being. Regardless, I was determined to continue this pattern in my desires to strengthen our marriage and bond with one another. My efforts were fruitless. Even today, I remember this story as if it happened yesterday. On the rare occasions I have had encounters with my now ex-husband, we laugh reminiscing about those days. His response is always the same, "Girl, are you still talking about that?" My response is always, "yes." This story, as well as the one of infidelity, are all etched in my memory bank of hurtful and painful events that occurred in my life and would change how I think and act.

Determined to be the wife I should be, I kept making dinner until suddenly he stopped coming home directly at night. His routine of coming home late became a pattern. I am not certain if I thought he was having an affair or not. All I remember thinking is that he had something to do that was more important than coming home to me. I thought possibly the honeymoon was over, as I heard others say about marriage when talking about how all of the argument-free, stress-free, and happily-ever-after parts of a new marriage ends.

This caused us to argue more as I sought answers to why he could not come straight home after work. I found myself increasingly irritated with him. It began to seem that all of our morning and late-night communication was filled with hostility, and it seemed like these arguments did not faze him at all. Where I do not remember the arguments, I am certain it eventually became about my believing there could possibly be another woman involved in these conversations. Not only was he coming home late at night, he was away more during the day, and weekends seemed to find him some place other than home. Then, when he was off work and home in the late evenings, Buck was fine being in another room at night while I was asleep in our bedroom.

Of course, I stopped cooking late-night dinners or often not cooking at all. I was becoming apathetic and disinterested in him. I had little regard for him in general. I had lost my desire to please him. And by this time, I was convinced he was involved in another relationship. One evening, I was asleep in our bed and he was awake in the room where he hung out at night. I woke up and it was dark, so I knew, having gone to sleep early, that I had been sleeping for a while. For some reason, I picked up the phone in our bedroom (there were no cell phones then). To my surprise he was talking to another woman. I interrupted the call by asking him whom he was talking to while the three of us were on the line. The woman hung up and my husband stayed in the front with no intentions of coming into our bedroom to explain himself. Of course, I knew now that a woman was involved.

I became rageful, argumentative, and very disrespectful of him with name calling and demeaning words (curse words). Any of these moments between us could have turned violent. One day, I said something so horrible to Buck that before I said what I said, I made certain the front door was open so that, when he came after me, I would already have a clear path to run from him and out of the house. I said what I had to say to him and he came after me. Thankfully, my home escape route worked.

This marriage came to a head one day when the verification came in person that he was actually having an affair. I was young and pretty naive about life, but somehow I was able to find out who the woman was he was having an affair with. My husband had gotten sick and had to go to the hospital. He was diagnosed with a sexually transmitted disease. The term he used evades my mind. However, that became another argument between us. Buck convinced me that this did not come from having sex and that it could have come from sitting on an infected toilet seat. I was still angry, but I believed him while at the same time still suspicious that he was lying. Then, I had the opportunity to talk to the woman. Either I had her number and called her or she simply called the house and I answered. Either way, I engaged her in a conversation.

She told me that there was no relationship between her and my husband. She repeated to me the same thing my husband said to me, "You can get a venereal disease without having sex." She added that they never had sex together, and as was the case with Buck, I believed her while at the same time suspecting that she was lying also.

Buck's relationship with this supposedly one woman was even more devastating to me than the food issue. Not only did I feel betrayed and hurt as a result of his behavior, but I also experienced health and embarrassing physical consequences related to him having unprotected sex. I was triggered by my father's infidelity as well as his incestuous relationship with me. It brought back memories of Daddy's infidelity while my mother did all she could to accommodate his needs, desires, and wants. I was triggered by my husband's cavalier attitude and the hundreds of lies he told proclaiming his innocence. I proceeded to go out of my way to prove my husband was lying, tricking him by saying I already had spoken with the woman (which was true), and that she had admitted to being in a relationship with him (which was untrue). Based on that information, I intimidated him into confessing, and he did.

My hurt turned into anger. These events alone triggered our constant arguments and volatility and caused me to not to want to have any sexual activity with him. I totally lost my trust in him and once again felt unsafe around him, both physically and emotionally. I felt, once again, in captivity. It also triggered my need to get revenge for what he had done to me. And I did. He never found out, but I returned the favor and had a sexual relationship with one of his friends in our house. We separated within the following year. He joined the military, and I became a single mom.

On reflection, I believe this marriage broke my naivete around the idea of the sitcom marriage. I came to some important conclusions that continued to impact my behavior. First, I no longer desired to be this *good wife*, nor did I desire to be a *good woman*. A good woman was the vernacular that men had on the streets who confessed to having affairs. The good woman was the one they loved at home, the outside women were the ones they had sex with while married without any intention of marrying them. The outside women were not worthy of marriage because their behaviors were not wife-material behaviors. My decision was to leave the good wife/good woman behavior model and go for what seemed to be my *more excellent way*. The more excellent way was to have relationships, but not have the burden of being a wife. The more excellent way was to have fun just being and doing whatever I wanted to when it came to relationships.

I decided that I would no longer marry, ever! My experience as a single woman showed me that single women are the ones who cheat with other women's husbands. They seemed to have the most fun. That fun became appealing to me. I developed an attitude of, "If you can't beat them, join them." I became attracted to this version of relationships versus the ideals of sitcom family life. This version seemed to be free of stress, sadness, and loneliness. I decided that instead of being the "married woman" being cheated on, I would become the "other woman." I guess in reality, if I compare this choice to criminality, I became the offender rather than the victim.

Although this was my first marriage, I immediately decided that married life was not for me. The triggers from my nuclear family and this marriage failure were enough to send me spiraling. I saw myself taking control of the decision to not be hurt again. The only choice I recognized was to become the outside woman, the free and adventurous woman, and the woman who could experience the joys of having affairs without the stress of being in a non-trusting relationship. This attitude surfaced and would live within me for many years. I never fully realized how this would hurt others. After all, I felt this life had to be better than the emotional pain I experienced through having an unfaithful, ungrateful, lying, and cheating husband. Switching roles post-separation sent me, once again, on a journey of escapism and a fight for a new kind of freedom. My one overarching goal was to not hurt anymore. Coupled with the *other woman* narrative, I adopted a familiar spoken belief that *all men were dogs*. I also set out to prove to myself that no matter how perfect a marriage seemed, the man will always ultimately cheat.

With this, the next year or so changed my direction to what I refer to now as *spiraling out of control*. Fueled with anger at men and disappointed with life in general, I engaged in the behavior of dating married men, proving that even if they claimed love for their wives they would have an affair, to becoming seriously attractive to men who were not emotionally available for me. The following scenarios demonstrate the reckless behaviors I engaged in during that period of time. Each name mentioned represents an aggregate of multiple engagements that indicated a pattern of behavior I had adopted.

I will name him Tim. I met Tim in a lounge my girlfriend and I visited quite often. He was not married, but he had a close and long-term on-and-off relationship. From the beginning, I knew they were obviously a couple. They both were familiar with each other's dance moves, and you could tell they had great chemistry together whether they were dancing or arguing. I knew that and had observed that. This made Tim my ideal person to prove my point about men's willingness to be unfaithful. Through manipulation, I got Tim's attention at various times when he was alone, and not long after that, we were in a sexual relationship together. Got him! Once again, I had proven my point. I felt as if now I was holding my little secret from the man's partner and that I knew things about her man she did not know. This gave me a strange sense of achievement.

I met him in a lounge also. I barely knew him when we began a sexual relationship. One night, I received a call from someone I believed was Tim, who asked if he could come to my house. It was late at night. Most likely, he had been out at the lounge and needed a place to land for a few moments, so he called me. I told him that he could come over. It was dark in the house, and I opened the door without turning on any lights, and we went straight to my bedroom. After an hour or so, he got up, dressed, and left. It was not until moments later that I begin to ponder and doubt whether it was Tim who had come to my house. My certainty turned to doubt. To this day, I do not know who I let in my house that night. I felt embarrassed, afraid, and shameful. However, none of these feelings gave me the motivation to stop. There seemed to be no limit or boundary to my behavior.

I got to the point of dating a married man under the pretense that we were in a real relationship, while all I desired to do was to get his phone number and tell his wife we were dating. When he arrived home, he caught hell from his wife so intensely that he called my parents to talk with me. My parents arrived at my door late one night. I let them in and to my surprise, they were there to confront me about messing with that man's wife. His presence initiated my anger at him and at his hypocrisy, and I immediately asked him out of my house. The nerve of him telling me anything about moral behavior! I was grown, and certainly my father was not going to grill me about messing with someone's husband or calling his wife. Surely, he was not there to do that! My mother was a tagalong trying to make certain I would be okay around my father. I never talked directly to her. My grown-ness was talking directly to him. They left with a life warning about my behavior. I was silent when they walked out the door. I never saw the guy again, but that was okay, there were plenty more cheating husbands where he came from. Some encounters were brief and others lasted longer. One in particular lasted several years. My conversation with any of these men prior to any type of relationship would always emphasize *no strings attached*. This meant, "You owe me nothing and I owe you nothing in this relationship." I was not looking for marriage or any type of committed relationship.

The fallacy, however, was that as much as my actions were designed to create a new me and to help me become that person who would never be hurt again, the tables were turned. I realized that I was only hurting myself and engaging in self-sabotaging behaviors. This left me with a sense of intense loneliness. I felt defeated and unworthy of a relationship where I was fully cared for. A part of my brain knew that I was a one-man woman and valued committed relationships. It was as if one side of my brain fully leaned into my newly created self, and the other side of my brain was always there to remind me this was not really the life I desired to live. However, the vulnerable part of my brain that knew the real me refused to set itself free to be that person. The voice very plain to me was the one stemming from the fortress I had built around that truth which only allowed that part of the brain to deliver the false messages that continued to bring turmoil and strife into my already sad state of mind. The sitcoms were no longer a helpful piece of my brain function, the music changed from romantic to songs of a broken and sad heart. And the *True Confessions* magazine vision was long gone.

The sad part of this narrative was that none of these sexualized encounters brought me any satisfaction, as my mind and body was so disconnected from receiving pleasure. This included the possibility of having a self-fulfilling sexual relationship with anyone. My mistrust of and hatred of men, coupled with the shame of my childhood experience of sexualized behavior with my father, blocked anything in me that would cause me to desire and act out any fantasy of enjoyable sexual relationships. What I was doing instead was allowing my body to be battered and used in the same way it was as a child. I was just there quietly, allowing my body to be used. My participation was absent. I had embodied my sexual abuse and become that person I hated. However, this awareness did not come close to stopping my quest. Trust issues, anger at men, and my need to avoid hurt and pain, along with other factors, were the catalyst for my continued behavior to the detriment of my mind, body, and spirit.

In a strange way, I felt safer hurting myself than trusting that others would not hurt me. This mindset gave me a sense of control over my pain. In my mind, even if I was hurting, I knew the source of my pain came from my actions and not the actions of others. This lifestyle continued to be my tactic toward survival. Just as with other addictions, I exchanged one style of toxic behavior for another. It did not matter how many tears I shed when I was alone. It did not matter that I felt as if my physical body was used and that I was becoming someone I did not recognize. I had no way of understanding or knowing that my childhood experience of sexual abuse was now being embodied in my relationship with men, as if I had inherited an abusive gene from my father. In the midst of engaging in self-sabotaging behavior, I managed to find places of happiness.

I had my son, Ozell. I loved him and he loved me. I had music, which had been my source of survival since I was young. There were songs for every feeling I experienced that would allow me to feel deeply and respond both with tears and feelings of elation, depending on the type of music I was listening to at any given time. Music continues to be my go-to when I need to live with various feelings or when I need assistance in changing my mood or behavior. I also had my sistergirl friendships. All of these continue to this day to give me life and hope. But these things never fulfilled my basic need to experience the love of a male. Therefore, my behavior continued in secret and unchecked until I met a man and eventually fell in love with him as I had grown to understand love.

His name was Wallace. I met him in a tavern that I frequented. We seemed to hit it off well. He liked to dance and so did I. He was fun loving and so was I. He seemed to be interested in me rather than my being interested in him. And he was eleven years older than me and much more attentive toward me than I had ever experienced. There was only one issue. Eventually, I discovered he was married. Because that boundary was still crossable for me, this fact was not an immediate concern. And, in this relationship, I was not a secret. I knew his family and friends. He had three children. The youngest son and my son were born the same month and year. Wallace often brought him over to my house because he was young and could not tell anyone about our relationship. I grew attached to him. Wallace and I went on vacation together. He spent nights at my house. The relationship seemed real, and I am convinced he did love me. I was as happy as I had ever been in a relationship. I felt that whatever was going on in his marriage, he chose to be with me. That was until I discovered that Wallace was not only unfaithful with me, but there were other side women.

Neither divorcing nor dismissing his other concubines was ever a consideration. He was clear how he was going to live and set up those boundaries of our relationship. One time, Wallace told me he wished he could put my traits into his wife. That hit me hard straight in the gut. It felt like a ton of bricks had fallen on me. He did not want me, he wanted his wife, but differently, and I was that model for different. I continued in the relationship while also being a pseudo-detective. I was tracking him down, attempting to catch him in unsavory behavior with women as if he were my husband and belonged to me. Those chases did prove what I suspected. He knew I was doing this, but it was like a game to him. I had been, for a time, faithful to him because I wanted to be with him. However, these events turned me back to self-preservation mode.

At that point in my life, I had begun to pick up new interests. Bowling in a league was one of them. Bowling helped me to engage in healthy competition, and I began meeting crowds who truly had a passion for the sport, and that was attractive. During this time, I met a kind man named Judge. Judge and I became friends and eventually it blossomed into a relationship. I was still committed to Wallace and felt I was in love with him. However, as was true of most of the men I met, Wallace was married. I needed to have something else in my life to fill that void I had been pretending not to have all along this *new me* journey.

Guess what? Judge was single! He had an apartment I could actually visit. He never came to my house, but I visited him. Visiting another man's house was an experience that I had never known, and it was wonderful having the freedom to do so. It is interesting that I never tried to have a relationship with Judge. He was nice, respectful, available, and great to be with. I guess the fact that Judge was actually available frightened me. He was available for me to pursue as someone in my life that I could be in a relationship with. Unmarried and available men were not suitable for my mind games charged with hate, anger, and revengeful behavior toward married men. Thus, Judge was not targeted in my then-dominant reality.

There was no real relationship between us and no real expectations from me. It felt great being with Judge because of his availability to me. He was actually single. Yet, if love was budding with him, I did not allow it to blossom. I was still holding on to Wallace, the one who was not available to me and the one I claimed to love. My relationship with Judge, which included a sexual relationship, helped me to not feel as lonely and it fulfilled that still-buried desire to have someone as my own. Another escape. The relationship was brief, we remained friends, and continued to bowl in the same league.

Soon after, I became pregnant with my second child. When I told Wallace I was pregnant, he had one question. He asked me what I wanted from him as a father. I responded, "To be a good father." And of course, that is what I really wanted. I had returned to my original false narrative, which denied any need for a loving, married relationship. Yet my denial of my real feelings resulted in more anger. My anger resulted in me searching for ways to let his wife know about me. I found ways to get her telephone number and began calling her and hanging up. I believe, as I had done before, I wanted to let her know that I was dating her husband. I wanted her to be angry and leave so I could be with him. I wanted to annoy her to avoid him having peace when he returned home. I was just angry that I did not have him for myself. Then it finally happened: I introduced myself to her as Wallace's girlfriend. In retrospect, I noticed this pattern.

Whenever I allowed myself to be vulnerable enough to feel loneliness and sadness, anger would emerge and I would do something stupid like bother the spouse of the person I was dating at the time. It was that mood that caused me to pick up the telephone and call Wallace's spouse. I gave birth to my daughter, Sharell, in 1975. With two children who I loved deeply, I became protective of them and decided I could not place them in harm's way with my crazy and careless behavior. In addition to being protective of my children, I had begun reflecting on and beginning the internal process of ending this relationship with Wallace.

For some reason, I decided to go to the Bureau of Vital Statistics to get a copy of Wallace's marriage license. When I received the license and read it, I could not believe what I was reading. While they were indeed married now, Wallace and his wife were not married at the beginning of our relationship. They were living together. He married her during our time in a relationship. Wow! That one really hurt, but instead of processing what I needed to feel about this, my anger and indignation kicked in.

This is when I knew I could also be a drama queen. I began to lie to Wallace about how I obtained the marriage license. I told him, while crying my eyes out, that his wife came by and left this in my mailbox as I shoved the license into his hands. I believe this was meant to be my last-ditch effort to make him angry enough to leave her. The hurt expressed was genuine even in the midst of the lie of how I obtained the marriage license. Being vulnerable enough to show that hurt in its reality was not an option for me. So, I guess this became my way of showing hurt. As the saying goes, *hurt people hurt people.*

The reality is, he was with her and I knew it. It did not matter that he was not married to her. In reality, he was married, although not legally. So, the marriage license did not excuse my choice to date him. I knew he had three children. And I knew this was a partnership that had existed for over twenty years. So, yes, it was all drama aimed at manipulation, which was successful. This is really when I began the reflection required to put in place a plan to turn my life in a new and positive direction.

I had a heart-to-heart talk with Wallace expressing that, although I was not ending our relationship directly, I was beginning the process of doing so. We both agreed to see each other less and less until it simply faded away. This was my first move in the direction of sincere reflection regarding what I wanted for my life and coming to terms with the fact I was not being faithful to myself. Although we continued seeing one another, we both knew the relationship was headed toward an eventual end. This was a major accomplishment for me. I found the strength to have that talk with him and become vulnerable enough to say it was not working for me. One other move I made was to reflect on what career I wanted to pursue. I was ready to return to exploring post-high school opportunities.

I had a high school education. After graduating from high school, I had no desire to pursue higher education. I thought about it but never pursued it. One day, I decided that I would apply to college and enrolled in the nursing program at Chicago State University. It was there where I realized I had a love for biology and other sciences. I was successful in school and had taken several nursing courses and engaged, as a student, in several specialized hospital sections. I developed experience in medical/surgery and neonatal positions as a nurse. My life was really changing and I felt it. I felt the change. I was in no way healed of anything, but I did find a path forward to feel more free of shame and self-blame over the choices I had made.

Pursuing a professional career was great for me. However, in the midst of it, I still had not totally lost my destructive self-sabotaging behavior pattern. I still wanted to see Wallace. Going back to school also served as an excellent way to distract me and slow me down from seeing him. I believe education, although a healthy option, became another way of avoiding realities, keeping my sanity by keeping busy. In addition to going to college and pursuing a nursing career, I was offered the opportunity to take the police examination to become a police officer. A year later, I became a police recruit with the city of Chicago.

The police officer position was my first career opportunity. When called to take the physical to become a police officer, I refused. My life was going halfway well. I did not want to interrupt this growth and development that was ridding me of my negative behaviors. I decided to continue pursuing my nursing degree. However—something that never happens within the department and that has not happened since—unsolicited, the police department gave me a second opportunity to take the physical and become a recruit. When the call came, I said yes to them and I thought to myself, "Why not?" I had not made the decision to take the job nor had any indication that I was really going to be hired. Having this second opportunity inspired me to follow through. The appointment was for me to report for the physical test, and if I passed, I would become a police officer. I went for the physical, passed the physical, and accepted the position of the police officer. This opportunity did not come without incident. I had a warrant out for my arrest for two misdemeanors that resulted in my arrest. But by the grace of God it was successfully resolved. I joined the department and postponed my education. I chose a career with a salary that would allow my children to live a viable life. On December 11, 1978, I joined the Chicago Police Department.

The years between the ages of eighteen and twenty-six were turbulent. I made many mistakes and would continue to do so for many more years to come. I continued in this transitional relationship with Wallace. I hurt others and others hurt me. During this period, I was not aware that the trauma I was experiencing was a result of my childhood abuse and its insidious effects on my behavior and my vulnerability of being used by men. Some of these effects, as I will mention later, were a lack of trust, difficulty in relationship building, decreased sexual appetite, and building a worldview that I believed would protect me from further harm. I was not at that level of sophistication and knowledge of what was occurring with me.

Still, I honor myself for even coming this far, and I contribute this to others who enfolded and held me close, my friends, family, and especially my mother. I still have lessons to learn, painful bridges to cross, and valleys I will experience. Now I will experience them with a little more knowledge, a little more strength, and a little more determination. I have learned how to proclaim and embrace my goodness while also feeling deeply how much I had hurt myself and others. I have not learned to fully forgive myself, and I still hold on to shame and anger. It is said that "water seeks its own level"—you attract who you are. I embraced the truth of this quote while owning up to my actions and who I was at that point in my life. Even then, this journey taught me that these levels do not define *who* I am, it just informs me of *how* I am. I was not what I ought to be, but certainly, I am not who I used to be. For this I am grateful!

Reflection: Trauma-Informed Pastoral Care Practices

Crisis situations, also known as crisis events, are different than an actual crisis response. However, a crisis event has the capacity to elevate into a full-blown crisis, whether the crisis occurred through violence in community, violence in our homes, violence within penal institutions, or global violence. Wherever the crisis situation originated, as it relates to violence it will inevitably lead to a full-blown crisis and trauma responses that can last a lifetime. I am not aware of any publication that ties both crises and trauma together. I believe in the case of personal and community violence it is always sparked by some time of crisis, and that crisis has a function. It can evoke more violence, and it can re-traumatize an individual or community based on past events. In these examples of crisis, the potential for both a crisis response and the resulting trauma is inevitable. Developing a trauma-informed pastoral care model can address both the crisis and the trauma to lessen the impact.

Here are three trauma-informed approaches to providing pastoral care to persons experiencing crises. Roslyn A. Karaban, a professor of ministry studies at St. Bernard's School of Theology in Rochester, New York, is certified in thanatology, the study of death, dying, and the care of families. In her book, *A Guide for Ministering to People in Crisis*, Karaban defines crisis as "an internal reaction to an external event and can be experienced by an individual family or a community."[2] In contrast, Resmaa Menakem, a licensed clinical social worker and author of *My Grandmother's Hands: Racialized Trauma and the Pathway to Mending Our Hearts and Bodies,* sees trauma as located in the body and refers to traumas as *retentions*. Menakem describes this retention as having lost its context.[3]

Shelly Rambo, assistant professor of theology at Boston University School of Theology is author of *Spirit and Trauma: A Theology of Remaining,* in which she presents various narratives of individuals who suffered a traumatic event, such as Hurricane Katrina. Hurricane Katrina violently and in a deadly way nearly destroyed New Orleans. Many of those who survived moved to other states, never to return. Survivors experienced trauma, and the memory of this traumatic event has never left them. In fact, it lives with them. In their minds, the event occurs over and over and never goes away. Rambo quotes one Hurricane Katrina survivor suffering the full impact of this natural disaster and traumatic event: "Things are not back to normal. People keep telling us to get over it already, the storm is gone, but after *the storm* is always here. It's always there."[4] Rambo categorizes this type of trauma as post-traumatic stress disorder. Her primary goal is to create a theology of suffering and what remains after. The book is dense and comprehensive where, at the end, she concludes what remains is love.[5]

Each of these books have so impacted my thinking regarding trauma and its impact on mind, body, and spirit that I refer to them in my course, "Pastoral Care in Times of Trauma and Crisis." The books remind me of the work laypersons, pastors, chaplains, pastoral care persons, and professors must engage in to provide appropriate trauma-informed pastoral care to victims/survivors of violence, including and especially victims/survivors of sexual and domestic violence. My work and language around trauma and crisis are deeply influenced by these authors. Each believe healing is possible. And while each has a different perspective of what healing looks like, all three provide ethical, moral, theological/spiritual, sociological, psychological, and historical frameworks for providing trauma-informed pastoral care.

2. Karaban, *Crisis Caring*, 3.
3. Menkem, *My Grandmother's Hands*, 39.
4. Rambo, *Spirit and Trauma*, 1–2.
5. Rambo, *Spirit and Trauma*, 132.

Consequently, trauma-informed pastoral care practices require preparation, information, and application skills. However, the key word is *trauma-informed*. As seminary professors, seminary students, laypersons, pastors, and chaplains, we are not required to be experts unless our educational pursuits lead to this specialty. Even if you have the expertise, know your role. As a pastoral caregiver, you are not acting in your position of expertise. What is required is that we be trauma-informed. To be trauma-informed requires reading, listening to the news, engaging in dialogue, fact-checking, and keeping an open mind to possibilities of care. With this knowledge, the hope is that you understand what trauma-informed care is appropriate. This knowledge lies with psychologists, sociologists, and other crisis-response trained personnel. We must collaborate with them to develop a culturally competent network of referrals in these areas of specialty. It also requires an acceptance of the basic principle that pastoral care is the role of the whole church and not simply the sole duty of the pastor and other designated lay leaders.

Pastors will have specific roles in offering trauma-informed pastoral care based on their relationship with victims/survivors, communities, and ties to outside organizations and structures. Where pastors have different roles in providing pastoral care, every member of the church should be considered a pastoral caregiver. In order to provide trauma-informed pastoral care practices with victims/survivors, perpetrators, and their families, there are pastoral qualities, values, skills, and principles one must have in order to be effective. In addition, in order for the congregation to fully lean into its caring role, the membership as well as the pastoral leadership must always examine and monitor their internal practices, which may actually re-traumatize victims/survivors.

Karaban lists seven qualities that are important in providing care at its most basic level before we can even speak of the values, skills, and principles also needed. These basics are respect, caring and compassion, prudence, courage, genuineness, assertiveness, and non-anxious presence.[6] At its most basic level, we have to rid ourselves of the temptation to judge others based on their race, class, social location, economic status, or who they choose to love. Karaban describes these as qualities necessary for being a crisis minister.[7]

---

6. Karaban, *Crisis Caring*, 35–39.
7. Karaban, *Crisis Caring*, 37.

We have the ability to project a non-judgmental presence in spite of our doctrinal, theological, and other biases that we have accumulated over time. If we are not able to perform this basic task, it would be better if we did not engage. It is the assumption that we as a faith community are present in caring for one another. We must be able to negotiate our inner feelings in order to care for one another. Karaban describes being caring and compassionate and concludes, "It is my assumption that we are in ministry because we care about people. When others are in pain . . . we are also pained and desire to help them with their pain."[8] Her statement on prudence helps us to understand that we don't have to be experts in this field to care. If a person is experiencing stress or is in a crisis, we have to be what she names as down-to-earth and have a pragmatic personality and resist our temptation to go off on tangents.[9] "Down-to-earth" in this context invites us all to provide basic comfort and care for those who are hurting. I have experienced laypersons and pastors attempting to be solution-oriented and desire to offer biblical principles that are at most times not necessary and, most importantly, not helpful to victims/survivors.

Practicality is what is missing in ministry to victims of violence. Practical questions such as, "Are you safe?" can be the most important questions you could ask. Another practical way to be present is to listen. Listening requires a skill called empathy. That involves listening to another's story without your judgments; that is, hearing that person tell their story and accept that story for what it is and not what you want to make it. Many of us have sympathy which simply refers to being sorry for someone. Empathy requires a different skill set. Karaban speaks of courage. Having empathy takes courage. Often when listening to the stories of others, our own triggers come to the surface as we remember incidents that occurred in our lives. We might be tempted to change the subject simply because we are not ready to have that particular conversation and the listening can cause distress. She cautions,

> Being with people in crisis is not for the fainthearted. As crisis ministers, we are called to listen to difficult stories of death and destruction that may seem overwhelming in helping people in crisis, such as battered women. We could be putting ourselves

---

8. Karaban, *Crisis Caring*, 37.
9. Karaban, *Crisis Caring*, 37.

in danger. It takes courage to listen to talks of trauma without giving in to despair.[10]

The final three qualities Karaban mentions are *genuineness*, which is similar to being prudent. And *assertiveness*, which again requires one having the ability to listen. And finally, having a *non-anxious presence*.

We cannot fake care. Victims/survivors can detect someone who does not have their best interest at heart or is struggling with their stories. Genuineness requires vulnerability and the ability to feel and express those feelings. Per Karaban, "We may temper our reactions as we provide counsel, but we do not deny we have feelings. We do not sit immobile as we hear of injustice and evil. We let people in crisis know that what they say affects us."[11] This requires a *non-anxious presence*, meaning we cannot allow our facial expressions or our behavior to exemplify fear or horror at what we hear.

Discussion

Look up the following and define:

- Trauma
- Post-traumatic stress disorder
- Vicarious trauma
- Compounded/Complex trauma
- Post-traumatic slave syndrome

How did your research inform how you will practice trauma-informed pastoral care in the future?

Activity: Referral List

Develop a referral list of at least ten culturally appropriate trauma-informed care specialists, along with their discipline, expertise, and how and to whom they would be most helpful.

---

10. Karaban, *Crisis Caring*, 38.
11. Karaban, *Crisis Caring*, 38.

Chapter 3

Sin, Shame, Guilt, and Dirty Stains

I KNEW BETTER. I learned better. I grew up better. My choices and behavior made no sense to me. Yet, I found myself making insane decisions that I knew, beyond any doubt, were totally wrong. My behavior was sinful, and I understood my actions placed me *out of a right relationship with God*. In our faith practice, to be out of a right relationship with God involved living a life that was contrary to the will God had for our lives. These thoughts were constantly going through my head with every negative behavior I found myself participating in. Before I reached eighteen years of age, these truths were already implanted in my psyche. There was never a time during my years of acting out that I was not reminded of these truths, whether it was through my memory, listening to preaching in church, or someone reminding me how my lifestyle was not according to the word and will of God. However, to read thus far one might believe I never saw the inside of a church or at least did not pay much attention to my spiritual life. On the contrary, to understand how my guilt operated and how, at times, it was denied and masked, here and moving forward it is imperative to offer some history that demonstrates many seeming contradictions between my faith and my actions within the contextual space of the Pentecostal church, especially from late adolescence into adulthood.

I was a church baby coming from a traditional Holiness family that was steeped in its faith. My earliest memories of going to church are when I was five or six years old. As I reflect on our family, I note that both my paternal grandfather and my maternal grandmother were founding pastors. My father was a founding pastor, also. Daddy pastored in several locations on the near north side of Chicago and he remained a pastor until 1967. Soon after I completed my first year of high school, we moved to the south side of Chicago, where we began worshipping again at his father's church, also known as our family home church, the church of my childhood.

As a young child, before my father left to become a solo pastor, I remember sitting in the front seat of my paternal grandfather's church and not being allowed to walk during services. If we left church, we could be assured that either my father, mother, or a member of the congregation would come to retrieve us and place us back in the spot where we belonged. I remember the outfits we wore, who attended, and the music we sang. However, what I remember most is the teaching, customs, and requirements of membership that were instilled in me as a child.

Growing up in the Black church Pentecostal tradition, I did know we were "Jesus only," meaning unless you were baptized in the name of Jesus, you were not legitimately baptized, and people who joined the church, if baptized in the name of the Father, Son, and Holy Spirit, had to be rebaptized. If you did not consent to being rebaptized, you could not participate in the ministries of the church and especially not in any leadership capacity. I knew before I ever read it in the Bible that there was one Lord, one faith, one baptism, and one God. The pastor added to this biblical proclamation, "And what's his name?" The congregation would loudly shout, "Jesus!" I heard preacher after preacher, including my father, proclaim from the pulpit there is no other way you can be saved but by the name of Jesus.

I remembered when you were baptized in the name of Jesus, you had to tarry for the Holy Ghost. And that Holy Ghost request to Jesus came with particularly required evidence—speaking in an unknown tongue. Tarrying on our knees was the preferred position to make this request. The seasoned saints who kneeled beside you instructed you to continuously say "Jesus" or "Thank you, Jesus" until Jesus entered your spirit and you began to speak in tongues. First, you said the words at a slow pace and were then encouraged to increase the pace gradually until you were saying the words faster and faster, which would lead into an ecstatic frenzied behavior that had you in a trance-like state speaking another language uncontrollably. When you publicly showed this "evidence" of speaking in tongues, you were declared and received as being saved and were now able to serve in the various ministries of the church. Only then could you proclaim victoriously these precious words, "*I am saved, sanctified, and filled with the precious gift of the Holy Ghost.*"

Did I ever experience this moment? Perhaps so, but without all of the drama others experienced. Or perhaps not. Perhaps I was simply doing what the culture expects of us in the church. After this proclamation, we were required to live lives of holiness. That is, as spoken about earlier, focusing solely on our relationship with God and not involving ourselves in the world, as we were often reminded to "be in the world but not of the world." I also remember as I was growing up being challenged by other adults who tested me to see if I was really saved.

Coming into adulthood, a work colleague of mine within the police department who attended a church of the same denomination located down the street from our family church, asked me a set of questions. He asked me if I was saved. I responded yes. He then asked me if I spoke in tongues. Again I responded yes. Then he asked me what language I spoke? Feeling irritated and judged by his incessant questioning, I refused to continue in conversation with him. It reminded me so much of my childhood experiences, as it related to the church and people who were judging me and my worthiness. This resulted in me always feeling unworthy and aware that I was denied the grace of pastors, preachers, and the saints who alone determined my worth.

This officer never engaged me again on this subject, but he had triggered my childhood trauma and left me angry, feeling worthless and ashamed—once again believing I did not pass his worthiness test. It is interesting that my pastor-father never challenged my nor anyone's worthiness within the church setting in his preaching and teaching. My feelings of unworthiness came only due to his abusive behavior toward me. Yet, he and others continued teaching the basics of what it meant in the Pentecostal church to live a life of holiness.

We knew those tenets well. They were basically located within the Ten Commandments, as recorded in the King James Version, the only Bible we were allowed to use. I refer to them as the *thou shalt nots* of the Bible, such as "Thou shalt not kill," "Thou shalt not steal," "Thou shalt not commit adultery," and "Thou shalt not use the Lord's name in vain" (Exod 20:2–17 KJV). I also knew the Scripture, "The wages of sin is death; but the gift of God is eternal life" (Rom 6:23 KJV). Unfortunately, I only heard in my mind the part about sin and death. I cannot recall hearing an emphasis on eternal life being a gift of God but only how these sins would result in damnation, condemnation, destruction, and eternal death in a fiery furnace named *hell*, as opposed to going to heaven where we could all sit at God's feet and receive our blessings. And, regardless of my father's allowing us to participate in secular activities, I continued to hear these messages loud and clear every moment of my life and with every self-sabotaging behavior I engaged in.

Although it seemed like, from my choices and actions, I had no concern about what was right and what was wrong, that was not true. Actually, for the most part, I had in many ways disengaged from the process of reflection or caring about my choices. It seemed as if I was moving toward destruction regardless of any consciousness of sin and its consequences. Guilt was forever before me as my church friends at the time fully bought into Holiness dogma and doctrine. My friend, Bethany, became the catalyst for my self-reflecting and becoming consciously aware of my sins.

Bethany came into my life in the early 70s. We worked together at a title and trust company prior to my joining the police department and developed a strong friendship. I guess she was my best friend, but I never referred to her that way. Bethany and I had a good friendship. We had fun together, participated in events together, talked about God together, and had much in common. We really liked one another. However, this friendship became strained in the mid-70s when I began dating Wallace. Bethany and I talked about everything, so it was only natural that she would know everything about my relationship with my married boyfriend, Wallace. Eventually though, her constant judgment regarding Wallace and me became intrusive and annoying.

Bethany was a person of faith and highly religious. It was her insufferable religious views she held that eventually resulted in ending our friendship. Once Bethany discovered I was dating and in love with a married man she became my personal preacher and judge of what I should do with my relationship. She never approved of Wallace and me being in a relationship, and I never asked for her approval. However, she was determined to convince me to not be in this relationship and insisted that I end it. I got it that as a person of faith and moral integrity, she would attempt to convince me to not be in a relationship with Wallace. What I did not expect was her judgmental attitude and the scare tactics she used in her futile attempts to sway me to break up with Wallace.

She used the same methods I grew up with in my childhood, which were shame-based, judgmental, and with condemning undertones. Bethany insinuated I needed to make a choice between having God in my life or Wallace. This choice did cause me to pause and think about whether I could let Wallace go so I could live into my holiness and free myself from the possibility of going to hell when I died. However, the contemplation did not take long. My choice, in keeping with the attitude I had at the time, was Wallace. Making this choice is when I began the private process of distancing myself from both Bethany and the church. It seemed as if Bethany made it her duty to persuade me to be more faithful to God and end the relationship. Her fast talking and preachy voice along with her perfect knowledge of the Bible deeply impacted me more than I wanted to admit it did.

My mind went back to some of the other Scripture passages and sermons I heard in my childhood, such as, *"Choose this day whom ye will serve"* (Josh 24:15 KJV), and *"No man can serve two masters, for either he will hate the one and love the other; or else he will hold to the one and despise the other"* (Matt 6:24 KJV). Bethany had successfully gotten into my head with all this Bible talk. My wheels of guilt and shame began to slowly turn. The last thing I remember her saying to me before we parted ways was reminding me that God could kill my boyfriend and kill my children because of my behavior. She warned me that God could even harm me and that I could really suffer because of the choice I made of being with Wallace. Bethany eventually faded out of my life, and I believe we were both relieved when this happened. This married man and the biblical warnings stayed on my mind. Wallace and I had already begun the process of breaking up, just on our own time. I intuitively knew that ending this relationship was the right thing to do.

Nothing much changed but the regularity of Wallace's visits and the ending of going on dates. Wallace still had keys to my apartment. He came over to my apartment approximately three days a week but stayed for shorter periods of time. When our daughter was born in 1975, he came over more frequently to visit with me as well as fulfill what he had promised me during my pregnancy: to be the best father he could. I loved those more frequent visits, our spending time together with Sharell, and going to his relatives' homes so they could meet her. He was a great father and cared for Sharell with gentleness and love. Wallace once told me his coworkers and some family members challenged whether Sharell was his baby. When I asked him how he responded to them, Wallace told them that it did not make any difference. He knew how much time we had spent together, and if she was not his, she should be. And that was the level of care he gave to Sharell, as if she were his daughter without any expressed doubts. His response was clear, concise, and sincere. I was moved by his statement because I believed him to be Sharell's father, regardless of my unfaithfulness in the relationship. I would not entertain Judge as a possible father to Sharell, although I did mention this possibility to him once.

One day in early January 1979, just one month into my police training career, Wallace informed me he was taking a trip out of town with his wife and children. Of course, I was not happy, but what could I do about it? I continued my training and was excited because I was also planning Sharell's fourth birthday celebration on January 29, 1979. Wallace took the trip and arrived home later that week. When he came over to my apartment, he seemed tired and exhausted.

Wallace, as he explained, had some kind of trip. His car had broken down and was at a place where it could not be fixed. He and his family had gotten a ride back home by a truck driver who allowed them into the back of his truck. It had been a miserable trip that raised his blood pressure, causing him to have severe headaches. Nevertheless, they arrived home safely. Still not feeling quite well, he visited the emergency room after returning home. The results of his visit did not consist of encouraging words for his health. The doctor told Wallace that his blood pressure was causing severe damage to his blood vessels and arteries and that he was *a walking time bomb*. The doctor and I encouraged Wallace to stop drinking. Wallace was a drinker, but not the fall down drunk kind of drinker. He was what many refer to as a functional drinker. He was able to work, carry on conversations, and drive. However, this did not stop the effect of his drinking on his health.

I remember a couple of weeks prior to his leaving town, he came to my house late at night. This had become his routine of late, and I was not happy with those late-night visits instead of days spending quality time together. On this particular night when Wallace came into my house, I had already fallen asleep and was awakened when he came inside. He came into my bedroom where it was dark and asked me immediately to take his blood pressure. Knowing that Wallace had high blood pressure, knowing that he had been drinking, and feeling sick and tired of these late-night visits, I angrily got up and, in the darkness, where I could only see a silhouette of him, grabbed the blood pressure kit and flung it across the bed where he was now standing and said, "Here, check it your damn self!" I immediately heard Wallace say, "Ouch!" and I knew I had hit him with the kit. I turned on the light and realized I had hit him in the head. He was bleeding profusely. I got up quickly, grabbed a towel, and began applying pressure on his wound until the blood flow ceased. When he realized the wound was not endangering him, he laid down and this time spent the night. The next morning, I examined his head and found a small-to-medium-sized bruise on the upper part of the side of his head. Other than that, he was fine, and our relationship continued as normal for us.

Before leaving, Wallace went through all of my record albums and asked if he could take a few of my blues albums home with him. He and I loved the blues, so this was no surprise. He actually took all of my blues albums home with him. I was remembering this particular night while he was telling me about the ordeal he experienced after being driven home in the back of a truck and his resulting emergency room visit. I strongly suggested to him to take it easy, rest, and, again, to stop drinking. He said he would, but the damage was already done. I saw him off and on after that day, but not much. Being a police recruit took up much of my time. I remember Wallace visited me on Christmas, but I do not remember seeing him. However, when I learned that I had to work overtime because of the wintry weather, I asked him to come over to watch the children for a couple of days. He agreed.

On January 16, there was a severe snowstorm that had basically shut down the city. That is, except for officers and certainly not for us police recruits. This was also the day Wallace was supposed to show up and watch the children. He never came. I was not upset about this, I just found someone to watch them, took them over to their home, and left for work. I reported to the training academy only to learn that as recruits, we were assigned to work the subway stations to shovel snow off of the tracks so that public transportation would not have to shut down. We worked all through the night shoveling snow and were not dismissed until well after one o'clock on the morning of the seventeenth. I arrived home and went straight to bed. A few hours into my sleep, I received a phone call from Wallace's cousin, Jane. Jane and I had become really close. We referred to ourselves as cousins. I knew her children well and they accepted me fully as family. Jane and I stayed connected and stayed that way until her passing in 2017. So, it was natural that she would be the one to call me.

When Jane called me, she asked me first if I was okay. I told her that I was and that I was asleep. I believe she was checking to see if I already knew. When she discovered I did not know, she went on to relay the bad news. Wallace had died. I immediately began crying uncontrollably. I could not believe what I was hearing and kept asking her if she was certain he was dead. I was alone in the house and I was in total shock. Filled with emotions, I asked her how he died. From what I can remember,

Wallace had been out, perhaps on public transportation, when he fell out on the platform of the train station on South 95th Street at Lafayette. Because of the weather, it took a long time for the police to arrive. After they arrived and examined him, they assumed that he was drunk, although as I understand it, he had not been drinking. This assumption resulted in them taking him to a detox center located approximately thirty minutes away. However, in the heavy snow conditions, it took them about two hours to arrive. He could have been taken to the trauma center not far away, and why they made this independent decision to drive two hours eludes me. A shorter trip to the trauma hospital might have saved his life. When they arrived at the detox center, they discovered that Wallace had not been drinking and determined that the smell they thought was from drinking was really due to the condition he was in. The ambulance drivers were told to get him to a hospital as soon as possible. Unfortunately, when they arrived at the hospital, Wallace was declared dead on arrival (DOA).

Jane talked to me for about an hour as we both continued to cry and reminisce about him. When we hung up the telephone, I immediately called his wife, Kate. The first time I called Kate, I was angry, mean, and revengeful. This time I called her because I felt that she must be mourning just as much as me, and even more. In some strange way, I felt empathy for her and needed to talk to her. I also needed to talk to someone who was close to Wallace, and she was the one. There were so many mixed emotions in needing to call her. The one thing I did not call her for was to be mean. I picked up the telephone and called her. I was surprised Kate did not hang up on me after she answered the telephone and discovered it was me. It was after 10 p.m. and, for good reason, she did not like me. Yet, she did answer, and we must have talked for about fifteen minutes. Our conversation was not an angry one nor was it friendly. Still crying, I offered my condolences and said some other words of comfort.

Kate did not respond to my words of condolences. Her conversation with me centered on how much I had hurt her over the years because of my relationship with Wallace. I listened to her. After she finished speaking about me ruining my life, I felt judged once again and began telling her how much I knew about her life and their history in the relationship. I believe she was stunned about how much I knew about her history with Wallace and how much I knew the relationship was not and had not been the best in the world. After that conversation ended, we hung up and I continued to cry. I called a police recruit male friend of mine and told him what had happened. He said in a caring way that he was coming right over. He arrived, hugged me, and then said, "Come with me and get out of your apartment for a while." Feeling alone and needing someone to be with, I immediately got dressed and left with him. I was unaware of where we were going nor was that a concern for me in that moment. We ended up at his house where I stayed for the rest of the night. I did not know what to expect and probably did not care what happened between us because, most of all, I did not want to be alone. He brought me back home the next morning. In retrospect, I believe he took advantage of this moment for his benefit and not mine, as spending the night resulted in our having sex. We never spoke about that night and what occurred with us again. Yet the grief I experienced was real.

Wallace's funeral was nearing, and I was debating on whether or not I would attend the services. I had heard from some of his friends that his wife said if I attended the funeral there would be trouble. I eventually made the decision that I would not attend the funeral out of respect for her and my love for Wallace. I really desired to attend his funeral and felt as if I was just as close to Wallace as any other woman, including his wife. What we shared was real, and I honestly felt I should be there. I ultimately decided not to go, in fear it would cause disruption, and he did not deserve that. I did decide to attend the visitation. Visitation was simply a time when the body was laid alone in the funeral home and people could come by between certain hours, sign the attendance book, and view the body. Nothing was happening during these times, and the family was not expected to be present.

I went to my parents' home. Both had been strong supports for me during this time. Mama was most verbally and physically supportive. Daddy was quietly supportive, but I knew beyond a doubt they were both there for me. The day of the visitation, my parents arrived at my apartment at the time we had previously arranged to go to the funeral home. We walked into the door of the parlor where he was, and I immediately began crying uncontrollably. They each comforted me and then followed slightly behind me up to the coffin. I stood there looking at him. There were no tears. I simply stood there quietly and reflectively. Then I noticed the scar on his right temple where the blood pressure instrument had hit him when I threw it at him in the dark. Regretting this had happened, I began to cry. I said to my parents, "Look, this is the scar I caused when I was angry and threw the blood pressure instrument at him." I never looked around at them but kept touching Wallace. All of a sudden,

I heard my father's voice, and he said, quietly, but loud enough for me to hear him, "That might be what killed him." I looked back at him in shock that he would say that, thinking to myself, *You mean I might have killed him?* At that moment, my mother looked at him and scolded, "Stop, Samuel." Mother and I both knew that he had ways of saying instigating things just for the effect. But I had already bought into his statement fully and now believed I could be a suspect for murder.

When they dropped me back off at home, this is where the grief turned into the acknowledgment of sin, shame, guilt, and dirty stains. I went from grief to feelings of guilt about the scar I put on Wallace's face. I felt the full range of shame for being in a relationship with a married man. Bethany had already warned me that God could cause Wallace to die. Now, in addition to his death, I might be the cause of his death. Certainly, this is what I was told. Wallace can die and I might suffer. Wow! Her prophecy came true. I should have broken up with him when she insisted that I make a choice. Wallace was dead because of me! I kept looking out my living room window, and every man I saw passing my house, in my mind, was there and watching my house for the right moment to come and arrest me for murder. After I finally decided I was not getting arrested and fully realized this paranoia was part of my mental stress and guilt, I slightly calmed down. But the guilt and shame remained. I was ashamed for making this choice, for betraying God, and for doing what I knew was clearly wrong. I wanted to make amends. I wanted to find ways to repent and prove to God I was sorry and that I had learned my lesson and would never again commit the greatest sin of God's commandments, adultery. I experienced guilt and shame for months and months. All I could think about was my friend Bethany and how she so powerfully warned me of what was to come if I remained in this relationship.

The day of Wallace's funeral was the worst. I was at home feeling horrible that I could not attend the funeral. There was no other place where I really needed to be than at the funeral services. But there was another person at the funeral who deserved to be there, his wife. What was I thinking? I had no place or business there. That was the most severe punishment I could receive. The acknowledgment that my choice to be with him ultimately ended up with the realization that I was not his wife. She was the one who ultimately had the condolences and empathy that real couples are deserving of, not me. I thought I was just a dirty stain in his life and was getting just what I deserved that night, to be alone at home with no real source of compassion guiding me through my grief.

Some days later, I cried again when I thought of the one thing we enjoyed together, the blues. All of my blues albums were in his home, and I no longer had access to him or the music we enjoyed together. All I could do was incessantly cry, all while feeling unworthy to cry and receive comfort. All I got were dreams that reminded me of my sins.

I must have dreamed about Wallace for months. My dreams were recurring and the theme never wavered. In my dreams, I would see Wallace and he was alive. I would see him, but I was not allowed to touch him. Intuitively, I knew this was the condition that I had to face if I wanted Wallace to be alive. He would come to me in dreams and I could not touch him. This was so painful to experience, yet I wished for the dreams to continue just so I could see him. The dreams eventually ceased, and he was totally out of my life. I promised God that I would never date another married man. I felt the need to prove to God, as part of this process, to marry again and commit myself to a legitimate relationship. These feelings of guilt and shame are what ultimately resulted in my second marriage, which was straight from hell. There was still more pain, shame, and guilt to experience.

Reflection: Providing Theological Clarity

When seeking assistance, some women victims/survivors of sexual and domestic violence were nurtured by pastors, clergy, and other faith leaders who did not or could not provide theological clarity on important texts regarding their spirituality and obedience to God. These texts spoke to themes such as forgiveness, suffering, repentance, and reconciliation. These, for many victims/survivors, were important in order to be faithful to the Scriptures and to God. Without offering theological clarity on the biblical text, victims/survivors may continue in abusive relationships thinking they are doing what God would have them to do. This decision could cost them their lives.

Many such women have heard and believed that they had to instantly forgive their abuser because of Jesus' teaching when asked by Peter how many times he should forgive those who sin against him. Peter impulsively threw out a random number equaling seven. Jesus' immediate response was, "'Not seven times but,' he instructed, 'I tell you, seventy-seven times seven'" (Matt 18:22 NRSV). Jesus' response has been interpreted over the centuries as meaning we should immediately forgive someone when they harm us. This interpretation is also signified through the Lord's prayer (Matt 6:9–13), which is the prayer Jesus taught his disciples. I encourage you to do more than to read a text and then take it literally without pausing to think what might Jesus be saying in these verses.

Recently, I was interviewed on a podcast, and part of the conversation was about forgiveness. I announced on social media that I would be speaking on this subject in a couple of days. The responses I received were fast and furious. The answer was consistently adamant that God calls us to forgive instantly. However, I do not subscribe to these texts being about when, where, or how forgiveness should occur. Women who are violated must hear from clergy that forgiveness is not required as an automatic response. Does Jesus call us to forgive? Does Jesus offer a timeframe by which we must forgive? And, the dreaded question: Does Jesus require us to forgive without being asked by the abuser? It is these types of questions we must reflect on as theologians. If we speak to others about what God intends, we are doing theology. Thus, everyone who goes further than what the Scriptures say is engaging in theological inquiry. And providing this type of theological clarity is an important part of providing pastoral-care practices that are trauma-informed.

Theologically, my response to the question of forgiveness is this, "No. Forgiveness is not the first act we should engage in when violation has occurred." Forgiveness is a process and it may take a lifetime to utter the words of forgiveness. Then there are those who forgive instantly and believe they should do so with all of their heart and their wills. To speak their truth does not mean it has to be your truth nor God's requirement. Furthermore, forgiveness requires repentance, accountability, and restitution by the abuser. I know this can sound strange to those like me who have been told differently over and over. Jesus, when he was being crucified on the cross, did not say to those who were harming them, "I forgive you." Jesus' response was, "Father, forgive them, for they know not what they do" (Luke 23:34). Perhaps Jesus was saying he was not able to forgive, but he knew a God who does forgive.

Victims/survivors may have grown up under self-sacrificing, stand-by-your-man (or partner) types of theology that call women to suffer and stick with their husband. God does not intend for victims/survivors to suffer although suffering happens. While Scripture teaches, "Blessed are those who are persecuted for righteousness' sake, for theirs is the Kingdom of heaven" (Matt 5:10 NRSV), this is not the type of suffering that is referred to in cases of domestic violence and sexual abuse. Redemptive suffering does not mean you must suffer when someone has violated your body. It does not mean you have to stay with him while you are being violated. Safety is what God intends for you, not violence. God's purpose is that we live life and live that life abundantly, not that we suffer (John 10:10). And even when forgiveness occurs in its proper time and context, reconciliation, meaning restoring the relationship, may not be possible. However, reconciliation in the Bible simply means finding a way to stop the violence.

I posit that reconciliation does not occur when the victimizer decides to stop the violence. Restoring the relationship depends on the victims/survivors participating in the reconciliation process. This is an example of bringing theological clarity to those for whom you provide care. One way to do this is to simply ask questions, such as: "Do you believe God intends for you to be abused and suffer?" I have made every attempt to counter these unhealthy narratives that place the sole burden on the victimized to forgive and fix the relationship. I countered this narrative as an advocate who speaks with women in shelters about these issues. I countered this narrative as an adjunct professor teaching about sexual and domestic violence to seminary students. I countered this narrative as a pastoral-care provider in a local care and counseling center, where I met many women victims/survivors who suffered from domestic violence, sexual violence, and clergy misconduct. I countered these narratives as a trainer for healthy relationships with FaithTrust Institute in Seattle, WA. And I countered these narratives by providing my expertise through the African American Domestic Peace Project. Over the years of service, each of these places helped to build biblically sound and theologically practical structure, context, and reflection.

When the additional subject of divorce came up, especially as it related to the Old Testament text that *God hates divorce* (Mal 2:16), victims/survivors are reminded that the text also declares that God hates violence. And that when divorce occurs, remember it was not the divorce that broke the marriage covenant, it was the violence. Rev. Al Miles, in his book *Violence in Families: What Every Christian Needs to Know,* points out also that the context of this Scripture only refers to men, and they had a specific charge centering around not leaving women unprotected. Referring to Matt 5:32 and 19:9, these verses were recited to prevent men from divorcing their wives and thus subjecting them to poverty and loss of social status, as women in Jesus' day derived those through men. In that era, Jewish women could not initiate divorce.[1] Frank Thomas, professor of preaching at Christian Theological Seminary, has consistently asked the following question that I have since adopted as my own: "To what end and for what purposes do people privilege some Scriptures over the other?"

Even though I believe students, and other recipients of the teaching and training, benefit from and were challenged to stretch their original thinking, I, as a survivor, only absorbed it cognitively and continued to not have the capabilities to incorporate the good news and the freedom it had to offer. Indeed, while it was easy to change my cognition, it was difficult to change my internal absorption enough to move even more toward healing and wholeness. I believe this to be true for many victims/survivors. More had to be done. Offering theological clarity would not be enough to undo the damage that had been done to many women. Yet, our challenge is to approach biblical text with caution. Refrain from using what we have learned from our youth without pause to reflect on the learning. When we refuse to learn, discern, and grow in wisdom and continue to disseminate information that harms and retraumatizes survivors, we are engaging in theological malpractice.

Not only victims/survivors, but women in general, especially women scholars who identified as Womanist theologians, began to interrogate, "Is the church, the Black church in particular, really a safe place for Black women?" This question continues to be examined, discussed, and critiqued in many Womanist circles. The call is for more critique of the Bible from the perspective of the overall oppression of women. We are challenged, in order to experience full liberation from oppression, to disconnect from the Western-born colonizer's patriarchal teaching, preaching, and practices that continue the cycle of violence sanctioned by a structure whose systematic abuse and structural racism intentionally destroys Black bodies.

Providing theological clarity to victims/survivors of sexual violence can facilitate eliminating or lessening the burden of shame, guilt, and blame, which often accompany traumatic experiences. Bishop Yvette Flunder, founding pastor of City of Refuge United Church of Christ (Oakland, CA), tweeted this message, which best emphasizes the value of providing theological clarity and ways others can benefit from doing the same:

---

1. Miles, *Violence in Families*, 66.

> There was once a "me" that would have sent the current me to hell without so much as a second thought. The current me has both regrets for those I wounded with religion and an obligation to spend the rest of my life as a healer myself, also had to forgive myself.[2]

Discussion

Providing theological clarity is an essential component in providing trauma-informed pastoral-care practices with victims/survivors of sexual and domestic violence.

> Get wisdom; get insight: do not forget, nor turn away from the words of my mouth. Do not forsake her, and she will keep you; love her, and she will guard you. The beginning of wisdom is this: Get wisdom, and whatever else you do get insight. (Prov 4:5–7 NRSV)

1. As you read and meditate on this passage, how does it speak to you regarding the importance of theological clarity?

2. In what ways did issues of shame, blame, and guilt plague you or others you have provided pastoral care for as a victim/survivor of abuse?

Activity: Scripture as Resource or Roadblock

- List particular Scriptures you have identified that can be used as a resource or as a roadblock for victims/survivors of sexual and domestic violence.
- Give an example of passages that can be used to reduce the shame, blame, and guilt many victims/survivors experience following acts of violence.

---

2. Bishop Yvette A. Flunder, Twitter post, August 8, 2020, 2:14 a.m. @BishopYvetteFlunder. Used with permission.

Chapter 4

I Made It to Hell

It is easy to put on the chains of oppression, but it can take a lifetime to take them off. This is the place where I found myself after the death of Wallace. I carried the weight of a broken heart as well as the guilt of my past and present behavior. These memories were too much for me to bear. Bethany's rebuke, "God could kill him [Wallace]," kept lingering in my thoughts. This was a prophecy fulfilled, and I could have avoided all of this by exiting the relationship. It was my fault. My dreams kept coming to remind me of my choices, and the only conclusion I could draw was that my dreams were a perpetual reminder of what I had done. My religious path, coupled with my lifestyle, left me with no other choice but to believe I was doomed.

I attended Sunday School. I listened to sermons. I knew the consequences of sin. Disobedience to this God resulted in war, famine, death, community and cultural violence, and/or destruction. For example, in the Bible there is a story about two cities. This story can be found in the book of Genesis. The two cities were Sodom and Gomorrah, and both were considered to be evil. Because of the evil in the cities, God destroyed them with "fire and brimstone" (Gen 19:24 KJV). However, God, through two male angels who looked like humans, went to the city to find good men who could be saved. The angels found only one, and his name was Lot. So he, his wife, and his children were led to the countryside and told to move forward but not to look back. Lot's wife yielded to the temptation and looked back anyway. Consequently, she turned into a pillar of salt (Gene 19:26). These and other similar stories exhibiting God's wrath were taught to us through sermons and Bible study.

For me, the God I served was akin to my childhood memories of the boogeyman. God was that larger-than-life boogeyman in the sky who sat, watched, and waited for me to sin so that I could be punished. I knew the consequences of sin very well. Still, I chose to live the life I led. So, if Lot's wife could be punished for simply looking back at a place where she once lived, what would be my punishment? Would more harm come to the people I loved? Would my children get sick and die? Would my family be harmed? What would my punishment be? I had siblings, parents, two children, and then there was me. What other price must I pay for my sins? How might I be punished?

I carried this burden for years, well into my grown life. Perhaps the totality of sins was unforgivable and the door was wide open for ample punishment. I felt the need to make amends more intensely after Wallace passed away, but I carried the burden of guilt long after his death. Life for me would never be a life of happiness. The only way out was to make amends. There were no real plans for making amends, and I had no idea of how to go about this process.

In the book of Leviticus, there were options for receiving forgiveness by offering what was considered a guilt offering. First, you had to be sincerely remorseful, and if the sin were taking money from someone, repentance could only happen when that money was given back with interest (Lev 6:4–5). Being sorry alone was not an option. In the Old Testament world, repentance required a deeper level of atonement that satisfied those who were offended. If I were truly sorry for all the sins I had committed, then I needed an act of atonement. I deeply desired to atone for my sins. But I also believed even making amends would never be available to me. My sins were unforgivable. It was difficult to conceive of how that would even be possible.

I was more convinced this was just my lot in life. I was doomed to a life of misery. My punishment was obvious to me. My lot in life was already written. I would be denied happiness, love, safety, and security. These oppressive chains hung tightly around my neck. Before I reached the age of eighteen, I was already socialized in these belief systems. However, unbeknownst to me at the time, becoming a police recruit would create a possible avenue toward receiving forgiveness and restoration.

I began my police career in December 1978. Wallace passed away in January 1979. The intersection of these two events offered me a way forward to make things right with God. Now it was about to happen! Greg, who was also a police recruit, would become my road toward restoring my relationship with God.

As a twenty-six-year-old young police recruit, I was excited to have a career that actually provided a salary, enabling me to take care of myself and my two children, as well as one that would bring me adventure and challenge. The training was both exciting and intimidating. Our weekly experiences included taking classes on policing, learning case law, shooting at the range, running, and other physical fitness challenges, as well as getting to know our recruit colleagues. We bonded as a group. We also formed separate friendships within this group. There were about five people I specifically bonded with, three were women and the other two were men. One of the men, in particular, seemed to be especially attracted to me. His name was Greg.

Greg and I became friends. Over the weeks and into January 1979, we spent time together. Sharing a meal in a local restaurant became a routine activity of ours, along with him making a couple of visits to my apartment where we listened to music and had fun conversations, which were usually about work. Over time, Greg's kindness extended even more. We were in the thick of the winter season and heavy snow was on the ground. I cannot remember if my car would not start or if it was stuck on the side street by my apartment, as most cars were. I called Greg and requested a ride. He lived all the way on the other side of town and, given the weather conditions, he was at least forty-five minutes away. Side streets were almost impossible to navigate, so Greg asked me to meet him on the corner. As police recruits, we all understood neither the weather nor anything else would be an excuse for calling off work. As police officers, we were essential workers. Snow days were not sleep-in days for us. If there was an active shooting, we could not run from the danger, but rather we'd run towards the sound of bullets. Greg made certain we both showed up on time. He did not do this just one day, he did it every day. His kindness, friendliness, and accessibility were beyond anything I had ever experienced in any relationship I was in. And he was single! At that moment the single implication was a passing thought. Or was it? I am certain seeds of possibilities were already beginning to take root.

During this time, Greg's acts of care and kindness increased. On one of these nights after shoveling snow, Greg asked if he could come upstairs for a while. After arriving in my apartment, Greg handed me a brown bag that resembled the bags delivered by the post office. The bag was sealed and it was addressed to him. Greg gave me the bag and told me it was a gift for me. The brown packaging was soft. I took the gift and thanked him for it. I did not open the gift until he left the house. Greg never insisted that I open it in front of him, so I believe my actions were appropriate. When I opened the envelope, I pulled out the most beautiful snowy white nightgown. The gown was A-line and about knee length. I laid the gown on the bed to admire it even more. Finally, I folded the gown back up, placed it back in its original packaging, and gently laid it in one of the dresser drawers, all the while thinking, "If he thinks I am going to bed with him, he's got another thing coming." The person I had envisioned wearing this gown for was Wallace. Wallace was the one who I wanted to see me all sexy, not Greg. And he was the one I loved, not Greg. Greg never said a word again about the gown. He kept doing nice things for me and being available whenever I wanted his company. Greg never asked me about the gown again, and his kindness to me never seemed to have a bottom. While I continued to see Greg, something happened where my life would never be the same again—Wallace died.

The guilt, shame, and blame I felt would consume me. I still needed to atone for my dating this married man, not to mention my prior sins. In March, three months after Wallace died, Greg began expressing his desire to be with me even more. His acts of kindness, availability, and friendship began leading me to believe he was the one fit for my atonement. I thought, "What do I have to lose? He is single, he is nice, he is kind, he is friendly, and there is nothing he would not do for me." The seeds that were planted earlier began to shape and form. The image was clear. Greg was my path to atonement. This was my opportunity to be in a real relationship that God would be pleased with, and I would be forgiven. "This is my opportunity to make amends," I thought. By marrying Greg, God would see that I was not dating a married man. Rather, God would see I was in an honest relationship, and that would bring me back in favor and in right relationship with God. I believed this was ideal. God would be pleased. I would be pleased. This is the type of man I knew I could live with knowing that he would cater to me in ways that no one else ever had. So, I begin to make the moves for this relationship to become one of a husband-and-wife team. We had a brief courtship. That August, seven months after Wallace's death, Greg and I married.

The wedding took place at the local North Star Lodge, No. 1 Prince Hall affiliated, where my father served as the worshipful master, the lead person. Daddy performed the wedding. The hall was filled with family, friends of mine, friends of my parents, church members, and members from my police family. My father was standing in front of the altar, and my husband was to his right. I walked down the aisle with my son and daughter, ages seven and four, respectively. Greg was already waiting for us. The next thing I recalled was my father pronouncing us husband and wife. I heard the sound of hands clapping and people cheering. All of a sudden and beyond my control, I began crying. I was crying the ugly face cry. I looked at my children and they were crying. I looked at my father and he was crying. I glanced over at my older sister, who is bipolar, and she was crying.

People came up to me, hugging me and congratulating me. They assumed they were witnessing my extreme happiness, when in actuality, I was in the midst of having a (albeit controlled) mini nervous breakdown. I knew at the moment of the pronouncement that I had made a mistake. My mind knew it! My spirit knew it! And my body knew it! I cannot remember if I kissed the groom! I cannot remember the rest of the reception! And whatever fun we had, dancing and greeting one another, was fake. There were pictures to help me remember parts of that day. I recall us finding an English basement rental apartment as our first home together. We lived there until we purchased our first house.

Both Greg and I together made a substantial income that allowed us to purchase our first home. I was finally able to purchase my first brand new car. Credit issues limited my choice; nevertheless, with Greg on the title, the car was new but lacked the amenities I desired with my first choice. In spite of this, I was pleased and excited to transition from older automobiles subject to breakdowns to a brand new car with a warranty. To my dismay and disappointment, one year from the date I purchased my car, it was stolen.

We had found our home. It was time to move from our first apartment. The night before we were to move, I packed the trunk of my car with cleaning supplies with the intention of going to the house early to do some cleaning. I left items in the car overnight so that I could wake up early the next morning, throw on some clothes, and leave right out. However, that morning I went outside only to find the car missing. I blinked my eyes, thinking something was wrong with my vision. I kept looking up and down the streets for where I might have parked the car, thinking perhaps I had parked the car somewhere else other than in front of the apartment. The car was gone. It had been stolen.

The insurance paid for the stolen car, but I did not receive any residual amount to put down on another car. My insurance covered the price of the car, but because of its value and my high rate of interest, purchasing another new car was out of the question. I was devastated. Not having the credit or extra funds to buy a new car, I settled on purchasing a car from a car lot that advertised, *"Good credit, no credit, come to us."* I felt as if I had gone three steps backwards. We both had to sign for a used car that had no warranty but, as with my new car, Greg understood the car was mine. He had his own vehicle. Yet I was grateful. I had a house, a husband, and two children. After moving in, everything seemed to be normal and almost better than normal. God was pleased, and what more could I ask for?

Our recruit phase had ended and we were off probation by the end of the year. This was a time of relief. On probation, you can get fired for any minor incident. Police recruits are not covered by unions. As a police officer and part of the union, life was different. One would have to find significant cause to even begin the procedure of suspending someone and eventually firing them. On December 11, we graduated from the training academy, received our badges, and were assigned to our particular police districts. We were still newlyweds and had only been married four months when everything began falling apart.

We were working on different shifts. Greg worked the overnight shift and I worked the day shift. I began noticing that when I arrived home from work, my two children, who slept upstairs in our large attic area, did not come down to see me. I would go upstairs to greet them. The attic was the perfect space for them because it covered the entire length of the house and was wide. They had their own beds and separate areas to sleep, and the room was well decorated. They had room for their toys and everything they could want was upstairs, even a bathroom. In addition to the children being upstairs, the house would be clean. I felt as if the weight of the world was lifted from having a mate that was so helpful around the house and with the children.

Greg's nickname for me was Doll Face. I am not certain how or why this name came into being, but he rarely called me by my first name. When I came in the door, he would greet me with a hug, calling me Doll Face. He would say something like, "Sit down and relax yourself. Everything is okay. We will eat soon." I thought to myself, "You mean I can arrive home to a clean house, change my clothes, sit down and rest while waiting for dinner? What a life!" I could hear the children upstairs stirring around and playing. They seemed to be satisfied and content. I would go upstairs and talk to them, but for some reason, they never came down, except to eat. My initial feeling was that of elation. How lucky I was to have a man who would go out of his way to ensure I could relax and not have to work hard. This behavior toward me was in addition to the continued gift giving, kindnesses, and the fun conversations we would have. I felt like I had died and gone to heaven. I have *never* to this date met anyone who was as kind and giving as Greg was. It was unbelievable.

After several weeks of experiencing this behavior, my elation turned to concern. Something in my gut was telling me this was not normal. I began to believe Greg was not making things easy for me: he was trying to keep my children away from me. But why would he do that? Responding to this concern, I began bringing my children downstairs to spend more time with me, watching television and just hanging out. It was during this time that Greg began changing his behavior. He was not as kind, friendly, or helpful around the house. This sudden onset of his behavioral changes made no sense to me. Yet, it was happening. Perhaps it did make sense. Perhaps I was in denial about his sudden change. Why? Because I was warned.

Months before we got married, Greg and I traveled to Ohio with my mother to see her mother's sister, my great aunt. My aunt, who was up in age, made a comment about him when he was not around. Her eighty-year-old brain that had signs of Alzheimer's disease picked up something about Greg that I had overlooked. She looked straight at me and then at my mother and said, "There's something wrong with that boy." Perhaps that was my very first warning from the wisdom of an elder. After arriving back home, I began to notice changes in his facial expressions. His looks began to transition from smiles to looks of displeasure and contempt, as if I had done something to upset him.

These looks indicated to me that he was not pleased with this routine, or perhaps I had done something else to cause these mood swings. In addition to these changes in Greg's behavior, he began leaving earlier than needed to go to work, and on his days off, he was hardly ever home. When Greg was home, he was disengaged and remained most of the time in our bedroom or on the telephone laughing and talking to friends about police work. It was as if the kindnesses and gift-giving person was disappearing and a new personality was developing. Knowing a little about mental illness from my nursing training, I believed Greg was developing some type of personality changes. I did not have a name for what I experienced from him. He was now becoming more like a Dr. Jekyll and Mr. Hyde. One moment, he could tell me how much he loved me and another moment his personality would switch. I felt uneasy around him and was becoming a little fearful of him.

The new personality (Dr. Jekyll) was more anti-me. He never said much to the children because his attention was always turned toward me. This did not change. But his attention toward me was more hostile. His tone of voice changed from soft to excessively harsh without a moment's notice. His acts of kindness eventually ceased. His attention shifted from me to his work in the department. All I could hear when on the telephone with his colleagues in the department was boasting regarding the many arrests he/they made, the people stopped on the street, the kinds of drug busts made, etc. Simultaneously, Greg was gaining more recognition from the rank and file in his district because of his aggressiveness on the street, his arrests, and his overall actions as an officer. As his personality changed, I began experiencing his actions as controlling, scary, and emotionally abusive.

Concerned even more for my children and their safety, I changed my work time from days to the afternoon shift so I could watch and manage their schedule firsthand. I began working the afternoon shift, 3 p.m. to 11 p.m. This allowed me to be home with my children during the day, send them off to school, and be home when they returned. By then, Greg was working varying hours because he became a member of the tactical team. The tactical team wore plain clothes and drove unmarked cars. They worked undercover and were assigned some of the most dangerous areas to work. Greg's hours were longer and his starting time varied.

By this time, in addition to the emotional abuse, I discovered he was having affairs with some of the women he served and protected. This was confirmed when I was diagnosed with a sexually transmitted disease. In the midst of his negative abusive behavior toward me, I never lost my voice. I confronted him on his behavior and challenged him to change. I accused him of having an affair with the papers in my hands proving my body had been infected as a result. Instead of confessing, he decided to shape the communicable disease as my fault, turning the tables and deciding to physically abuse me for having an affair. This was the point of escalation into both emotional and physical violence. We would have volatile arguments, and the physical abuse would continue. Usually, it was pushing and shoving and always some type of threat involving his gun. On one occasion, he nearly broke my wrist. It did not matter what the argument was about, because he just used those situations as an excuse to be physically and emotionally abusive.

The escalation continued and the blame increased. He went from calling me Doll Face to describing me as "the mouth." He would say, "It's your mouth." He declared he even dreamed at night of my mouth. I think it was these statements along with the abuse continuing that convinced me that not only was he an abuser, but he was also crazy. Those angry faces he would make, the look of rage in his eyes, and my belief that he would follow through on any threats he would make, warranted my distance from him as well as my silence. I was becoming more and more afraid of him. By this time, I also was coming to the reality that I really did not love him. I regretted encouraging him toward marriage. I knew that marrying him was a huge mistake. However, I never made the choice to leave him. By now, I was too afraid to even think about divorcing him, and there were also other reasons for not moving toward a divorce. I did not want to fail in marriage again, as I had chosen to marry him as an act of atonement. This was a promise I made to God. How could I ever back down on that commitment, even though the abuse was escalating?

One day, I was upstairs cleaning the kids' room and Greg came upstairs simply to provoke an argument. I would not even have a conversation with him for fear of a physical attack. Regardless, he literally grabbed my arm and demanded, "You better talk to me." I then asked in a mild and non-hostile voice, "What do you want me to say?" What I remembered next was getting up off the floor at the bottom of the stairwell. He had pushed me down the stairs. My wrist felt as if it had fractured, and I was in pain. I never reported this incident to the police. By this time, I was truly afraid of him. He had turned into a different person.

My best friend, Rhonda, was probably the only one who knew the extent of my abuse as well as the only one who understood the extent of his craziness. She was an officer, also. Rhonda would make certain to show up at my house on a regular basis, as if to dare him to try and mess with me while she was around. She introduced humor so that I was not stressed all the time. And she provided a listening ear for what must have seemed an endless disoriented rattling. Yet, unlike me, she was fearless. She was supportive and loving and her empathy toward me was unmatched. I was the opposite: confused, afraid, paranoid, in fear of my life, and feeling as if I was losing my mind. I felt as if I was living in hell. This was not a case of making amends for my sins, this was an extended punishment from God who was obviously not finished asserting God's wrath upon me. Although I was not dead, I was fully convinced I had made it to hell.

Greg's behavior continued to escalate and become even more erratic. He stole my police uniforms out of our closet, and I had to miss work to buy new ones. He manipulated the machinery in my car so it would not start, leaving me stranded while he was out doing whatever. He poured water over me just because. And I never said a word. I was completely silenced with fear. The escalation was so far out of the norm of excuses for men abusing women. The false narrative regarding my mouth was no longer an excuse for Greg's abuse. Greg would become physically abusive without any of his sought-after verbal indicators from me. I believed the only way that I was going to get out of this marriage was to kill him. I thought about this for a while, and one night I convinced myself to try. My plan was to shoot him and then act as if it was self-defense. After all, I did feel as if his abusive behavior never stopped even when I was asleep. It would not be a fake display. It would be filled with the reality of the situation. I did not feel safe, awake or asleep.

My fear for my physical safety caused me to considered killing him before he eventually killed me. However, although today there is a psychological term for this behavior, in the Department it would be a crime that could cost me my career and everything I held near and dear to me. I continued living in the depth of fear for my life as well as for the life of my children. I was trapped in an abusive relationship and was convinced this would eventually cost me my life.

Greg was working the overnight shift. He was preparing to leave for work as soon as his partner arrived to pick him up. I was sitting in our living room on the couch wearing my nightgown and housecoat. The couch was located in the living room just to the right of our front door. I was quietly reading a book and anticipating him leaving so that I could get a peaceful night's sleep. By this time, Greg's partner was waiting for him outside. His rage and violence had become more unpredictable. As he headed toward the door, without any prompting from me it suddenly happened. Greg grabbed me off the couch and literally dragged me with him out the front door. I felt him coming toward me and could see out of the side of my eyes that he was heading for me. I was not certain what he intended to do to me after he forced me outside of the house. Greg's partner failed to exit the unmarked car to assist me. Instead, he simply rolled down his window and beckoned Greg to come on to the car. Greg let me go and I fell on my porch. I stayed there until they drove away. I was not injured. After making it back into my house, I sat on my couch crying profusely. I knew I should have left then, but I was still afraid.

I kept crying and thinking about how his partner never got out of the car to help me. He never got out of the car to confront Greg. He never called for additional police protection. He never asked me if I was okay. He was a police officer, and he never did anything. I could have gotten shot! I could have died that night, and he never got out of the car! He never got out of the car! I lost my respect for him and I do not think it was ever recovered. Although we share today's social media space as friends, it is only because of our collective history; but we rarely engage one another.

I was in emotional pain. I felt as if the other officer was a co-conspirator with Greg toward my demise. I was angry at him and angry with my husband. I had all of these feelings, yet, once again, I did not leave him in spite of this traumatic experience. This man was crazy. I began thinking about what would be next. What is next in store in his twisted mind for me? What needs to happen that would convince me to leave this man? Well, it did not take long for both of those questions to be answered. The escalation continued.

It happened on a weekday during the evening, slightly before it became dark. We were sitting quietly in the dining room when Greg began talking to me out of the blue. Nothing had occurred between us, not even a small disagreement, because I always walked on eggshells when he was around. Out of the blue, he said to me something to this effect, "You know I always wanted to make my mark on someone. I think it will be you." He went on to tell me how he had been having more dreams about me. In his dreams, he was dragging me out of the house and attaching me to the back of his car and dragging me up and down the street until I died. His eyes and look were indescribable. It felt as if the devil had finally appeared in hell with me and was ready to end it all. I felt terrified and believed this was the day I would die. I had never seen him look more determined to mortally harm me. I was frozen with shock. I felt paralyzed and could only stand still and intensely listen to him. He continued telling me how he had been waiting to do this. Then he pulled out his automatic pistol, pointed it at my head, and pulled the trigger. The gun did not fire. It was either the gun never had bullets inside the chamber or it had misfired. However, I knew I had to get out of that house.

I am not certain how I did it, but I suddenly developed the energy to get up and run. I found my way out of the house and ran for my life. I kept thinking he might be chasing me, but I would not look around. I left my children in the house with him and did not think about the possibility of him hurting them. I even left my weapons in the house. All I knew was I had to run for my life. I ended up in a tavern and I told the employee what had happened and that I was a police officer. Feeling anxious and afraid, I pleaded with the owner to call the police. He must have seen the urgency and fear on my face. He called the police. I was still convinced I was being chased, so they allowed me to hide in the bathroom. Two White police officers arrived, and I explained to them what occurred in my house and that we were both police officers. Initially, I told them all I wanted was to collect my children and a few things out of my house and I would leave. I did not know where I would go, I just wanted to leave. The police drove me to the house. As we were walking up my stairs to the house, Greg opened the door and greeted them as if they were his best friends. And what he said to them at the door really blew my mind. He spoke to the officers and invited them into the house. Sounding as if he was relieved when the police officers arrived, he proceeded to tell them how I had pulled a gun on him and threatened to kill him. As he was speaking, he handed the officers my weapon. I was speechless and could not believe the lie he told right in front of my face.

By this time, I did not know what the hell had just happened. One of the officers asked him to move so that we could come in. The officers listened to Greg's story again as Greg went to describe in dramatic terms how I got angry at him and pulled the gun and ran. His story did not sound believable to me, but I wondered if the police actually believed him. I was the one who ran for my life. Yet it seemed they were more concerned with listening to his story than mine. My mind recalled the incident at the police station when I went to Greg's district of assignment and talked with his supervisors about Greg's abusive behavior and all they could talk about was how wonderful of a police officer he was and the amount of arrests he made. My mind went back to his partner and how he silently sat in the unmarked police car as he observed Greg violently drag me out of the house and did nothing. Now in my own home and with the police present, I felt vulnerable to continued violence.

While the officers and Greg continued to engage one another, I began to feel as if what happened to me did not matter. I felt disregarded, disrespected, and unprotected as a woman officer by the officers seemingly lacking concern for my safety. The officers began writing up the report and, at some point, the officers decided we should be separated into different rooms. I was in one room with one of the officers and Greg was in another room with the other officer. I told my story and I assumed

Greg told his story again. The officers left their respective rooms and conferred with one another and then came back to talk to us separately again. I am not certain what the officer said to Greg, but I do know what the officer I spoke with said to me.

The officer advised me to adjust my report stating this event never occurred. He went on to explain writing two separate reports with competing accusations could start a long investigation and get the police all in our business. By the time this officer finished telling me all the trouble a report would cause, I took the officer's advice and did what was suggested. I told the officer the event never occurred. They talked to us for a while and then left. The officers never asked Greg to leave or check to see if I still desired to leave. My husband must have said the same thing on his report, because several weeks later we both were given a three-day suspension for filing a false report. I was young on the job and stressed. I realized I was given the wrong advice from the officer.

After the suspension, I pulled the report to see what happened in that process to get me suspended and discovered these White officers, instead of discarding the initial report, as I initially believed was the action they would take, wrote the report of the gun and then filed a supplementary report. A supplementary report is a follow-up report to the initial investigation to offer additional information. Consequently, contrary to their advice, they actually reported the incident and then manipulated me to say it never happened.

I did spend another night at home and lived through it. The next day, however, I began making plans to leave. I instructed my children to start packing quietly upstairs and that we would be leaving that night. They looked so happy and worked quietly that day putting their things together. I planned to pack what little I was taking, at the last minute. I was able to get a moving truck and two men, one a police officer friend and a friend who was a civilian employee, to do the heavy lifting. In addition, I got my older sister, who was in a manic state, and her husband to help.

Everyone knew to arrive at 10 p.m. unless it was not safe for them to come. After being nervous all day that something would go wrong, the night came and Greg did leave for work. (Sigh.) The plan was in motion and everyone showed up as expected. I was so fearful during this time because I just knew that Greg would, as he had previously done in other situations, circle and come back home. Over time, I grew to believe that he could read my mind and that he knew what I was going to do and would respond. So, my fear of him circling back home to some might have been considered me being paranoid. But my experience had taught me that my paranoia was healthy paranoia. I wanted them to move fast to avoid any possible blood bath where my family and police department friends would be harmed. We got the truck loaded with no incidents. My family and the police officer went home. I got the children in the car and followed the civilian employee to his home, where we stayed in his basement apartment until I found an apartment for us. I had finally left hell, so I thought. My children were out of this environment. I had made a giant step toward freedom.

Making this step to leave my abuser seemed like it took a thousand years. Yet, the strength it takes to leave an abuser is to be celebrated. Many people could not understand why I did not leave sooner. That was a great question. I had a billy club, a gun, mace, and a whole gang of officers to come to my rescue. Even though I had all of this, I could not access the ability and strength to leave. I was a victim of abuse. I had lost my power. And there was nothing in my sacred history with the church that gave me permission to leave. I only left because I was concerned for my children. I was still scared. I was still a victim of abuse. I was still stuck in a religious cage that had me trapped. I was still the victim of deception by the White police officers who I now could not depend on for service nor protection. Yet, I was free. At the same time, there were so many more webs of entanglement, which seemed as if they were insurmountable barriers.

Still, I cannot deny, there was victory in my ability to leave.

Reflection: Forgiveness and Domestic Violence

Archbishop Desmond Tutu wrote the foreword for Robert D. Enright and Joanna North's book, *Exploring Forgiveness*. In the foreword, Archbishop Desmond Tutu explains, "Forgiveness is taking seriously the awfulness of what has happened when you are treated unfairly. It is opening the door for the other person to have a chance to begin again."[1] This framework has been a guide I have followed to get to a place of forgiveness with my abuser, Greg.

First, I worked with all I had to get to this place of thinking about forgiveness. I engaged in a ritual of self-forgiveness, and there were plenty

---

1. Enright and North, *Exploring Forgiveness*, xiii.

of things I needed forgiving *for* in my history. I called this process thus far the "letting go" stage of forgiveness.

The second stage resulted in me receiving complete forgiveness from God in my choices. Although I realized the harm was trauma-related, I needed to feel God's healing love in this process. Last, paraphrasing Tutu's words, my heart was open to forgiving my abuser. However, it was the gift I would offer him if he asked. It was the letting go stage that facilitated my heart opening to forgive Greg. And for me, this was as far as I believed I needed to go with obeying God. It is important to note that if I never got to this point, I believe God would honor me just as well.

Gratefully, Greg and I had a chance encounter where I was able to confront him for what he did. We had more conversations and finally he asked for forgiveness. The gift was there and I offered it to him saying, "God does not want you to suffer for all you have done to me, no more than God wants me to suffer for what I have done to others." That conversation ended and he walked out of my office door.

This is how I navigate forgiveness. There was no real repentance as I knew repentance to be. There was no accountability on his part or desire to confess openly to his violence and treatment of me. He offered no restitution. He eventually died. I felt safe for the first time through his death. Unexpectedly, posthumous restitution came from his mother who returned everything Greg had stolen from me and given to her to store away.

Researchers agree it takes an average of seven times for victims of domestic violence to finally leave their abusers. And in the midst, people continue to ask the question, *"Why doesn't she leave?"* First, caregivers need to remember that to ask this question is a subtle way to blame the victim for her own abuse, thus producing another avenue of shame. However, learning how to be safe in an abusive household, and even garnering the strength and will to leave an abusive home, are the first of many navigational challenges toward the victim figuring out how to be safe. The trauma victims experience during this phase is the beginning of navigating these paths in silence. Trauma is a journey most victims/survivors take in silence and isolation. In addition, research has shown that leaving an abusive relationship can be lethal for the victim as well as her family.

According to the National Coalition Against Domestic Violence (NCADV), 72 percent of all murder-suicides involve an intimate partner.[2] And the United States Department of Justice reported in 2007 that intimate partners committed 14 percent of all homicides in the United States. The total estimated number of intimate partner homicide victims in 2007 was 2,340, including 1,640 females and 700 males. And it must be noted when it comes to homicides, a study of intimate partner homicides found that 20 percent of victims were not the intimate partners themselves, but family members, friends, neighbors, persons who intervened, law enforcement responders, or bystanders.[3]

In addition, violence against Black trans women must be included in these statistics. *The Harvard Civil Rights-Civil Liberties Law Review* reports regarding America's treatment of Black trans women:

> Violence against Black trans women has been accurately described as a pandemic within a pandemic. And this summer, six transwomen all under the age of 32, were murdered in the span of nine days. Their deaths are part of a horrifying pattern. Hate crimes against transgender and gender non-conforming individuals have been on the rise for years, with the number of murders in 2020 already almost surpassing that of 2019. Of the 26 victims so far this year and the 27 victims last year, the majority have been Black trans women under the age of 30.[4]

Research further suggests that women with disabilities are more likely to experience domestic violence, emotional abuse, and sexual assault than women without disabilities. Women with disabilities may also feel more isolated and feel they are unable to report the abuse, or they may be dependent on the abuser for their care. Like many women who are abused, women with disabilities are usually abused by someone they know, such as a partner or family member.[5]

These statistics alone are both horrifying and disconcerting and require caregivers to focus more on the safety, health, and welfare of victims/survivors rather than engage with victim-blaming questions. There are a plethora of reasons why women remain in abusive relationships with their intimate partners. However, the better question would

2. See "Statistics."
3. Catalano et al., "Female Victims of Violence."
4. Forestiere, "America's War on Black Transwomen," para. 1.
5. See the United States Department of Justice's Office on Women's Health: https://www.womenshealth.gov/.

be, "Why can abusive partners commit these crimes with impunity?" The average citizen on the street who chooses to harm others will face the possibility of arrest. There is never a question as to why their victims did not run. We must learn to ask the right questions that will facilitate being effective caregivers. This way the pastoral care offered will be focused more on accountability of those who choose to harm others.

Although sexual violence fits into a category by itself, sexual violence can occur in a marital relationship. Pastors and faith leaders use 1 Cor 7:3–4 to justify a husband's right to sexual privileges: "The husband should give to his wife her conjugal rights, and likewise the wife to her husband. For the wife does not have authority over her own body but the husband does; likewise, the husband does not have authority over his own body, but the wife does." Theologian and ethicist Marie Fortune in her book, *Keeping the Faith: Questions and Answers for the Abused Woman*, exegetes this passage to affirm that both the husband and the wife have equal sexual access to one another. However, Fortune points out that this access is not *at-will* as "both partners have a right to expect sexual activity with the other and both have a responsibility to respect the wishes of the other."[6]

Rape is the legal definition for sex without consent, including within a marital relationship.

Discussion

A friend and colleague, Oliver Williams, professor of sociology at the University of Minnesota, founded the Institute on Domestic Violence in the African American Community. Other colleagues and I were a part of this organization. Later, Williams turned over the reins of this organization to another colleague of his and created the organization African American Domestic Peace Project (AADPP), which I and several colleagues from the institute joined also. We continue to provide ministry needs across the United States. However, while serving with the Institute on Domestic Violence in the African American Community, several of my colleagues and I, under the direction of Williams, created a guide for providing care around domestic violence for the African American community. The primary writers of this were Dr. Sharon Ellis Davis, Minister LaDonna M. Combs, and Rev. J. R. Thicklin.

---

6. Fortune, *Keeping the Faith*, 18.

In the foreword, Thicklin admonished, "There is a great responsibility that we have as pastors and ministers to embrace our mandate to serve as stewards to our congregations. It is not only our commission, but it is our duty to fulfill it both in word and in behavior. As preachers of the Bible, we must acknowledge that its message of liberation transcends race, color, creed, and gender."[7] Also highlighted here, Williams offers five action plans based on the understanding of the recognition that faith-based groups and organizations have strong relationships with communities of color, older women, women with disabilities, and immigrant communities. These plans include the following:

1. Committing to making the problem of violence against women a critical concern.
2. Ensuring that faith-based environments are safe to allow victims of violence to discuss their experiences and seek healing.
3. Developing strategies to address the needs of all women and girls exposed to violence.
4. Drawing on the resources of secular victim services, as well as advocacy and abuser treatment programs, to enhance community responses to violence against women.
5. And, helping to secure financial support for religious, spiritual, or faith-based groups and organizations developing responses to violence against women and children.[8]

Thicklin first recognizes that there are many African American male allies, preachers, and professors who have joined forces to advocate for victims/survivors and hold abusers accountable within AADPP. Second, although this manual speaks specifically to African American women, it is also an important resource for those victims/survivors, advocates, students of religion, and professors, because issues of sexual and domestic violence transcend race and gender. Third and most important, it emphasizes the five action plans for churches and faith-based organizations. A copy of this manual as well as a DVD of pastors preaching can be obtained from the African American Domestic Peace Project (www.aadpp.org).

---

7. Williams, *Speaking of Faith*, 2.
8. Thicklin, quoted in Williams, *Speaking of Faith*, 5.

Activity: Commit to Act

Using the five action plans highlighted by Williams at the IDVACC, develop a plan that emphasizes ways by which these goals can be achieved.

1. How will your church commit to making the problem of violence against women a critical concern?
2. How will you ensure that faith-based environments are safe spaces for victims of violence to discuss their experiences and seek healing?
3. What are short-term and long-term strategies to address the needs of women and girls exposed to violence?
4. How will you partner with secular victim services, as well as advocacy and abuser treatment programs, to enhance community responses to violence against women?
5. What national, local, and philanthropic resources are available, and how will you secure financial support from them for religious, spiritual, or faith-based groups and organizations developing responses to violence against women and children?

Chapter 5

Prepare for War in Times of Peace

I HAD A FRIEND who worked in the medical section of the police department. The medical section was located in the training academy where recruits came to train to become police officers. The training consisted of exercise, physical fitness tests, range instruction, and academic rigor that would lead to an associate in applied science (AAS), a degree in law enforcement. The building is also used for officers and other command staff who are often detailed from their normal duties to receive specialized training to enhance their skill sets for particular assignments. There is hardly ever a time when some activity is not occurring within the academy. The academy also houses the Chaplain's Unit and was staffed by police officers who are also ordained clergy. These chaplains take care of police officers and members of their families, especially when officers have been killed or seriously injured in the line of duty. The medical section is where officers report when they are ill and have to file paperwork for a medical leave of absence. This is the place you report to for evaluation of your condition, and if you are able to return to work, continue on medical leave, or if the illness persists, begin the process of going on disability until such time as an officer is ready to retire.

It was in this section of the training academy that I met a police lieutenant who I referred to as my friend. Professionally, he was referred to as Lieutenant Bold. Officers do not usually refer to other ranking officers as a friend. The reality is that the department is a semi-military organization, which means people usually refer to ranking officers by their title and last name. First names are not usually used in this semi-military environment. Depending on their gender, ranking officers are acknowledged as "sir" and "ma'am." However, I thought of my lieutenant friend as a friend.

Lieutenant Bold did not necessarily feel the same way nor think of me as a friend. For me, especially within the police culture, coupled with my being a victim of abuse *by* a police officer, my trust factor in this environment was low. The qualities exhibited by the lieutenant were very rare in an environment where I felt unprotected. I had already experienced police officers who did not believe my story and made light of my accusations of abuse, offered advice that caused me to be suspended, and one particular officer refused to come to my rescue when he witnessed me being abused outside my home while reporting for duty. So, other than my best friend, Rhonda, who was a police officer, I shared very little with others out of fear of not being believed. But, in my mind, Lieutenant Bold was my friend. He was someone I believed I could trust. He was someone who I believed actually seemed to care about the several times I had to go on medical leave due to my emotional or physical state while living with an abuser who I believed was capable of harming me and my children or even causing our demise.

My friend, Lieutenant Bold, stood about six feet tall, had a dark complexion, and probably weighed 250 pounds. His build was more buff than heavy. His uniform was the same as most officers, with the exception that his shirt was white instead of blue. This color automatically indicated that he was a supervisor. The bar on each side of his white shirt indicated that he was a lieutenant of police. In addition to his dress, which commanded respect and attention, his stern and strong facial expressions and overall countenance gave me the impression that he was all about business. My visits were for those purposes only. I was there because I was reporting due to being on the medical. Although Lieutenant Bold was the commanding officer of the medical section, I was not expecting to encounter him during my daily visits. My absences had everything to do with the abuse I had encountered and the resulting physical and emotional distress I was experiencing. It was not seen as a good thing to refer to yourself as having psychological issues. Consequently, emotional distress was the next best thing, but even saying this was risky, and officers might be placed on leave pending psychological evaluations. As a result, any time I called in sick, the reasons were described as headaches, migraines, and severe stomach aches.

Going on the medical is the same as calling in sick from your job. You call your unit/district of assignment, notifying them you are ill and will not be coming to work. What might be different is after calling in sick, you have a short window of time where you, in addition to your unit of assignment, notify the medical section with more details. Within the medical section, there are procedures to follow. If requested by them, you will have to go into the medical unit in person or call them. It was the medical section that determined how much longer you could stay off work. This decision is made in conjunction with the officer, the officer's physician, and the medical section personnel. It is not looked upon favorably by the unit of assignment if you called in sick for too many days. It is more favorable to be off sick for a longer period of time than to be seen constantly going on medical leave.

It was on one of those visits where I had the opportunity to meet and have conversations with Lieutenant Bold. I had made several visits to the medical section. During that year, I had become a familiar face to the personnel, including the lieutenant. He seemed to relax more and would refer to me by name when I approached the front desk where he usually sat. Lieutenant Bold began to exhibit a friendlier attitude and his curiosity peaked regarding my visits, as he would ask me general questions to break the ice toward more specific questions regarding my visits. Soon he made himself available for me to have conversations with him by inviting me to have coffee in the cafeteria. As a victim of abuse, I was at first fearful that he was making a pass at me, and that made me uncomfortable. I felt uncomfortable because I did not trust my own judgment. I was afraid if he asked me for a more personal relationship that I would consent and live to regret my decision. However, despite the fear I was experiencing, I agreed, hoping that he would allow me to speak my truth to him off the record and confidentially, and that he would not involve the police in my business to any greater degree than it already was. I was grateful that our conversations unfolded just as I had hoped.

Lieutenant Bold provided me with space to talk freely. These conversations were where I began to feel safe with him and share with him all that has happened between me and my abuser. He took the time to listen without making comments or providing me with an authoritarian police-type lecture. He simply listened. I found myself seeking out more time when I was off duty to find opportunities to talk with him. I always referred to him during these times as "Lieutenant." Yet, for me, he had become a friend and confidant. I trusted him. The relationship never turned into anything sexual because he never approached me in that way. If he did ask, I knew I would have said "yes." At that time, if anyone was nice and caring toward me, I felt obligated to sleep with them. My boundaries were weak. I did not know that our conversations would eventually yield the best advice I could have received and would be the stimulus to help me to navigate what I had no idea would come next. And little did I know that the drama was not even half over.

I made the decision to divorce my husband Greg even before I left our home. I had already visited one attorney for advice. I was just too fearful to follow through. But now, I was ready to begin this process. I needed a lawyer that would not be intimidated by my husband's irrational and volatile behavior and who also was familiar with the department, its general orders, rules, culture, and procedures. I found all of these qualities in retired Lieutenant Laws, who was recommended to me by Lieutenant Bold. Lieutenant Laws was African American and also a lawyer. I knew Lieutenant Laws but not personally. I reached out to him and eventually met with and hired him as my divorce attorney. The divorce proceedings had officially begun.

Greg, who I now referred to as my estranged husband, received the divorcing documents via the United States Postal Service. I had left our marital home, and he was staying there alone. We both received our first documents that gave us the date to make our initial appearance. Greg showed up all triumphant looking, as if he did not have a care in the world and acted as if he was happy to see me. He looked at me in the waiting room, smiled, and with a smile on his face, spoke, "Hey there Doll Face." Wow! I was back to being *Doll Face*, and not the *Mouth*. Afraid of him and intimidated by his presence and words, I barely looked at his face. I smiled or quickly said, "*Hi.*" By that time, both our lawyers were present, and we were called into the courtroom.

Greg's attorney was a tall White woman with long reddish hair named Gates. The sound of her high-pitch voice indicated that she would dramatize everything regarding our proceedings, and she did. After my lawyer, Laws, read the divorce petition to the judge, which included expressing my intention to divorce my husband, as well as the stated grounds for the divorce (physical, mental, and emotional cruelty), Gates went ballistic. After hearing Laws offer to the court the grounds for divorce, Gates loudly proclaimed she was appalled. She was appalled that she received the papers late. She was appalled that my attorney and I had put her client "through the ringer." She was appalled by everything. To this day, my friend Marsha and I jokingly express how we are "appalled" whenever we hear something we do not like. After this first proceeding, I left the courtroom disappointed. I was not disappointed over the divorce proceedings. I was disappointed over my lawyer's performance in court. Greg's attorney, with her flare for dramatics, seemed to have the energy I expected from my attorney. I wanted him to sound harsh. I wanted his presence and demeanor to say, "*Listen to me! I am a police lieutenant and attorney.*" I wanted his presence, voice, and attitude to inform my husband, his attorney, and the judge that we were not here to play games. Instead, my attorney was soft spoken and did not seem to have any fight in him, and that was disturbing to me. I just knew at that moment I had made the wrong choice for an attorney. But it was too late for me to change attorneys. I wanted my divorce.

Soon after this date, we were granted another court appearance. This court appearance was to address the second petition my attorney filed to grant me custodial rights to move back into the home with my children until the final decision was made through our divorce agreement. Eventually, my attorney advised me to change the petition to "Irreconcilable Differences." He simply believed it would speed up the process of my divorce. And he also stated that the original grounds would be difficult to prove, since I had little to no formal documentation of these violations. In my mind, I thought, "Here we go again with my passive attorney." But aloud, I agreed and the document was changed. On our next court date, the judge granted the petition.

Prior to arriving in court, my attorney told me to not expect possession of our home to be granted on a temporary basis since Greg was already living there. Consequently, I was surprised by the judge's decision. Greg was ordered to evacuate the property because I had children and they were already attending the local schools. My two children and I moved back into the home. I was relieved to be back home. My children were still going to school, and it was a great inconvenience getting them to school. My children were able to continue their routine and feel some kind of normalcy even in the midst of their fear, confusion, and concern for me. Their well-being was an important part of my having some sense of sanity.

The next morning, I began my search for a locksmith to change my locks. I finally reached them and made an appointment for them to come to change all the locks on my door. They arranged to arrive between 1 p.m. and 4 p.m. Somewhere between these times, they arrived. The locksmith began with my front door. He had barely taken the top lock off of the door when my estranged husband showed up. He was wearing his plain clothes and had a gun around his waist. He was wearing his badge. He looked as if he had just got off of work and was simply arriving home.

The locksmith was unaware of our circumstances. I did not think there was any reason to explain our situation to him. He began shouting at me and shouting at the locksmith, telling him how this was his house and he had no business changing the lock on the door. Greg began interrogating the locksmith asking, "What are you doing changing locks on my door? This is my house? Did she tell you to change my locks?" I could tell the locksmith was as fearful as I was at the moment. In a low voice, I told the locksmith that we were divorcing and that I was granted permission to temporarily live here until the divorce was final and the house matter was adjudicated. The last thing I wanted him to do was to stop changing my locks. Greg walked back to his car and left. He had done what he came to do. The locksmith, sufficiently terrified, cared nothing about my pleas. He then gathered his tools and left. I believe Greg left the area because he knew he should not be there and was probably afraid I or the locksmith might call the police.

Calling the police was the last thing on my mind, and getting in trouble with the Department was never on my mind. The only thing on my mind was getting back into my house so I could have some sense of normalcy. I sat down on the stairs and in the midst of my fear and frustration cried for the next hour. After I settled myself and my children arrived home, I sat with them for a while, fixed dinner, and got them settled in bed. I stayed up most of the night thinking about this incident. I was convinced, even more, that somehow Greg knew what I was thinking and doing every moment of the day and that was how he knew to show up at the house at key moments.

Before I hired Lieutenant Laws, and while Greg and I were still sharing our home, I visited a divorce attorney for a consultation. When I arrived home that evening, Greg moved close to my face, his gun lying on the table where we were standing while wearing a bullet-proof vest. This intimidating look usually demonstrated on the street was directed toward me. His voice sounded as if he was conducting an interrogation, rough and quickly talking, as he questioned my whereabouts, stating "I know you went to see a lawyer, didn't you?" I remember thinking, "How in the hell did he know this?" I told him that I was not divorcing him simply to avoid a physical confrontation with him. This inteminading behavior is another reason I wanted him dead. In every phase of our abusive relationship I believed my life was in danger. But, after this incident with the locks, my fears escalated exponentially. I felt both paralyzed and helpless as to what next steps I should take. That morning after my children left for school, I called my friend Lieutenant Bold from the medical section and he agreed to meet with me.

Lieutenant Bold, as usual, listened intently to me telling him the story regarding the divorce proceedings, my being temporarily allowed custodianship of our home, and my estranged husband being ordered to leave the house. Then I shared with him all that had occurred the day my door locks were scheduled to be changed. I told him this story while tears were rolling down my face. I sensed he felt the fear and terror I was experiencing. Yet, he continued to let me express myself with very little comment, just affirmations by nodding his head and other short expressions. Finally, when I finished talking, he looked at me for what seemed like forever. He had that look I spoke about earlier, intimidating, stern, in command, and serious. However, this time, I did not experience him in the same way. I saw this look differently. It was a look of care and concern. He looked at me and offered the advice I needed at that moment. He spoke these words, "Sharon, prepare for war in times of peace."

Prepare for war in times of peace. These words may sound superficial to some, but they were powerful for me. His words echoed in my mind in ways that activated my thinking brain and inactivated my lower brain that caused me to be paralyzed and not able to make decisions. It shook me to my core and went through me like a lightning bolt recharging me into action. Yes, I was still both fearful and afraid, yet I had awakened to the realization that this abuse pattern was not over simply because I filed for divorce and was awarded exclusive temporary sole legal rights to be in our home. Showing up unexpectedly to our home where he had been ordered to leave was only the beginning of what was to come. *Prepare for war in times of peace* meant I needed to plan for survival and start the process of expecting the unexpected. *Prepare for war in times of peace* was a wake-up call I heard loud and clear. Ironically, this was the last time I actually contacted my lieutenant friend. During this time, he actually became ill and had to go on medical leave, never to return to the department. Eventually, I heard he had passed away. I was in for the fight of my life. My energy went into taking care of my children, working to financially support my family, and navigating the craziness I would experience over the next year.

Although my lieutenant friend was gone, I will always remember the rock he was for me at such a crucial moment in my life. He will never know how those words shaped me. These words continue to live inside of me. They continue to push me into survival mode whenever I feel threatened. His voice is a tape that will never be erased: *prepare for war in times of peace.* And I did. My first action was to move out of my home. I first contacted my attorney to tell him what happened while I was attempting to change locks and that I did not feel safe being in the home. I told him that I had to leave the house because I was threatened by Greg. His presence was threatening, his personhood was threatening, and his conversation with the locksmith was threatening. My attorney advised me that he would file another petition and get a court date to address that issue. I packed up what few things I could gather for my children and myself, placed them in the car, and left. I returned to the place I originally stayed when I had fled from my husband.

I was informed by a friend that when Greg discovered I had left, he moved back into the house, regardless of a written legal order to vacate the premises. By this time, I was fully engulfed with my duties in the crime laboratory of the police department, where I had been previously detailed (working in another unit besides patrol). I had also moved into my own apartment, where I had direct access to the lakefront. The forensic work I was doing was intriguing, and that work was a welcome distraction from thinking about what my estranged husband would do next and when he would do it. I felt relatively safe for the time being. I had my own apartment by the lake, which provided a tranquil setting and gave me space to breathe. I felt safe at work in the crime lab.

The crime laboratory was located on the fifth floor of the headquarters (main section) of the department. After exiting the elevator to the fifth floor, you would encounter the front desk. The front desk was similar to the front desk at the police districts. It had a long counterspace, and officers worked behind the desk. They had several duties. One was to screen people who came into the lab to ensure they were there for official police business. The laboratory sections were to the right of the elevator and extended down a long hallway. This hallway stretch was home to several units that tested crime scene evidence. There was the crime laboratory section, the drug testing section, the photography section, and the fingerprint section. All of these were specialized sections whose main duties were to examine evidence and testify in court as experts within the court system during trials.

The unit where I worked was the crime laboratory, which examined evidence from crime scenes, including rape kits, clothing, gunshot residue, microscopic evidence, electrophoresis, and other testing. To enter this space, you'd have to come through a door and, again, there is counterspace. Officers who enter that space often come to collect information about a case or to drop off a subpoena or evidence for us to inventory and examine. Then there are the spaces where we sat to do our examination of evidence. Two long desks, separated about six inches apart, sat on either side of the room, making space for the eight serologists (the title we were given). These desks were there as our desk/exam tables. In the front were various technical instruments we used for testing. The back contained rooms on each side of the laboratory. One room housed our rape kits and a large space that contained other evidence. The other side contained space to do our electrophoresis and analysis work with blood, semen, saliva, and hair samples. Today, DNA testing has replaced most electrophoresis tests. Needless to say, I felt protected in the lab by my coworkers. I felt protected by the space and by the protocols to enter the lab. One day, despite all of the security measures in place, I managed to receive an unwanted surprise right inside of the crime laboratory, which was nothing short of embarrassing.

One of my coworkers in the crime lab got my attention and pointed me to the front desk. I walked up as usual to see what the gentleman desired. Immediately, a delivery man dressed pretty casually with a big smile on his face lifted up a bunch of colorful balloons and began singing some songs that spoke of love, forgiveness, and wanting me back at home. After he finished, he handed the balloons to me and left. Everyone in the laboratory knew of my abuse and pending divorce. My coworkers were very supportive of me. They knew intimate details about me and my estranged husband. I recall the time when I called in sick because I had developed an infection in my pelvis, and the doctor described it as having puss in my tubes, which they later translated, to my surprise and embarrassment, as a communicable disease Greg had given to me. They joked around and called me "puss tube." In spite of my embarrassment for even telling them what was wrong with me, I still felt supported by them, and I was eventually okay with their teasing. My smile, which I had developed the ability to maintain in times of stress and duress, hid all those feelings that were buried deep inside of me. I had learned to press on no matter the circumstances.

Consequently, after the singing telegram incident, my coworkers simply followed suit and began to proclaim to one another and to me how I should go back to my husband after him making such a grand effort to reconcile. I endured the rest of the day with those kinds of remarks until it was finally time to leave the laboratory. On my way out of the building, I stopped at the front desk and asked them why they allowed this person to come back to my unit. Their response, with proud grins on their faces, was, "We thought you would appreciate the surprise." Really, I thought to myself. I never responded to Greg to acknowledge this visit. I just wanted my divorce. Not long after this incident, my lawyer called me to let me know the courts had scheduled an emergency session to address the house situation the following week.

Our court date was 10 a.m. the following Wednesday. Both attorneys, Laws and Gates, were present when I arrived in court. Greg appeared just as we were about to begin our hearing. When the judge asked why he showed up at the house, Greg denied being there. When the judge asked him why he was in the house and I was not, he became animated as he lied about why he was living in the house. With his eyes really big (which was his I'm-telling-you-the-truth eyes) and his facial expressions, he seemed to signify how concerned he was for the safety of the property and he told the judge that I had abandoned the property, took all the furniture from the home, and the house was empty. He testified to this lie with a straight face, as if he really believed this occurred, knowing it did not. He then said he moved back in to make certain I would not come back and take what was left. The judge listened while my attorney remained silent. I was sitting there waiting to see if his lawyer had any appalled statements to make. She was silent also.

The judge looked over at me and began questioning me. "Did you abandon the house?" I answered, "no." "Did you take any furniture from the home?" Again, I said that I had not and explained that all of the furniture was gone when I arrived at the house. He finally asked me if I wanted to return to the house. I declined. By this time, I did not feel safe after the initial event when I moved back home with court orders. However, I did explain to the judge I had possessions in the home I needed to recover. He asked me what I desired to recover, reminding me that I could not have access to any of the property at this time because that part needed to be adjudicated. I told him I had a great number of books in the house, clothes in the attic for my children, and clothes and other personal items I needed to retrieve. The judge then granted Greg permission to stay in the house, and we all agreed on a date I could return to the house to retrieve my property. We left the court without incident.

The next week, when I was assigned to go to the house to recover my belongings, I asked my best girlfriend to go with me. I did not plan to be in the house long. I just wanted to grab my stuff, put them in boxes, and leave. I asked my girlfriend, Rhonda, to go with me because I knew him enough to know that he would not act a fool or attempt to hurt me in front of her. His persona was to make everyone on the surface believe he is the best guy in the world. And he did that with precision. My girlfriend never saw him in any other capacity other than his nice, kind, and welcoming behavior.

Greg opened the door to the house when he saw us arriving, greeting the both of us with hellos and smiles. You would have thought we were his special guests. When we walked into our home, I was surprised to notice that all of the furniture was gone from the living room, dining room, and kitchen. The house was empty. I never said anything to him about the furniture. I knew he would say something insane, and I had one goal in mind, to get in and get out. My girlfriend and I went down to the basement to first retrieve the books that were in a long bookcase along the north wall. In front of the bookcase, approximately ten feet out from the shelves, were all types of bottles (milk bottles, liquor bottles, soda bottles, etc.). There were so many, I remember thinking to myself and ultimately asked my girlfriend why these bottles were on the table. She shrugged her shoulders as if to say, "I do not know." Other than those items, the large portion of the basement had nothing in it, either. I began moving the bottles out of the way so that we could lay the books on the table, pack them up, and bring them upstairs. The rest was even faster. I threw things in bags and never acknowledged the missing items I noticed. Nothing mattered more to me than to get out of that house and get away from him ASAP. My estranged husband in his grandiose way grabbed a box and began helping us out of the house. My girlfriend engaged in the task of thanking him for his assistance. I had that smile plastered on my face. We drove off and I felt a sense of relief. But that sense of relief would soon turn into fear and frustration. I'm reminded, *prepare for war in times of peace.*

I was not aware of the term *domestic violence* back in early 1979 when the abuse occurred. However, I did see some movies where there was fighting in relationships. The abuser was usually the man, and I knew enough to notice a pattern of behavior. I did not know the dynamics of domestic violence and the shapes and forms that could take place within the relationship. This expertise came much later. I did know, however, that leaving an abusive relationship could cost you your life. I did know that power and control was at the center of abusive relationships. And I did know that leaving an abusive relationship could drive the abuser to take your life. What I did not know was that rather than taking my life, which was always my fear, he would attempt to destroy my character and my livelihood.

Not too long after my visit to the house, I arrived at work early, as I normally do. I would take different routes to and from work to avoid being followed by Greg. *Prepare for war in times of peace* was constantly in my thoughts. I was intentionally early for work to get there before anyone else so that I had a moment to breathe before anyone else arrived. I also prepared coffee for everyone who arrived later. I poured my coffee and sat at my work table to relax, leaving the lights off for the calming effect. Later, officers would arrive, folk would begin talking and filling the space with laughter, and then we would buckle down and begin a day's work. It was approximately 10 a.m. when an officer from the front desk came into the crime laboratory. My desk was located in the front of the office where I sat working. My best girlfriend, Rhonda, worked there also. She shared the desk next to mine in the laboratory. The officer motioned at me to come to our front desk and I complied. He informed me that an officer/investigator from the Internal Affairs Division (IAD) wanted to see me. I informed my supervisor and then went to the lobby area and took the elevator up to where the IAD was housed.

The department had two investigative units. One unit is the Office of Internal Affairs (OPS), which investigated citizen complaints against officers mainly from the patrol division. The other unit is the IAD, whose job is to investigate officers who were believed to be involved in activities outside the law. That department is run by officers and it was rumored that these officers loved their jobs and loved investigating officers. "They are not your friends." I heard these words over and over from various officers. And it was not a good thing for the division personnel to call you to their office.

So, imagine how I was feeling called to IAD. On the outside, I was cool and calm. Internally, I heard churning inside my stomach and it felt like at any second I would lose control of my bowels. A supervisor, Sergeant Cousins, walked in and greeted me. After affirming who I was and asking me if I was estranged from my husband, the sergeant began to tell me why I was there. He began by saying there was a complaint filed against me. The complaint stated that I went to my mother-in-law's apartment and placed a Molotov cocktail in the back of her door. I listened to him stunned. In my mind I felt as if I was once again in a movie. I thought this could not be real. This could not be happening to me. I found some solace in knowing the complaint contained lies. I did not commit this act. After my denial, the supervisor went on to say my prints were found on the bottle. The supervisor went on to inform me there was a note inside the bottle. The note contained multicolored letters cut out and pasted on the paper. They were arranged on the paper to read, "Death to you bitch and your family." After reading those words and being told my prints were on the bottle, I could no longer hold the smile to imply that all was well with me. Tears begin to flow from my eyes. The bottle and note were evidence that I could be criminally charged for and immediately suspended over. I cried and cried and the tears did not stop. I had not committed this act.

My mother-in-law and I had no real relationship and I barely knew where she lived. The neighborhood where she resided was not one I would travel in at night to place anything on her porch. To my surprise, the supervisor did not have the look of suspicion on his face and seemed to have empathy for my situation. But he had to do his job. I would not return to work that day. I had to go to the police station to be charged for this crime. Although I was never placed in the lockup, I was detained and fingerprinted. After being processed, I was allowed to leave after the prints cleared. I could not believe it. I was under a full-blown investigation.

I met once with the detective assigned to the case. During his interview with me, he asked me, "If you didn't do this, Sharon, how do you think your fingerprints got on the bottle? " This question hit like a brick. Suddenly the lights came on in my head. I began to recall my visit to our house to retrieve my belongings, mainly my books. I recalled seeing all of the bottles on the table and remembered touching them. "Damn!" I swore aloud. It was that moment I realized what had occurred. I began telling the detective my whole story of abuse, which ended with me coming to the house and touching the bottles.

My abuse story with a police officer was no longer a secret. The news would spread far and wide. Some of that spreading came from my estranged husband who told his sad story to whoever would listen to him to garner support for his side of the story. The others came from police having access to case reports and as a result of sheer gossip. The detective seemed to believe my story. However, even if he did not believe me, I had given him a reasonable explanation for how my prints got on the bottle. At the very least, their evidence had holes in it, and the state's attorney who was the ultimate determinant of criminal activity would more than likely not approve the charges. That charge was eventually dropped; there would be other charges.

During the next several months, I got hit with accusation after accusation. I was accused through an anonymous complaint of stealing drugs out of the crime laboratory. I was investigated for that. However, because of the way the drug unit is secured, most of the supervisors knew I could not have stolen drugs from it unless I actually worked in that unit. I was accused of going to my husband's girlfriend's house in the projects replete with criminal activity, going up the elevator, and knocking on her door. She opened the door and I allegedly pulled my weapon, pointed the gun at her, and said, "Bitch, leave my husband alone."

What was so disturbing about this complaint for which I was also charged was that her daughter, who was about ten or eleven years old, was her witness. She told the officers that she saw me do this. Now, I am not certain if my estranged husband put someone up to do this or not. I am not certain if they both set me up together and dragged her daughter into this. All I knew is I did not know this woman, nor did I know where she lived. And I could not identify her daughter if she were standing right in front of me. I certainly would not have been in the projects for any reason other than as part of my police duties, and I was not even working in the patrol cars at this time. This investigation did have feet. There was a witness. And who knows? The investigators might very well bring the case of the Molotov cocktail back for another look.

By this point, I was so physically and mentally exhausted. I felt traumatized and I had started to believe that perhaps I was committing these crimes. Perhaps I was falling asleep and waking up in my sleep to commit these felonies. My attorney, Laws, already aware of these various accusations and charges, advised me to go take a polygraph test. I immediately refused because I was well aware that the polygraph test reacts to emotions and could result in my failing the test. And I was aware that pathological people could be void of both feeling and fear, take the test, and pass in spite of his/her guilt. And the only good use of a polygraph test within the department was to garner a verbal admission of guilt. Otherwise, the test was not even admissible in court. I absolutely refused to take the polygraph on my own accord. My attorney tried to convince me again, arguing that if I passed, it might put an end to the accusations. And if I failed, no one would ever know that I took the test because it was privately done. I refused to take the polygraph test. Period!

The accusations continued. The IAD reached out again. This time it involved arson. This took place at my estranged husband's residence, the home we used to share. His sister was the witness this time. She supposedly witnessed me coming to the home, setting fire to my husband's vehicle, and burning it up. Again, this was added to the multitude of charges I already had. And the detectives informed me that the car was actually burnt up. Here we go again, another case. I was an emotional wreck. I just knew I was going to get kicked out of the crime laboratory, and I knew I was on the verge of getting fired. So, I took my attorney's advice.

I went for the polygraph test. The results of the test were devastating. The man who administered the test came back, took a seat, and looked at me with disdain in his face and said, "The polygraph test said you did these things." He hardly said a word but kept looking at me with an accusatory expression until I left. I will never forget the look on this man's face. I felt hopeless. My attorney told me not to worry about it. He looked me in the face and said, "Sharon, you didn't do it." By this time, I was dating another man I met while bowling in a league. We seemed to like each other. Paul was tall, and I felt that if my estranged husband saw me with him, he would think twice about doing anything to me.

Around this time, Greg had stolen my car from the parking lot of where I lived. The car was in both of our names. Since he wrote the police report when it was finally recovered, he was the one called. I never saw the car again. I purchased another used car that was now in my name only. However, in the midst of what I was going through, that car was the least of my concerns. He now knew where I was living. I no longer had a place where I could be at peace. But I had a boyfriend. Paul knew some of my story and was kindhearted. I needed someone who could, first, help me stay safe and, second, be my witness and alibi. We agreed that I would move in with him. There was another event that never reached the level of these other offenses I had been accused of. However, I did have an alibi who would say I was with him. I learned at this time that family members and friends would not make reliable witnesses and would probably lie for you.

I then developed another plan. I asked the crime laboratory director if I could work midnights, (11 p.m. until 7 a.m.). I asked to work this shift because these were the hours when I would be accused of committing some type of crime. My premise was that working these hours would provide me with the opportunity I needed to prove my innocence. This request was an unusual request and I believe, if approved, I would be the first person to work these hours. The personnel within the crime laboratory were very supportive of me during this process. The crime laboratory consisted mostly of civilian personnel and very few were officers.

The director of the crime laboratory and my supervisor thought it was a good idea and allowed me to temporarily work this shift. I worked in the crime laboratory on the graveyard shift for three months. And guess what? I was not accused of a single crime. *This was not good*, at least, that was my thinking. Now the people on my job will start believing that perhaps I am guilty. However, their opinion was the opposite. They believed, as I did, that Greg may have been following me and somehow knew I was working this late-night shift.

Unlike the rank and file who worked the patrol division, there was never a time when I felt unsupported by the officers and civilian staff nor did I feel judged. I am not certain how much I could have remained in my right mind if the situation were different. Working in this space brought me a sense of peace and safety. I was grateful for those eight hours I spent daily.

Eventually, as the accusations poured in, we both were ordered to take the polygraph exam. This time I had no choice. I had to schedule an appointment. I was so nervous about getting the same results that I followed a colleague's suggestion to visit a hypnotist to lessen my anxiety about the test. When I visited the hypnotist, I was concerned that when I blanked out as a result of being hypnotized, the examiner would take sexual advantage of me. This is a fear I kept to myself, but it was a real fear. However, during the actual process, I never felt as if I was under any hypnotic control and I sincerely believed this was a scam of a profession. I completed the process and went home. The next day I arrived to take the polygraph. I was less nervous not because of being hypnotized, but as a result of having participated in this process previously.

Participating in this examination was similar to the one I took previously. The results this time came out slightly different. I did not commit these crimes but they decided I knew who did the crimes. As for my estranged husband's results, he passed. Through all of this, my supervisors and coworkers in the laboratory stood by me, supported me, and helped me in any way they were able to while I had to navigate my way through this ordeal.

The officers from the IAD took a liking to me. And where they could not help me navigate the system, they warned me in advance when another accusation was brewing. I developed friendships from both the IAD and the Office of Professional Standards who advised me and affirmed their belief in my innocence. It was very important to be believed. Although both of these units performed their duties with integrity, I was never formally arrested/charged, suspended, in jeopardy of losing my position in the crime laboratory, or at risk of being fired. However, many rumors and suspicions persisted within the patrol division. One of my friends, who was also a police recruit at the same time Greg and I were recruits, expressed it best: "Sharon I swear, if I did not know you, I would have believed everything Greg said about you." This is how smooth and manipulative Greg was. There were those who were supportive but my lived experience felt differently. The command staff, in general, demonstrated support with superficial words that I interpreted as, "Good luck." Yet, none of them demonstrated their commitment to justice in helping me in any way navigate my way through this ordeal. Interestingly enough, today people believe police cover for police. That may be true for patrol officers, but as for the rank and file they were willing to discipline officers unless there was substantial proof of innocence. In the unit where my estranged husband worked, the expressions of support for him continued with both the officers and command staff.

The command personnel never took my concerns for my life seriously. Nor did they express any empathy regarding all of these false accusations. They continued to support rather than challenge him because he made plenty of arrests that made the department look good. I experienced the department through the lens of what many women of any race often experience as the *good old boy department*. This means many experienced the department as a patriarchal and misogynistic environment, especially as it related to promotional opportunities and other types of support for them. In that type of sexist environment, I felt as if the men experienced a greater level of protection. Yet, there were times during my experience where I felt racism as it related to my estranged husband.

It became obvious to me during this second phase of Greg's abusive behavior how many of the White command staff were getting frustrated by Greg's ability to get away with his tactics of accusing me of crimes and of committing department violations. He was outsmarting the ones who were really in control in the department. My estranged husband was outsmarting them, and they did not like being outsmarted by a Black man. They intuitively knew he was behind the orchestration of these incidents. The command personnel's empathy slowly began to lean my way. I really believed they wanted to catch him in these acts and work to have him fired. I sensed my receiving their empathy was less about me and more about this Black man's cunning ability to escape their wrath and judgment. Consequently, I felt not only sexism but also racism actively being played out in these investigations and accusations. Their actions were more covert.

They would say things such as, "This asshole will not get away with this." I knew this anger, frustration, and passion they were exhibiting had nothing to do with me, but about this Black man getting away with these criminal acts. Intuitively, I both knew and felt this as truth. This is why many Black women today refuse to report abuse. They are afraid of what would happen if their husbands, spouses, or partners got into what is now perceived to be the racist actions of police. These same biases are being played out today. And to be clear, I never desired my husband's arrest or him being fired. I simply wanted the abuse, violence, and accusations to stop.

My divorce finally came through, and my ex-husband Greg stayed in the house and allowed it to go into foreclosure. The judge allowed him to stay there because I did not feel safe returning to the house. There were serious bills that he did not pay that bill collectors were calling me about. After telling them my story (in short form) and explaining that through court orders he was to pay those bills, the collector said, "Don't worry, we will find him; we will never bother you again for these bills." They never did call me again.

My parents were supportive of me but knew very little about what I was going through. There is a reason for my silence. I was afraid for their safety, knowing he would target them also and might try to harm them. I had my siblings and I had my best friend, Rhonda, by my side. Her mother thought I was going crazy, and she rightfully believed that I would drain her daughter to death given the emotional and mental toll this had taken on me too. Yet, Rhonda saw me through. I will forever love her for being there with me during these times. And my attorney? He did alright. In the end, I was quite pleased and proud of his support and litigation on my behalf. As crazy as my husband acted, Attorney Laws would often reassure me that he was not intimidated or scared of Greg and that he "knew his type." As for Rhonda, we remain friends to this day and have supported each other through our life circumstances. And as for my friend, Lieutenant Bold, I am eternally grateful.

Yes! I had support, but there was one thing I never had the opportunity to do: prove my innocence. This certainly left me feeling scared, shamed, and with continued feelings of guilt, as if the rumors were true. Having to live with others who believed I could be that type of person was heartbreaking. That was the scar I felt would hurt for a lifetime.

As for Greg, I was determined to dismiss his name out of my mind. I did not desire to call him by his name. Where he was once Greg my friend, who became Greg my husband, then Greg my estranged husband, and Greg, ex-husband, I referred to him now as *my abuser*. Unless absolutely necessary, I was determined to erase his name from my lips when I decided this would be how I see him and refer to him even today. For me, he has no name. His name, Greg, represents to me all that I experienced. Things died down but nothing was ever proven. I remained afraid that on any given day, he could kill me and get away with it. The one main thing I learned in this process was to *prepare for war in times of peace*.

Reflection: Navigating Systems and Institutions of Power

In 2000, I was admitted to a PhD program at Chicago Theological Seminary with a focus on theology, ethics, and human science. The human science of choice was sociology. I had to take sociology courses and chose to take them through the University of Illinois, Chicago. One of the courses that caught my attention was: "Is the Criminal Justice System Racist?" Even before I registered, I thought to myself, "Yes, of course, it's racist." The course was fascinating.

As students, our individual assignment was to prepare a final paper through researching statistical information to prove our hypothesis or to just do the research and discern its conclusion. We were responsible for research from the point of arrest to prosecution and determination of guilt. The main focus was on police and judges within the system. The results, for me, were alarming. Based on my research, there were no signs of racism within the department or in the courts. Statistics showed that across the spectrum, police officers of every ethnicity made an equal amount of arrests. It was the same for judges. The interesting thing about the judges was that Black judges tended to convict and sentence Black people even more toughly than White judges. One of the sociological explanations for this was that perhaps Black judges' hope and desire was for Black offenders to see the errors of their ways and change their behavior. It was suggested that perhaps Black judges even wanted to teach the Black convicts a lesson because of the resulting embarrassment for themselves and the community. However, what there was evidence of was the existence of discretion. When White officers and White judges had the discretion to arrest or sentence, Blacks suffered the disparities. This was the result of the research. However, did this put an end to the possibilities of racism? Definitely not.

What statistics had not proven is what we recognize today. We know that individuals can be racist in the ways discretion is used. However, what has been ignored in the data collected was how racism was built into the criminal justice system. Policing and historical antecedents to the criminal-justice system were instituted for the purpose of policing enslaved Black people. Is a criminal justice system racist whose internal structure was built on a racist foundation? Perhaps it is true that a system built on racism and racist practices must be dismantled and not simply reformed. This is the question we must seriously debate, discern, and make important decisions on—what would police reform look like if the criminal justice system is not dismantled? If it is to be dismantled, what is built in its place?

When I was a child growing up on the near north side of Chicago, our favorite pastime was walking the streets of Chicago with both the girls and boys who lived in the surrounding neighborhoods. As I grew older, the pattern was different, but at a younger age it was always about walking through the neighborhood, talking and laughing in groups, and just generally having fun. That was until the appointed time when police cars entered the neighborhood. Someone would holler "Police!" and with no hesitation, consultation, or communication, we would all begin to run. Whether I was actively involved in the walks or simply watching other children walk, the pattern was the same. Hearing someone in the group yell "Police!" triggered the running process immediately. When the police would show up, it was not to stop us. We were children. It was not to arrest us or to harass us. It was something about the name *police* that struck enough of our collective nerves to act out trauma while at the same time not feeling endangered or necessarily afraid. In fact, we laughed while running, and the police never chased us. They were obviously familiar with this routine. Lately, I have given deep thought to this ritual in our low-income community. When did this running attitude begin? How did it begin? Where did it begin? What incident in our communities sparked this ritual? And what history was behind it?

It was during the late 60s, and as I grew older during the 70s and 80s, when I began to understand more history related to my questions and how crime within the Black community became an excuse for further oppressive actions between citizens, by the police, and through legislative acts. Street crime was high indeed. Urban life took place in the streets. As youth, we ran the streets. I realize now we were not acting in a vacuum. We were collectively acting out our parents', older siblings', cousins', etc. lived experiences. On the other hand, there were other parents, aunts, elderly people, and so forth asking for the police to intervene and stop the crimes. These varying attitudes continue to exist today.

On September 13, 1994, President William Clinton signed the Violent Crime Control and Law Enforcement Act of 1994.[1] It was passed on a bipartisan vote and overwhelmingly disrupted urban communities, had serious implications for the likelihood of Black men being arrested and convicted and weakened the Black family and community. Michelle Alexander, author of *The New Jim Crow: Mass Incarceration in the Age of Colorblindness*, offers an extensive account of the historical contexts that brought about the New Jim Crow.[2]

The Clinton Crime Bill provided a tremendous amount of funding to police departments to fight street crime and eliminate drugs from urban areas. Targeted especially were Black men and persons who were described as criminal aliens. This became the "Three Strikes Rule," which came with a life sentence if you were convicted three times. The Act also created sixty more offenses by which offenders could receive the death penalty, including killing law enforcement officers. The Act further provided for hiring over 100,000 law enforcement officers. This violent control bill was deemed the largest crime bill ever passed in United States history and had a price tag of 9.7 billion dollars.[3] The purpose of Alexander's book was to debunk the myth of why these bills were established and to document the harm they do to communities. Alexander writes, "I have a specific audience in mind: people who care deeply about racial justice but who, for any number of reasons, do not yet appreciate the

---

1. Catalano et al., "Female Victims of Violence."
2. Alexander, *The New Jim Crow*.
3. Catalano et al., "Female Victims of Violence."

magnitude of the crisis faced by communities of color as a result of mass incarceration."[4]

There is not enough space in this reflection to do justice to Alexander's extensive work, and I invite everyone to get a copy of her most recent edition and read it carefully. She offers statistics that prove how Black and Brown men were targeted and their representation in prison as a percentage of the population far exceeds Whites. In her introduction, she speaks of her own personal family being attacked by the Klu Klux Klan to remind us that "In each generation, new tactics have been used to achieve the same goal—goals shared by the Founding Fathers. Denying African Americans citizenship was deemed essential to the formation of the original union."[5]

Alexander's premise is that from enslavement, through the Jim Crow era, the civil rights era, and up until the present day, the overall goal was to keep the caste system in play; the so-called *war on drugs* was simply the way to maintain it. Alexander notes it succinctly: "The drug war is the new Jim Crow."[6] I believe the beginning of the twenty-first century has brought on a new revelation and awareness that the control of Black bodies has always been the agenda of legislative practices, police practices, and prisons. Navigating these systems has been an increasing struggle to save the lives, communities, mental health, health care, and economic empowerment in Black and Brown communities. From enslavement to the industrial prison complex, new ways are still being devised to control Black and Brown bodies; these include police killing of Black men and women with impunity. Such violence has produced generational trauma that lives consciously and subconsciously in Black bodies. The consequences of the trauma it produces not only passes from generation to generation, but also pasess from body to body.

In his book *My Grandmother's Hands: Racialized Trauma and the Pathway to Mending Our Hearts and Bodies*, Resmaa Menakem speaks to this transfer from body to body. He shares how trauma is like a contagious disease and is not something similar to a toothache, which is individualist in nature. He explains, "When someone with unhealed trauma chooses dirty pain over clean pain, the person may try to soothe his or

---

4. Alexander, *The New Jim Crow*, viii.
5. Alexander, *The New Jim Crow*, 1.
6. Alexander, *The New Jim Crow*, 3.

her trauma by blowing it through another person using violence, rage, coercion, deception, betrayal, or emotional abuse."[7]

I experienced this phenomenon while teaching seminary students in a course titled "Is the Criminal Justice System Racist?" During our class time, we were scheduled for a field visit to a transitional house where formerly incarcerated people stayed for a while to get acclimated as returning citizens. During this time, we had the privilege of meeting with several men who were residents. One young Black male told his story of going to jail. He began by admitting he was wrong and had committed the crime of robbery. He also told the story of being a child and observing his home and the deplorable conditions in his neighborhood (broken glass, broken-down homes and apartments, and broke people committing burglaries and robbing Black bodies). Not understanding why these conditions existed, he decided that he would adjust his life to making money as others in the neighborhood through robbery. This young man's body caught the contagious and violent dirty pain that landed him in the prison system, which only assisted in destroying his opportunity to survive and enable his family to survive.

Interestingly enough, the Violent Crime Act that unleashed 100,000 police into urban Black and Brown communities never cared about the conditions within communities that were major causes of violence in the community. How can you ever navigate and trust a system that dehumanized you since the era of enslavement, saw you as only partially human, never making equal protection its goal, and that thrives to this day? The relationship between Black citizens and White police, in particular, has never been one of trust because of the continuing practices of the New Jim Crow now manifesting itself in mass incarceration, as well as the recent rash of police killings of unarmed Black citizens, still occurring in 2021. This is beginning to look as if it is an impossible fate because White eyes see the inhumanity of Black and Brown people; seeing them as threats, dangerous, and in need of being controlled, while seeing White police officers in particular as the *good* guys deserving of respect, trust, and appreciation for fighting the *bad* guys in the community. Is any relationship with officers possible under these conditions?

This chasm between police and Black and Brown citizens may never be filled. What then? Menakem draws from the work of David Rosenbloom, professor of public administration at American University, and

---

7. Menakem, *My Grandmother's Hands*, 37.

concludes, "White-body sees itself as fragile and vulnerable, and it looks to the police for its protection and safety. It sees Black bodies as dangerously impervious to pain and needing to be controlled. And the Black body sees the White body as privileged, controlling, and dangerous."[8] Where policing is concerned, Black bodies are consistent about how they feel around police who gather in groups. There is no conflicting or competing thought. In this scenario, there exists a consistent, non-conflicting picture, "The Black body sees police as a controlling and occupying force."[9] Where in general, police understand that protection is to be offered to everyone, for the most part police see Black bodies attached to these adjectives: "dangerous, disruptive, controlling, superhumanly powerful and impervious to pain."[10] In these all-too-frequent situations when police encounter Black bodies, they see its mission as one that should "control and subdue."[11]

Thus even today, we experience control through the imprisonment and killing of Black bodies by the police. Is there really a reliable and trustworthy way to navigate a system which is so broken? Can we legislate racism? Can enhanced police training eliminate White supremacy and change the eyesight of police whose actions toward Black men and women continues to resemble slavery when unfounded fear of Black men and women was connected to rapes, lynchings, and other violent means of control? Is there a way out of this quagmire of structural racism, systemic oppression, intergenerational oppression, and the divided country we have become? How long must Black citizens and their allies continue to say "Black lives matter!" and "Say his/her name!"?

The latest public outcry is to *defund the police*. Instead of investigating its meaning, implications, and possibilities, political pundits have used this statement to further divide people, convincing them that the Black Lives Matter movement seeks to destroy the entire police system so they can become better criminals. In a recent online sermon by Rev. Dr. Bernice A. Powell, a retired United Church of Christ executive staff for over twenty-two years and the former president of the World Council of Churches, she mentioned something to be considered as we use the phrase "We are divided as a nation." She reminded us through Scripture

8. Menakem, *My Grandmother's Hands*, 27–28.
9. Menakem, *My Grandmother's Hands*, 27–28.
10. Menakem, *My Grandmother's Hands*, 27–28.
11. Menakem, *My Grandmother's Hands*, 27–28.

that we are not divided. We are torn apart. For Powell, divided indicated something evenly split in half.[12] However, torn apart indicates an intentional act that leaves no possible way to pull the pieces back together again. We are a nation that is torn apart.

Black and Brown people are navigating systems that are insurmountable. Survivors of sexual and domestic violence, even when in fear of their lives, are refusing to call the police. The cry for defunding the police has caused apologetic voices to rise to say that is not what they mean. How are we to move forward? Some say it's a matter of re-allocating funds, and others declare we need to continue to look at other ways to train police and take measures to reform the police. Or is this idea dead on arrival? Whatever happens in this age, we cannot give up on demanding justice, speaking truth to power, and protesting. Certainly, in this time of trauma and crisis, we cannot give up the fight. The future of our children is at stake. The lives of our sons and daughters are at stake.

My friend Sharon Stolz and I have known each other for over forty years. She has to be the most long-standing friends I have. We are both United Church of Christ ordained clergy. We connected when the Church Women in Society, existed and we were both members of this gathered community. We may not consider ourselves best friends, but we are buddies and have shared in many conversations and have had honest discourse around our politics, theology, family, and children. I call her children, who are adopted from China, my nieces and receive picture updates. We have journeyed together. I asked her to provide me with a quote that speaks to who I am. She emailed me this statement. "Sharon lives with a fierce hope, and an expansive love for others which also does not pretend that injustice is anything other than injustice. Her commitment to the truth deepens the argument for being alive."[13] I am deeply moved by the ways she saw me, because sometimes I feel as if I should be doing more. We, no matter our race, ethnicity, gender, or economic or privilege status, must do our part. We are in the urgency of now. And our call gathers at the virtual table, or tables of your choice, to not lose hope. There are more people than we know working towards justice and liberation both globally, nationally, statewide, and within communities. Discover what your work is and let your talk guide your walk. Together we can.

12. Powell, "Sermon."
13. Sharon Stolz, BSW, MDiv, in email correspondence with the author, April 3, 2020.

Discussion

In chapter 1 of her book *Decriminalizing Domestic Violence: A Balanced Policy Approach to Intimate Partner Violence*, Leigh Goodmark, professor of law and director of the Gender Violence Clinic at the University of Maryland Carey School of Law, describes her reasons for working to decriminalize domestic violence. She lays out the early antiviolence movement's work to make intimate partner violence a crime and explained how the crime was listed as similar in purpose to other crimes. When the anti-violence movement was not getting the results, they formed a research group to leverage their political power to connect with the state toward the enforcement of police arrest of abusers. Goodmark further argues that the legal system "failed to deter intimate partner violence, and the harms of criminalization are significant enough to justify abandoning the use of the criminal legal system in cases of intimate partner violence."[14] Thus, her argument for decriminalizing domestic violence.

I joined a task force that meets via conference calls. The force consists of people from various professions, such as law enforcement officers, attorneys, social workers, and other public service providers. We have ongoing conversations regarding the rally to *defund the police*. Our goal is to share our varying perspectives and figure out where we should go from here. We have decided to hold a different type of gathering with younger people in the lead, as opposed to hearing our older voices. The premise is to bring new ideas from younger people because ideas from the past have outlived their usefulness.

Activity: Build Coalitions, Gain Understanding

1. What organizations, focus groups, or gatherings are you a part of that are examining these current issues and seeking solutions?
2. What are your personal thoughts about the defunding the police clarion call?
3. Police reform seems to be the wave of the future. In what ways would you see police reform aligning with justice, which is the ultimate goal for the criminal justice system?

---

14. Goodmark, *Decriminalizing Domestic Violence*, 12.

Chapter 6

Contradictions in Church and Circumstances

I AM A GREAT woman, not a good woman. The term *good woman* has negative connotations for me. Whether it was within the faith community or society in general, by the time I reached the age of twenty I realized becoming a good woman was something I would never achieve. My earliest notion of becoming a *good woman* came from biblical teachings about the Virtuous Woman, often referred to as the Proverbs 31 Woman, described in Prov 31:10–31. This text begins with a stinging question, "Who can find a virtuous woman?" (v. 1). This statement alone insinuated that whoever this woman is or whatever values she exudes, she would be difficult or impossible to locate. Then came the prolonged descriptions of her character and values (vv. 11–31):

> The heart of her husband doth safely trust in her, so that he shall have no need of spoil.
> She will do him good and not evil all the days of her life.
> She seeketh wool, and flax, and worketh willingly with her hands.
> She is like the merchants' ships; she bringeth her food from afar.
> She riseth also while it is yet night, and giveth meat to her household, and a portion to her maiden She considereth a field, and buyeth it: with the fruit of her hands she planteth a vineyard.
> She girdeth her loins with strength, and strengtheneth her arms.
> She perceiveth that her merchandise is good: her candle goeth not out by night.
> She layeth her hands to the spindle, and her hands hold the distaff.

> She stretcheth out her hand to the poor; yea, she reacheth forth her hands to the needy. She is not afraid of the snow for her household: for all her household are clothed with scarlet.
> She maketh herself coverings of tapestry; her clothing is silk and purple.
> Her husband is known in the gates when he sitteth among the elders of the land.
> She maketh fine linen, and selleth it; and delivereth girdles unto the merchant.
> Strength and honour are her clothing; and she shall rejoice in time to come.
> She openeth her mouth with wisdom; and in her tongue is the law of kindness. She looketh well to the ways of her household, and eateth not the bread of idleness Her children arise up, and call her blessed; her husband also, and he praiseth her.
> Many daughters have done virtuously, but thou excellest them all.
> Favor is deceitful, and beauty is vain: but a woman that feareth the LORD, she shall be praised.
> Give her of the fruit of her hands; and let her own works praise her in the gates.

Although this text, due to the Old English vocabulary, is difficult to read, the King James Version of the Bible was the only legitimate version in my Pentecostal upbringing. Anything else was not the Bible. The Bible I grew up with was emphasized as the *Holy* Bible. The King James Version of this Bible was also read literally, meaning it was inerrant, *not adding to it and not taking away from it*. This is how, even as a young teen, the text was presented in the preaching and teaching of the church. This particular text, which was generally preached by male pastors on Mother's Day but could be referred to at other times, tended to highlight women's relationship with their spouses. The verses I remember hearing most were, "The heart of her husband trusts in her and she will do good and not evil all the days of her life. Her children will rise and call her blessed. Many daughters have done virtuously, but the virtuous woman excels even that" (31:11, 12, 29, 30). Overall, the character and values of the virtuous woman are strong, faithful, submissive, honorable, hardworking, and beautiful yet modest. She must also be a good homemaker and a good wife.

This is how I heard this text preached for most of my life, and from various pulpits I continue to hear similar interpretations. As I grew older and as a young adult, the women older than me seemed to value this text and were excited to hear it preached. Part of me wondered why this was so, since it always struck me negatively; but I was certain that I was subconsciously buying into the narrative as well. In fact, it was this ideology that framed the wife I imagined being for my husband while making plans for leaving my parents' home. I was determined to become a good woman as described in the text. A good woman was a woman to be praised.

Although my engagement and ultimate marriage to Buck was part of my escape plan from sexual, physical, and emotional abuse in my youth, the underlying values of my marriage were influenced by sermons I recalled of the Proverbs 31 Woman. Consequently, in this marriage I cooked, cleaned, and served dinner on the table, whether it was for breakfast or late at night after Buck arrived home from work. I was faithful and honored him as my husband, as well as engaged in other positive behaviors to rise to the occasion of being a good wife. All of these efforts yielded a husband who was unfaithful and caused medical harm to my body. It yielded a liar and a cheater. It yielded revenge on my part. Ultimately, it yielded a divorce and a determination that I would never allow any man to garner that much faithfulness and commitment from me. Buck's infidelity felt like another violation upon my body. In turn, it stripped away residual naiveté. I realized that being a *good girl* or a *good woman* would not protect me. In order to protect myself, I had to become the one in a position of power, or so I thought. Being a *good woman* was not really working for my defense mechanism to become the cheater instead of the cheated.

It is commonly said that hurt people hurt people. I was determined not to ever experience infidelity, but I had never taken time for myself to heal from the wounds of my childhood nor my marriage. This left my heart full of rage and revenge. I desired to prove that all men were incapable of faithfulness in marriage and to make others feel the pain that I had felt. I spent years developing unhealthy relationships, short- and long-term, with men who were emotionally unavailable; they were engaged or living within committed partners in established families. I was wrong and strong in my commitment to have multiple relationships at a time and to engage in sexual escapades that not only disrespected others but did further damage to my higher self. I did all of this and continued professing Jesus as my personal Savior.

The decade between leaving the church of my childhood at eighteen years old (1970) and joining my home church, Trinity United Church, in

Chicago (1980), did not mean I was totally absent from the church. I visited several churches randomly but could never find one I was willing to join. By 1975, I had two children, Ozell and Sharell, and began attending church more often. In 1977, I finally joined an African Episcopal Methodist (AME) church, where both of my children were baptized. I have their baptismal certificates to this day. I never attended a new members class. I never received any instructions on the baptism of children. I never joined a ministry or remember meeting or socializing with any member of the church. As quickly as I established my membership and got my children baptized, I left. There was never any follow-up call regarding my absence or well-being of my children and me.

Subconsciously, I believe this short journey of visiting churches and eventually joining one was my effort toward reconnecting with the church and possibly with God. There was a connection between my joining the church and my children. I wanted them involved in the church and at least baptized. This act was gratifying to me. Yet, there was no solid reason for my presence and certainly church membership did not stop my self-destructive behavior. I was living a life of contradictions. My actions were incongruent with the faith I professed, even if on a superficial level. I was constantly faced with the sins of my past and present. I was haunted by guilt, shame, and feeling unworthy but was not influenced to change my behavior or explore emotional healing. Guilt and shame just gave birth to more guilt and shame. The guilt was grounded in the teachings of the church as well as by men within the community. The shame was reinforced by my failure to be the *good woman* I was taught to be or to find ways to honor my self-worth.

In the circles of men, there was a common theme regarding who they would marry and others with whom they would just date and have sexual relationships. These relationships were fun and enjoyable to them, and some of them truly liked the women they dated. However, the women who provided fun, pleasure, and desire were, according to them, not marriage material. The women they would potentially marry, as they consistently expressed, would be a *good woman*. The film that represented this reality for me was the movie *Ray*, released in 2004.

Legendary blues singer Ray Charles, played by Jamie Foxx, married the love of his life, Della Bea Robinson, played by Kerry Washington. Ray was an over-the-road and well-known blues singer and was away from his wife and their son for lengthy periods of time. While over the road, Ray engaged in sexual relationships with several women he hired as background singers. He eventually developed a stronger relationship with Margie Hendricks, played by Regina King. Margie was in love with Ray and believed Ray was in love with her. Ray never wavered from his commitment to Bea, as he referred to his wife. No matter how much Margie tried to build this love relationship with Ray, he would always assert Bea's name as the one he loved. Margie realized she was his over-the-road wife and longed to be *the* wife. At some point in the movie, Margie, frustrated by Ray's relationship with his wife, referred to her as Ray's "precious Bea."

Margie's commitment to Ray was best seen in the scenes revolving around his struggle with heroin addiction. After a horrifying experience, Ray had withdrawal symptoms where he relived terrifying and horrific reviews of his traumatic childhood. He relived his brother's death for which he felt responsible. He relived the moment he became blind. He relived when his mother sent him away on a bus to a special school to learn to navigate his blindness. She knew that she could not take care of him in ways that would help him thrive as a blind man. Reliving these traumatic moments while going through withdrawal was depicted as Ray being overtaken by uncontrollable shakes, body distortions, and long periods of incoherent ramblings.

Margie was with him through it all. As she lay in bed with Ray, holding him tight, calling his name and speaking soothing words of support, Ray suddenly turned around and looked at her. Disoriented by the physical exhaustion of this experience, Ray mistook Margie for his wife and asked, "Bea?" This for Margie was the straw that broke the camel's back. She got up, grabbed her personal belongings, and left. Margie's realization that she would never be good enough for Ray nor ever replace Ray's *precious Bea* was a pivotal and painful moment in her life. This moment exemplifies the similar pain women might feel when realizing they are not good enough nor would they ever become wife material.

The men I talked to about this double-edged sword confirmed that this was reality. The term *good woman* must have been a universal proclamation and an already established term, as it was a consistent theme with many men I encountered, whether or not I was in relationship with them or simply in conversation with them. It was just reality in the minds of the many men I knew who spoke with sincerity. They were willing to sleep with these women but not marry them. They would marry a *good woman*.

But where did this patriarchal privilege originate? My best answer and assumption was that these men heard the same sermons and teachings I had from within the walls of the church. They learned early about the virtuous woman and how these types of women would benefit them. They already understood that the woman described was created for their betterment and would be the ultimate woman they would eventually marry. They would marry the woman who took care of them, was pure and moral in her behavior, who looked after their needs, who was faithful, and who they could trust. These virtues are what was described as the *good woman* men would ultimately marry in spite of their own prowling sexual behavior. As a survivor of intimate personal violence, I could be considered a risk for marriage yet perfect in the category of the fun life.

The term *good woman* plays itself out in 2 Samuel 13, which tells the story of the rape of Tamar, the daughter of King David. It seemed because of her royal lineage, Tamar would fit into the good woman category and deserved by default to be a wife. This would ensure her safety and stability and enhance her pedigree. However, things changed after she was raped by her half brother, Amnon. He looked upon his sister as beautiful and he fell in love with her. Amnon was so in love with Tamar that he cooked up a scheme to rape her in spite of her being his sister. She pleaded with him not to, but he raped her anyway. After he raped her, he no longer had a desire for her and his love faded. Tamar asked him to at least marry her because now she was no longer viable as a mate for any other male, and she needed a husband as her covering, which was custom in this context. Instead of Amnon marrying her, he raged at her and kicked Tamar out of his quarters. Raped and discarded, the abuser left his victim abandoned in the world to fend for herself. Even after her brother, Absolom, vowed to get revenge upon Amnon, he told Tamar to keep silent and to live out her days in his home. Tamar's story ended there. Tamar was no longer a *good woman* even though being raped was not her fault. Society regarded her as damaged goods in the eyes of men who would have otherwise scrambled to marry her and be son-in-law of the king. I am certain the notion of a *good woman* originated in biblical stories like this one. I am certain that then as well as now these stories were passed down as culture, law, and lore. The contemporary church inherited a colonized version of this mindset steeped in cultural beliefs and male hegemonic practices.

The story of the woman caught in adultery in John 8:1–11 is another example of how patriarchy and misogyny define a woman's worth. Jesus was out doing the ministry of his calling when suddenly a bunch of men showed up dragging a woman to Jesus. Interrupting his teaching, they demanded that Jesus obey the law and stone to death this woman who they caught committing acts of adultery. These men demanded her death because, according to the law, she was not faithful to her husband, and the penalty was to be stoned. Not only was the woman caught in the midst of adultery not seen as a *good woman*, but this also justified her life to be taken away from her. The problem in the text is this: adultery requires the participation of the man and the woman. However, the man who had sex with her was not dragged alongside her in public humiliation and indictment. Both the man and the woman were engaged in adulterous behavior, but only the woman caught the case. The man got a pass. It is likely that the men in and out of my life were groomed by this biblical/historical church tradition, according to which women were regarded as unworthy because of unsavory behavior attributed to them but not to men.

Despite the reality of the particular situations of many of the women within the sacred text and real life who were raped, used, and abused by the very men who saw them as unworthy, the men were now willing to destroy the woman's character. Despite the men being recipients of pleasure during these sexual escapades, it was by default the women who were deemed unworthy. These were the aggregate of men who somehow saw themselves worthy of the *good woman* and were unwilling to settle for anything less. Consequently, in all of my sinfulness, woundedness, and anger, I saw myself as the unworthy one and never judged the men's participation in sexual dalliances with me the same way. Further, there was little to no accountability in church and society for the immoral actions of men engaged in the same behavior. Regardless of the guilt and shame I experienced, none of these feelings encouraged me to follow a different and healthier path in the choices I made. I willingly entered into these relationships, although none of them brought me any real sense of peace and joy.

I am always careful when explaining this confusing and contradictory part of my life to not leave anyone believing that I was miserable in my choices. I was not someone lying prostrate on the ground pleading, as the biblical figure of Paul, for God to take this thorn out of my flesh (2 Cor 12:8). No! I laughed and danced while engaged in these behaviors, entertaining neither guilt nor shame. I was not outwardly repenting for my sins, but when the music faded and the lights came up afterwards, inwardly I knew my behaviors were wrong and not pleasing to God. Most of all, I knew deep down within that I was not the person I was obviously pretending to be. Life experiences had convinced me and verified that I was not a *good woman*. So, I thought, why should I continue to attend church? I was replete with contradictions surrounding the woman who willingly acted out, on the one hand, and the one who I knew I was on the inside, on the other. The stronghold of church teachings that played out in society had convinced me there was no virtue in my womanhood worthy of praise and honor.

The guilt, shame, and the after-effects of my actions increased, and eventually I felt lost and alone. I felt like my life was a fraud. Even in the midst of educational achievements and success in my career, I felt like a fraud. Even as a survivor of sexual and domestic violence, and as a child of the church, I felt like a fraud. Even with my love for Jesus, my attempts to attend church, and having my children baptized, in the depths of my soul I felt like a fraud.

My sexual and domestic violence experiences were not real.

My faith in God was not real.

My being a victim of interpersonal violence in my family of origin was not real.

My education was not real.

Nothing in my life felt real. I was a fake and a fraud pretending that I was better than the person who was presenting herself over these years. How could I ever think differently about myself when I was so happy in the midst of the life I was living? How could I possibly have two very different versions of myself? One of them had to be a fraud. I decided the surviving part of me, as well as the bettering part of me, was a fraud. I determined that I was not worthy to be in the spaces of the sanctuary. I concluded that I was not worthy of any committed and loving male relationship because I did not fit the model of a *good woman*. I had no virtue. I was a fraud.

My dislike and disdain for the Proverbs 31 Woman was equivalent to that declaration of many Black people who, post enslavement, loved Jesus but decided they would not include the clause, "Slaves, obey your master" (Eph 6:5) as essential Scripture. I totally dismissed this passage as not relevant to my faith and decided I would never use the term *good woman* or *virtuous woman* in any statement regarding women. I also decided if I were to attend a Mothers' Day service, I would not remain for a sermon that was derived from Prov 31:10–31. Despite this avoidance, I still longed to be found worthy in God's sight. I still longed to believe God loved me in spite of me. I still longed for someone to see through my pain and the walls of mistrust and deceit I had built. I longed for someone to break down those walls so that my partner and Jesus could see me for the person I knew was buried deep inside of me.

How then did I see myself deep inside? I began seeing myself as a *great woman* rather than as the *good woman* I had dismissed from my consciousness. I saw myself as faithful in relationships. I saw myself filled with integrity. I saw myself as the best wife anyone could ever have. I saw myself as a family person. I saw myself as a *one man's woman*. I saw myself as the total opposite of the woman I was presenting in relationships. Deep down inside, I saw myself as faithful to God and pleasing in God's sight. This image was totally incongruent with my lifestyle. I took full responsibility for my choices and consequences. Yet, the tears, pain, shame, and guilt of my actions coexisted with longing for God in my life. Somehow, I convinced myself that I was not that horrible of a sinner, and the real fraudulent person was the one who acted out.

I lived with these contradictions for many more years, although the quality of men in my life changed for the better. By the quality of men, I meant then they were educated and employed in semi-professional or professional careers, as was I. Consequently, this meant I was growing by making better choices. I realize now I was engaging in class bias and that education, financial means, or status in life does not determine your value. Quality is measured by the content of your character. Even with this awareness, and although I was not acting out, seeking revenge, or trying to hurt others, some of my patterns of behaviors had not improved. I continued to pretend that I was not seeking to be in a committed relationship.

This lack of agency and fear of expressing my authentic self continued to hold me captive to this cycle of shame, self-blame, guilt, sleepless nights, and other behavior that carried even deeper internal consequences. I continued to mask my need to be loved completely and give that love in return in a mutually rewarding committed relationship. During my healing process, I continued to wear this mask and wear it well. Eventually, joining Trinity United Church of Christ (UCC) became one of the best decisions I ever made. Joining Trinity was the beginning of my journey toward authenticity in my behavior, discovering my worth, and finding my authentic self. I embarked on what was to be a slow journey.

I was in college studying for my bachelor's degree in nursing when one of my classmates and I happened to engage each other on the topic of church. I mentioned to her how I had been basically absent from church but was ready to find a church home where I could genuinely join and become active. She immediately recommended that I visit Trinity UCC, her church home. She had so much excitement about the church that I became curious enough to ask where it was located. Her evangelistic style of excitement was my only impetus to visit. After one or two visits, I decided to join. I joined Trinity for many reasons.

I loved everything about my new church home where Rev. Dr. Jeremiah A. Wright Jr. served as pastor. I loved the music. I have always been a lover of music, both sacred and secular. Trinity UCC had the best music ministry my heart could desire. The songs were inspirational, diverse, electric, and spoke to my heart. Bible study was more than just a preacher standing at the pulpit speaking as if it was Sunday morning with little or no engagement from the attendees. There was an entire ministry dedicated to facilitating Bible study, training the teachers who consisted of clergy, laypersons, and deacons, and offered several Bible study opportunities twice a week or more. Bible study was a dual engagement of the Bible and of various books related to the particular courses that were offered. I remember participating in classes such as "Inspiration of the Scripture, Revelations, Space for God," and others that challenged both our minds and spirituality.

Sunday preaching was spectacular. Pastor Wright spoke to the head and the heart and connected what was occurring in the world to biblical text. I would leave Sunday worship with the understanding and anticipation of finding ways to live out my faith in the world. In other words, I was able to understand the world differently than from my understanding in my upbringing. In my early days of the church, the *world* was someplace you should not participate in due to the sinfulness of humanity. Conversely, during my time at Trinity, I discovered how my faith calls me to engage the world to be a voice of liberation, hope, and calling forth a just world. I became more than just a Sunday member.

Baptism was different, as well. My Pentecostal method of baptism was by immersion. My new church sprinkled water over the candidates for baptism. This took some getting used to. However, it did not take long for me to adjust to this new way of receiving Jesus as Savior. We did not routinely practice baptizing babies; however, if requested, the leadership did not have any problems with infant baptism. Additionally, there was the confirmation class where when children reached a certain age they would engage in biblical studies, denominational polity, storytelling, and the meaning of personal acceptance of Jesus into their lives. Preteens were then responsible for developing their own relationship with God.

Trinity UCC is a well-organized faith institution, and I was excited to make it my church home. This time, I had every intention of becoming fully engaged. I not only attended Sunday worship and taken Bible classes, but I also attended revivals, volunteered to fold bulletins for the hundreds of people who worshipped, and eventually I went through the proscribed training and became an ordained deacon of the church. There was one surprise, however. My father had also joined Trinity, and neither of us knew the other was a member.

Trinity had three services. Therefore, it was easy not to see people you knew. After my father joined, it did not take long before my mother and siblings along with their children joined. My mother Annelle, who was an organist at the church where my father previously served as pastor, eventually joined Trinity's sanctuary choir. My father became part of the ministerial staff, and my siblings—Gloria, Peggy, and Linda—participated at their own level of comfort. As for me, Trinity UCC became the springboard for ministry opportunities inside and outside the walls of the church. My father and I got along. I was happy he found a place where he felt he belonged. It seemed like a good period for our family. We had found a church home outside of our former denomination and were in the same worship space of our individual free will.

Would this transformation be enough to break down the walls of my self-defeating behaviors that stood between my greater self and the self that acted out? Could I live into my image of being a *great woman*? Could I stop being a fraud? Could I actually develop a close relationship with God? And would I completely experience the grace, mercy, and forgiveness of God? These are the questions I faced as I continued to develop a real desire to live into the realm of God not just in words but in how I negotiated life. I was determined to do so not as a *good woman*, but as a *great woman*!

Reflection: Exploring Black Liberation, Womanist, Feminist Theological and Biblical Scholarship as Tools of Navigation

Shortly after earning my master of divinity degree and eager to do ministry, I volunteered with Evergreen Park Ministries Care and Counseling Center in Evergreen Park, Illinois. The ministry was established in

1988 by Howard Vandenberg and the founding director of Evergreen Park Ministries, Rev. Bruce Pangborn. This was known as the shopping mall ministry. Vandenberg's vision was to provide pastoral care to those shopping within the mall, as he believed many people shopping may, at the same time, have some type of depression and need care. During my time as a volunteer, Vandenberg offered me an opportunity to be paid, as he felt that was the right thing to do. I began working more hours. The location of the ministry provided shoppers with opportunities to stop by simply to see who we were and what we were about. They discovered the services we offered were free and by appointment only. Shoppers came by for services.

One of the clients I remember well. She was in a domestic and violent relationship that included both mental and physical abuse. I will call her Betty. Betty and I discussed ways in which she could be safe because the abuse she described had the potential of escalating. On her next appointment, I engaged in safety-type conversations again. I expressed concern that she could be in danger and asked if she had given thought of a place she could go, if necessary. Betty redirected the conversation and said she needed to ask me a question. I followed her lead and listened. Her question centered around solidifying our conversation about safety and finding a safe place. Betty wanted to be certain I was affirming that she could leave her home where her abuser lived to go somewhere else to be safe. I assured her that she could. Betty, while packing up her belongings, then declared she could no longer allow me to counsel her because what I was saying to her was against her religion and that was something she would never do. Then she walked out.

Betty's response reminded me of conversations I have had with many victims/survivors of sexual and domestic violence. Their responses often centered on their faith practices and belief systems based on their relationship with their church. I was saddened by this because I remembered so well the ways I was bound and did not know it because my faith teachings tended to favor caring for and nurturing the husband in spite of his abuse.

One familiar phrase I remember was *standing in the gap*. What this meant was that abused women should stay in abusive relationships and pray for their husband until Satan releases him from whatever was making him abusive. This phrase insinuated that women had the responsibility to stay and fix the relationship. After all, male pastors would frequently ask, "What did *you* do to make him hit you?" Implied by the question was that if you started the abusive incident, it was *your* responsibility to fix it. It was messages like these that caused Betty to be confused as she heard contradicting statements by me as a pastor and by her pastor. This type of language can bind your spirit for life, leaving victims/survivors without any clear choice but to suffer in silence

As a lover of music, I often share with my students lyrics both sacred and secular that also can be heard by victims/survivors to stay in abusive relationships. Sacred music consists of music that challenges how unworthy we are with lyrics such as "I'm not worthy of all your blessings." And secular music consists of music that announces when we have problems in relationships to "try everything, but don't give up." Between sacred and secular music, the lives of many women of faith, especially those suffering from sexual and domestic violence, are replete with contradictions that facilitate women not leaving abusive relationships and heightening the likelihood of being murdered by their spouses.

Trinity UCC is where I was introduced to a more liberating biblical interpretation, contextual explanations, relevance for today's living, and reflective and reflexive theological analysis. Where I was once full of the *personal salvation* dogma, I was now being introduced to a God who challenged *systems and principalities* and held oppressive systems accountable for their collective sins against humanity. During those early years as a member, I had no idea it was Black liberation theological thought influencing Trinity's leadership and making a difference in my learning and practice of ministry. I came to know, love, and understand the God who hears my prayers, loves me unconditionally, and charges me to go out and share with others while challenging the evils in our society. This was the essence of Black liberation theology introduced in academic settings by the father of Black liberation theology, Dr. James Cone, and that was practiced and lived out in everything I learned within my church setting. All I knew was this was a pastor who preached in such ways that my father, Rev. Samuel Lee Ellis, began wearing dashikis. This was something I had never witnessed before! I began wanting more and more to hear this gospel preached and taught that was freeing my spirit.

While accepting a call to ministry and attending seminary, Pastor Wright met with seminarians in the lower level of the church, which then was located at 400 West 95th Street, a.k.a. the Old Trinity. Between my pastor and seminary, I became aware of Black liberation and feminist theology, which I experienced as pathways toward breaking the contradictions and confusion about who God is, who God calls us to be, the nature of God in relationship to God's people, and more. I discovered the methodology of the scholars, preachers, and pastors who practice these frameworks to provide ways for victims/survivors to navigate their way and avoid or heal from the guilt, shame, blame, and feelings of unworthiness.

However good, nothing is perfect. Feminist theology was not quick to be inclusive of the plight of Black men during a time when Black men were suffering economic and racial oppression, mass incarceration, and being murdered by police. Likewise, Black liberation theology was not as fast to lend itself to liberating Black women. This lapse in inclusion by both catalyzed the emergence of womanist theology to bridge this gap.

Theological deficiencies and discoveries were experienced by seminarians when I taught the course "Domestic Violence in the African American Community." My personal goal was to highlight some of the key issues, factors, and behaviors within the Black community which, besides the need for power and control, were more nuanced than indicated on the pattern and control wheel. Ironically, my class was equally filled with both White and Black students with a couple of Asian students enrolled. We had been in session for at least two weeks, discovering the pattern of the power and control wheel, when it came time for me to add different keys to the well-established and thought-out wheel. I began by asking the class, "What do you all think about me adding to the narrative of domestic violence in the African American Community? Would you be willing to engage for a while in how issues of racism, unemployment, housing, and poverty might impact domestic violence in these communities?"

A young White woman who had been silent the past couple of weeks raised her hand. I acknowledged her and she stood as if she had something major to say. Her emphatic response was, "No!" and she further said, "and this is my contribution to this class." Although the conversation continued, her statement left me in a daze. What I experienced with the White feminist students was their unwillingness to engage in anything other than the standard conversation. They were not willing to consider the intersectionality issues in Black communities. As my colleague and friend, Brenda Burney, would say, "They just wanted to sing the same song but in different keys." Time has passed. Conversations are changing. And I pray we all will continue to connect with the multiplicity of issues in communities of color as we consider viable solutions to ending gender-based violence against women.

We must consider the multiplicity of quality-of-life issues that have the possibility of being the answer to our prayers for victims/survivors of domestic violence and sexual abuse. Addressing each brings unique, quantifiable value to the table that liberates and empowers. Most importantly, each brings the humility and commitment to be critiqued by the other and transformed in the process. The following are examples from each category.

United Theological Seminary's Doctor of Ministry Program allotted time during the week, referred to as plenary, which follows the opening worship on Monday morning during our one-week intensive. On January 29, 2019, Lisa Hess, a faculty member, and I were both invited to be leading lecturers. Hess lectured on the intriguing topic, "Conscious Feminine Leadership." She spent a great amount of time examining her thoughts around its meaning, which was more complex than I could note at that moment. However, I captured some of the values she provided for us, which helps define for me feminist thought and the lessons and blessings it brings to theological and biblical scholarship. Those values were transparency, hospitality, nurture, and capacity to hold paradox.[1] One of the values that attracted me in that moment was the mention of the *capacity to hold a paradox.* What an effective navigational tool. Oftentimes, victims/survivors have to hold the contradictions they learn in biblical teaching and understand that there are many interpretations of the same passage while grabbing hold of the original intentions that move one to God's love, faithfulness, joy, and forgiveness.

There will be times when survivors of sexual/domestic violence must choose to leave their church community. Should this occur, that loss has to be mourned. Rev. Dr. Edward Smith Davis, conference minister of the Southern Conference, reflected to me, "Navigating the theological waters all too often has us ascribing things to God that are not specific to God." However, it is a reality and is embedded into the theologies of Black folk religions since enslavement and can be expressed in any church of all denominations and misunderstood and seen as a contradiction. We live with paradox, as it is called faith in what God can do, in spite of the plethora of ways the belief systems of Black persons were challenged by the actions of individuals who bought into the oppressive structures that disregarded the lives of Black people.

---

1. Hess, "Conscious Feminine Leadership."

Cone, in *The Cross and the Lynching Tree*, helps us to live with the paradox in seeing that "God could make a way out of no way in Jesus' cross as being truly absurd to the intellect, yet profoundly real in the souls of Black folk."[2] In JoAnne Marie Terrell's *Power in the Blood?*, she sought to understand the significance of the suffering and oppression of Black people and its connection to the atonement. She asks, "How is the gospel message of the Atonement, or reconciliation of sinners with God through Jesus Christ, to be construed by Black people, who are similarly persecuted and simultaneously indicted as sinners?"[3] This question causes Terrell to seek understanding of how this liberative work finds room to claim the identity of being Black and Christian. The cross in the African American experience, as well as *power in the blood*, both demonstrate the paradox we live with daily.

Cone makes an important claim about who God is and whose side God is on in exegeting Luke 4:18-19. Being under the guidance of the Holy Spirit, we are empowered to speak freedom from oppression and offer sight to the blind and release to captives. If this is what Jesus proclaimed as his mission, such is ours. Cone understands this text this way, "In view of the biblical emphasis on liberation, it seems appropriate but necessary to define the Christian community as the community of the oppressed which joins Jesus Christ in his fight for the liberation of humankind."[4] For victims/survivors, this offers the opportunity for our reframing of the message of being caught up in traditional messages of hell and damnation to embrace freedom and release of whatever is holding us in capacity. This newfound freedom and release from what has caught victims/survivors up, disabled their vision, and held them in bondage, is now a message of hope offered by Jesus through the power of the resurrection.[5]

Womanist scholar Mitzi J. Smith in *Womanist Sass and Talk Back: Social (In) Justice, Intersectionality, and Biblical Interpretation*, embodies the spirit of womanist theology that frees the voice of women, especially marginalized women, and frees them to talk back to theologies that bind Black women, as well as share in the remedies. Smith, exegeting the story of the Samaritan and her encounter with Jesus in John 4:1-42, "uses the

---

2. Cone, *The Cross and the Lynching Tree*, 2.
3. Terrell, *Power in the Blood?*, 7-8.
4. Cone, *A Black Theology of Liberation*, 3.
5. Cone, *A Black Theology of Liberation*, 3-4.

framework that prioritizes and values the voices and experiences of black women and communities of color."[6] She goes on to argue that "too many readers have treated Jesus' revelation about the Samaritan woman's domestic history and current living situation as the most significant part of the narrative . . ."[7] However, what Smith argues for is that both Jesus and the Samaritan woman recognize how water becomes a human right in the midst of oppression. Contemporary relevance is demonstrated by the Michigan government continuing to refuse to fix the polluted waters in the predominately African American populated city of Flint.[8] Water is a human right. And the woman got to share in that conversation and its demands for justice.[9]

All of this writing and scholarship are fundamental to victim survivors navigating the text toward developing for themselves a liberating theology. My pastor always speaks to the context of a passage before its interpretation and application. He insists that "a text taken out of context is a pretext." For me it is more about truth-telling, confession, and our call to love one another. This liberating love does not carry the weight of guilt, shame, and blame; and an absolute remedy is offered by the leader or pastor. Navigating the waters of theology is also about asking God for clarity on what to do with any mistakes or sins that may keep me out of relationship with God. In that the process is sacred and moves me and others toward wholeness, however that may look or feel, I have put to bed prescriptive theologies that serve to force feed with scare tactics and that walk back and forth seeking who can be devoured. Our call is always to love, and love moves us toward justice.

Discussion

In her book, *Asking for It: The Alarming Rise of Rape Culture—And What We Can Do about It*, Kate Harding, who describes herself as a proud feminist, explores the term *rape culture*. This is the idea that has been

---

6. Smith, *Womanist Sass and Talk Back*, 3.

7. Smith, "Water Is a Human Right, but It Ain't Free," 4.

8. The Flint Water Crisis made headline news in 2014 when environmental justice groups confirmed toxic levels of lead and other chemicals in the water supply. The various health issues resulting included critically high levels of lead in children. To date (2021), the city water supply continues to be politically charged and environmentally compromised.

9. Smith, "Water Is a Human Right, but It Ain't Free."

around since the seventies as ways culture allows women to be harassed, shamed, and blamed for their rape, while the offender suffers little to no consequences. Harding describes the seven characteristics of rape culture that have been around since the end of the twentieth century: she asked for it; it wasn't really rape; he didn't mean to; she wanted it; she lied; rape is a trivial event; rape is a deviant event.

Coupled with these categories that contribute to rape culture are rape jokes. "A crucial element of changing destructive cultural norms is to associate the negative behaviors with a loss of status and desired behaviors with a gain."[10] Other dangerous actions and attitudes fall under the category of blaming the victim. These include asking the rape victim what she was wearing, asserting that boys will be boys, and normalizing the rape- and slut-shaming.

How can pastoral care providers, through our faith traditions, values, and norms, help to debunk these myths while helping victims/survivors know the rape was not their fault?

Activity: Collaborate to Eliminate

- What will you do, as a pastoral care provider, to advocate for victims/survivors?
- What is your plan to collaborate with agencies outside of your faith community to mitigate further emotional harm and eliminate rape culture norms?

---

10. Harding, *Asking for It*, 41.

Chapter 7

Me, My Mind, My Body, and My Home— All Depressed

THINGS WERE GOING PRETTY well in my life now. By well, I mean I was finally divorced from my abusive husband, was moving toward being less afraid because Joel and I were together, and I felt more protected just by his presence. However, lingering behind my new sense of safety and security with Joel was always a constant internal fear that Greg, in his narcissistic and sinister behavior, would cook up another scheme that could get me arrested or cause me to lose my job. I was learning to live with embarrassment, negative rumors, and lies spread by Greg that had permeated the department. I also realized I needed to adjust to the reality that my story will never have the opportunity to be adjudicated within the police environment. Some would insist on being blamed for the criminality I was accused of and rumors would never end. I would likely have to live with that shame and reality for my entire career.

In spite of these realities my life was going well. I was secure in my career as a police officer now and the department respected my professional work. As a police recruit with the courses taken in the training department I earned my associate's degree in law enforcement. Later, while working in the department's crime laboratory, I was afforded flexibility in my work schedule to attend college to complete my bachelor's degree. I was able to do so debt-free, courtesy of the department's tuition reimbursement program. And by 1983, I was very active in my church where I was discovering new ways to listen, discern, and teach the word of God.

Under the leadership of Pastor Wright, I was exposed to excellent preaching of scholars such as Rev. James Forbes, former pastor of Riverside

Presbyterian Church in New York, and Rev. Dr. Renita Weems, professor of Hebrew Bible at Vanderbilt School of Theology. The congregation was exposed to Black liberation theologians such as Dr. James Cone, the author of the book *A Black Theology of Liberation*. Pastor Wright, who in his own right is one of the most prolific pulpiteers and prophetic preachers of this century, regularly invited esteemed scholars to Trinity UCC. He ensured his congregants were not simply able to receive the gospel of our faith but were also equipped to critique and offer practical implications of our faith. I was part of a community that encouraged loving God with both mind and body while being *unashamedly Black and unapologetically Christian*. It was in this space where I solidified my faith in God through Jesus Christ and was introduced to the God of justice and liberation.

Although I had been raised Pentecostal, I had found a place where I could be both Black and Christian. I found a place I believed was relevant *to* the world, as opposed to being *in the world but not of the world*, as one of defining tenets and practices of our faith. The holiness required of our faith is manifested through not allowing our carnal bodies to be aligned with the world. To be carnal-minded means you enjoyed the pleasures of the world rather than focusing on the things of God. Particularly for women, being carnal-minded tended to have sexual undertones. This carnality included dressing sexy—practically anything viewed by the pastors and saints as appearing to be attractive. A woman's carnality was further compared to Jezebel as shameless, Potiphar's wife as a seductress, and Mary Magdalene as a sex worker.

Jezebel was often described as a corrupt, sexual, seductive, shameless, and morally unrestrained woman (1 Kings 19). Potiphar's wife was often described as conniving for seducing Joseph and falsely accusing him of rape when he rebuffed her advances (Gen 39). Even today, this Scripture is one of the excuses given for not believing women who claim they had been raped. Mary Magdalene was an avid follower of Jesus (Luke 8:2–3) and described by many preachers as a wealthy woman. However, known for having seven demons cast out of her, Mary is characterized by some clergy as a prostitute. Growing up in the church, I heard many references to one of those demons cast out of her as her negative sexual behavior. Could this in reality be character assasination since she was also wealthy, successful, and had influence as a follower of Jesus?

In contrast, Trinity UCC fostered a spirit of engagement with the world and theologies of liberation and empowerment. I was introduced to a Jesus who was brown and not the usual White Jesus I had come to know with long, lightly colored hair, an off-white robe, and sandals. This Jesus was on television, pictured and framed in churches from my childhood, and became the image of the one who I prayed to in times of distress. Prior to joining Trinity, I never thought about Jesus as any other color but white. After meeting this brown-skinned man with curly black hair and viewing his picture within our church context, I can no longer picture Jesus looking any kind of way except as described within the Bible (Rev 1:14–15) with woolly hair and a dark skin tone. That is the Jesus I came to love, worship, and adore.

I was introduced to a God who cared about our human experiences and was there to meet people at their point of need. I discovered my church to be an environment where I could be both Black and Christian during a time when the question was being asked: Why the Christian Church? I became part of a community where I could love Jesus, grow in Jesus, increase my faith, all while I simultaneously fight for justice within our society and call out social ills and racism for what it was. I found a home. I had a newfound freedom. I came to know Jesus in ways that countered all I had ever learned. Jesus was not just concerned about my personal sins. Jesus was concerned with the sins of the world. Salvation and liberation were seen as one in the same and not something we earned, prayed for, or tarried hours to receive: it was a gift of our baptism. This Jesus was counter to my childhood understanding and was accessible to me even in my sinfulness. But alas, even with all of these newfound discoveries over the years that certainly increased my faith, I was still plagued by those older childhood teachings that continued to dominate my thoughts relating to sin, hell, repentance, and judgments relating to how I should live.

I first discovered my judgmentalism right in my new church home. I noticed as I became active in the church that women were dressing in short dresses, very high-heels, fancy earrings, makeup, and red lipstick. They boldly broke all of the dress codes that would guarantee their journey to hell, especially those women who dared to wear red. As I scanned the congregation and the choir, it was no surprise when I thought to myself, "They are all going to hell." Their attire brought to mind teachings from my childhood regarding women such as Jezebel, who were often viewed as morally depraved and unrestrained. This description was often given to women who refused to play by the rules of male patriarchy. These rules required women to dress a certain way, speak a certain way, especially when in public, and behave in ways approved by the pastor, the one who was usually the main influencer within the church setting.

I remember figuratively pointing my fingers towards various groups of women, judging and critiquing them negatively for daring to trespass dress rules. On New Year's Eve, the women were all dressed up in their robes prepared to worship as we collectively brought in the New Year. But underneath their choir robes, the *Jezebels* were dressed to go out into the world and party right after the benediction. This was my judgment. I had no idea that I was projecting my past guilt onto these women. I did not understand at that moment. I attempted to work out my salvation and discover myself in this newfound environment called the church. Yet, there was another incident that was even more telling about my understanding of what was meant for one to join the church.

The standard way to join the church in typical Black Protestant churches was to walk down the aisle and give the pastor or those designated your hand, indicating you wanted to be a part of the church. This invitation to join Christ was marked by the preacher saying, "The doors of the church are open." One day in 1980, I walked down the aisle and joined the church. After attending new members classes, I became a full member of the church. However, before the official service of welcoming occurred, I found myself walking the aisle for the next three Sundays after the sermon when the invitation to Christ was extended. After my third time walking the aisle, my pastor finally noticed me as a repeat walker during this time and obviously decided I was confused. Consequently, on this third effort to walk the aisle, Pastor Wright interceded. He took my hand and brought me and placed me in the hands of a person who was part of the Newness of Life Ministries. From my memory, this ministry was the group of persons who helped new members to acclimate to the church and receive spiritual guidance. The person I was introduced to helped me understand I did not have to walk the aisle of the church every Sunday and that I was a member and had met all the requirements to be brought in on the first Sunday and officially given the right hand of fellowship by those who would come around to welcome me. This particular Sunday was very defining for me, as I knew why I kept walking the aisle.

In my upbringing, walking down the aisle was not necessarily to join the church. Walking the aisle was the confession that I was not saved and I had a desire to be so. We were then taken to the back room for a change in clothes to robes and sheets to prepare us for baptism.

ME, MY MIND, MY BODY, AND MY HOME—ALL DEPRESSED

Afterwards, we were placed on our knees to tarry (pray) until we received the Holy Ghost. This was to be verified by the saints by speaking in an unknown tongue. Each time I walked the aisles of Trinity United Church of Christ, I still believed that, even though I had acknowledged being saved, I was not saved. I was walking the aisle for my baptism and prayers toward being saved. Later, I had a revelation. I had not really bought into the God I had met in my new church home.

I was still attempting to please the God who required so much of me that I could never reach *His* (God's) perfected expectation, and therefore I was stuck in my sinful state for life. I had to do so much to earn *His* (God's) love, affection, forgiveness, trust, and affirmation. Yes, even in the midst of my newfound relationship with Jesus, the voice of the God of my childhood and the God of my liberation and salvation, who I had come to love, were at war with one another within my self-understanding and my awareness of who I was in the middle. These are more of the contradictions I was living with as I questioned if I was worthy or unworthy before God and the people to be called a Christian.

There were times when I saw myself as worthy and at other times I couldn't shake feelings of unworthiness. I referred to these competing voices as tapes that played loudly in my head. The latter judgment was the loudest and left me longing for validation. In the midst of this longing, I was judging others instead of myself. I projected my guilt onto the members of my new church so I would feel better. In the midst of judging others and proclaiming to be in Christ, I had another revelation; I was sitting in this church while cohabitating with Joel, a.k.a. *living in sin*.

Joel stood about six feet tall, which was one of the things that attracted me to him during the period of my abusive relationship with Greg. We met at the bowling alley. Eventually, we became a team along with other friends we had in common. We bowled together for several years. Joel worked in a factory where car motors were manufactured and remained there until his retirement. He was ten years older than I, and he was born and raised in Brookhaven, Mississippi. Several of his family members currently live there and one sibling resides in New Orleans. Joel had two children from a previous marriage. His daughter, Geraldine, lived with her mother and the son, Jerry, who was severely handicapped, lived in a group home. Joel was a family-type man and not the type to run the streets or play the field. He was not the woman-chasing type of man. He never graduated from high school; however, his salary far exceeded the salary of many college graduates. This was common for most people who worked in factories. Joel's values and actions centered around taking care of his family and working. He was an all-around funny and stable person.

Prior to our moving in together, Joel and I had separate living arrangements. I lived on the southeast side and he lived on the southwest side. However, I found myself semi-living with him as I needed the protection and surveillance of Joel during the time I was being accused of several crimes by Greg. These crimes occurred during times when I did not have a witness to speak to my whereabouts or be my alibi. After the abuse and the drama surrounding my now-finalized divorce, I decided to give up my apartment to officially move in with Joel. We spent a couple of months in his apartment until we located a larger space to live. This, for me, was when Joel, my children, and I officially became a family. But for me, what we were was a family living in sin.

Initially, this felt great. Ozell and Sharell attended the school across the street from our new apartment and all seemed to be well. Never in my wildest imagination did I ever consider that I would find this relationship problematic. Yet, there I was, newly divorced, living partnered in a new relationship, and, as the tapes in my head played on loop, I was living in sin. *Living in sin* was a prominent message of my childhood. Marriage was the only covenant to enter if a man and woman wanted to live together. Shacking, as it was referred to, was against God's will for our lives. Any other arrangement that has a man and woman living together was referred to as living in sin. We were a full-fledged family. I was/we were living in sin because I was not married to Joel. This had to change. And it did.

Initiated by me, Joel and I began to talk about our living arrangement. I did not share my theological stance on why we needed to be married. I just told him we needed to be married and he agreed. There was no holy talk about God, sin, or being in a right relationship with God. It was as if he understood what I was saying and why I was saying it. The conversation was not about love, either. How we truly felt about each other did not seem to be the catalyst for our marriage. The implied message, I am assuming for us both, was that marriage should happen now that we were living together. We began this process by deciding we needed to purchase a home. We secured a real-estate agent and began the home-buying process.

When I broke the news to my parents, they seemed to be happy for me. Afterall, this was now my third marriage. I expected to be questioned about my choice, but the general reaction from both family and friends was one of joy for me and relief that someone was in my life that was more stable. Joel and I found a house and within a few months we relocated. The house was not far away from our apartment, so we allowed the children to remain in the elementary school they were attending. The next step was to plan our wedding. Joel and I began planning for this day. We decided to have a home wedding to make it simple. We set a wedding date in August of 1984, three months after we moved into our home. One of my friends, Mary, the one who allowed my children to stay with her and attend an elementary school by her house during my abusive relationship with Greg, volunteered to make the cake. My father agreed to be the officiant. We invited about fifty of our friends and family to join us for the ceremony and reception.

Joel and I liked each other very much and had plenty of laughs together and good times enjoying each other's company. By then the word love had come up between us both on varying occasions. I believe we really thought we were in love. At least I did, and to that end, the most important part of the planning for me was to make certain the right music would be played for our walk from the bedroom to the kitchen, passing our guests to arrive where my father would be standing to perform the service. And I found the perfect song. The song stirred up happy feelings in me. The song generated sensations of love on the inside of me. There were tears of happiness when I played it. The song made me feel as if I was truly making a brand new start, and that felt good. Those love feelings grew every time I would listen to the music. The song was "Love Ballad," by the group L.T.D., with Jeffery Osborne as lead singer. It is about the feelings you have when you discover you have really found love after claiming love before and the difference in how this love made him feel. This love is as described indescribable and could only be explained as in this particular stanza: "Though it's not the feeling I had before, it's much much more."[1] Yes! I believed I had truly finally found this love.

The wedding day was beautiful. Our home was decorated with fresh flowers, and an arch was erected near the kitchen for us to stand under. The children were all dressed up. Joel wore his black suit, and I wore a white knee-length dress. The day looked and felt festive as family and friends began to arrive. After some preliminaries, the wedding procession began. The wedding song was cued, and Joel and I walked to our place

1. L.T.D., "Love Ballad."

under the arch while our wedding song played. Ozell and Sharell followed closely behind. My close friends and associates who knew my story came out to support me. They knew my story and were happy believing, as did I, that this one was the real deal. The music was appropriate for this feeling and many of the guests were crying tears of joy. Others were most probably teary-eyed because the song was just a wonderful love song that touched the heart. Our families were present, friends were present, and people from our new neighborhood came to show their support.

My father, as in my past two weddings, was teary-eyed while officiating the ceremony. Both Joel and I were misty-eyed as we said our vows and were pronounced husband and wife. The festivities were lively as we ate, drank, toasted, mingled, and danced. The weather was warm, so the crowd covered both the inside of the house and outside. As people began to leave, others began helping us to clean up before they left. The festivities were coming to an end.

When everyone left, my husband and I took a seat on the couch in the living room while the children went their separate ways to their own spaces in the house. However, there was something unsettling to me about our behavior on the couch. There seemed to be no real connection between us. No debriefing of the day. No hugging. No kissing. These inactions could have been passed off as simply being tired from the day's events. And of course, that probably existed, but something strange and ominous lingered.

We sat close. But it seemed as if we had just completed something perfunctory and now that was over. I felt empty. I was not certain how Joel felt. I never asked him. Yet nothing about our presence on the couch felt like we were madly-in-love newlyweds. We were not angry at each other. Things were simply strange between us. I felt it. I believe he did, also. If I had to describe what it felt like, I would compare that moment to a movie where the couple had guests over and had to pretend their marriage was wonderful. But, after the guests left, they went back to their very unhappy relationship. Within a few minutes, our doorbell rang. I got up to open the door, and it was our neighbors from across the street.

She came in with a bottle of wine and offered it to us, explaining that she could not make the wedding but wanted to bring us some wine. She noticed that the crowd had left and thought it was a good time to bring the wine. Cheerfully, she handed us the bottle of wine with a twinkle in her eye telling us that she thought we would enjoy this together tonight. Joel and I smiled, received the bottle, and she left. I sat the bottle on the counter and we resumed the same posture we were in before the neighbor arrived. For me, this was strange. Even years later, this moment continued to haunt me as I believed perhaps this was a telling moment that might have questioned the authenticity of our love for one another. I failed to exhibit any happy emotions during her short visit and neither did Joel. Was there something going on with Joel, or with me, or with the both of us we failed to detect? I could not figure this out. We seemed to get along pretty well with one another. Certainly, as the relationship continued, there were some moments that were challenging, and those moments usually related to my children.

Joel lived with me during the second half of my abusive relationship with Greg when I was being accused of several criminal acts by him. He knew most of my story of abuse. The one thing I absolutely knew was how I would not tolerate him mistreating my children. I had previously set one boundary regarding them that was non-negotiable. I asked him, no matter how terrible things get with his discipline of them, to never physically or sexually violate them or put them out of our house. He nodded as if he agreed. However, over the years, he continued in a controlling way to make the children obey his every command on simple things such as insisting that they not put sugar on their grits even when I would remind him this is the way we, meaning the three of us, have always eaten grits. I would tell him not to try and change the way my children ate.

Other occasions involved forcing Ozell to clean up his room and insisting that my young daughter cook for him when I was not around. While none of his requests were unreasonable, there was always the issue about Joel's constant insistence that these things were done when *he* wanted them done without any flexibility. Joel had his ways and his ways were the way. He controlled when they would go outside and when they needed to come in. The children in the neighborhood would tease my children when they saw their stepfather coming down the street to collect them due to their refusal to come home at the designated time. The neighborhood children would laugh when they saw him coming, warning them that Joel was coming to get them, "There comes your dad again." When Joel walked out of the house, his presence caused feelings of respect and fear from the neighborhood children.

I remember one Fourth of July when the children of the neighborhood gathered around our house located at the end of the block. Because of it being on the corner, there was much more space for the neighborhood children to gather, whether Ozell and Sharell were out there or not.

On this night, they had obtained some fireworks and enjoyed setting them off. The next morning, Joel went outside and noticed the sidewalks and streets encircling our home were littered with trash. He walked to every house in the neighborhood, and before I knew it, all the children were outside cleaning up the mess from the night before. Around Joel, no child was left behind. They were all under his authority and they danced to his music. Again, none of these things in and of themselves were disturbing. However, how he consistently treated my children was beginning to wear on me. His behavior was filled with orders, rules, and unnecessary strict disciplines and lacked sufficient demonstration of love and care for my children.

I began to feel some of this authoritative behavior as he began challenging my decision-making. He believed that I was allowing my children to *just do what they wanted to do*. This mainly related to my assertion that he was not going to change a habit of theirs established over the years. I accused him of attempting unnecessarily to control my children. Joel gave orders as if he were the sole authority figure in the house and things were going to go his way. This led to many short-fused arguments that ended up with me challenging his demands. This was beginning to wear on my patience and on the tolerance of Joel. Certainly, this behavior was part of his overall personality that began to show itself as we began living together in marriage as a family.

Joel would treat my friends like this, also. He seemed to find joy in simply ordering people around. There was a sense of entitlement in his behavior that made him believe his actions were appreciated as he ordered my friends around. It was neither cute nor acceptable behavior and certainly I would address these feelings. As the children got older, we began to adjust to his behavior by behaving the opposite of what he expected of us.

Ozell and Sharell had graduated from elementary school and by this time we were our most authentic selves when Joel was not in the house, especially if he was out of town. We would order food, eat it on the floor of the living room (which was not allowed) while talking, laughing, and watching television. Oh, and about dishes, we did not wash them. We would save all the cleaning responsibilities until the day Joel would be due to arrive back home from out of town. We would, while laughing, go into rush mode to have the house clean when he arrived. We had fun. Fun! That is what seemed to be missing as a family, fun! This was my first revelation regarding our wedding day blues, this relationship was void of family fun. We had a relationship where there was no fun! Joel and I did not know how to be a family together. He looked at fatherhood as making certain he had control over but not necessarily love for our newly formed family. And yet there were other things brewing. I felt as if I had no joy. Actually, it felt like a strange sadness was taking over my whole body.

I did not feel as if I was becoming depressed. I still could laugh, love on my children and friends, work, attend school, and basically function and have fun when outside of the walls of my house. It was coming back home where the sadness would show its face. Eventually, I had to face the reality that something in my life was not right. Upon reflection, I had plenty of reasons to be depressed.

In January and March 1984, my brother-in-law died suddenly from a heart attack and, shortly after that, my mother's aunt, who was the eldest and closest family member on my mother's side of the family, died. My father, who married Joel and me in August, suddenly died in December of that same year just a few days before his sixtieth birthday of complications from back surgery. Before these events, I spent the prior three years living with Joel on and off while seeking safety from the abusive relationship with Greg that almost cost me my life and my career. We were fully living together by 1982. I found myself in a live-in relationship arrangement with a man I had never fully expressed love for, and now I was married to him.

By 1991, I had been in the department for twelve years and married to Joel for seven years—not including the two years or so we were living together. A year after Daddy died, in 1985, I answered my call to ministry and enrolled in seminary to study for my master of divinity (MDiv) degree. Answering a *call* is based on the understanding that God has called you into ordained ministry. I was a full-time student and a full-time employee of the police department. I worked the overnight shift and attended seminary during the day and evenings. In addition to my full-time department duties, I became a part-time St. Jude Chaplain. St. Jude is the Catholic patron saint of hopeless causes. St. Jude volunteer chaplains were responsible for the police services of a loved one or a family member of an officer who had died or been killed in the line of duty. These are short words and prayers conducted during the wake of a funeral or during visitation hours if the services are done within a funeral home. Officers join this service and line up in front of the family while the St. Jude chaplain speaks words of comfort ending in the Lord's Prayer. Then the chaplain, followed by the officers, greets the family and leaves. I served in this capacity until 1991, when I was appointed by the superintendent of police as a full-time chaplain. I served the department in that capacity until my retirement in 2010.

During this time, I was also very active in my home church. By 1985, I had entered seminary while simultaneously training at my home church to become an ordained deacon and later a Bible study facilitator. My son, Ozell, graduated from high school in 1990 and joined the National Guard. It was during these years (1985–1995) leading up to my daughter Sharell's high school graduation when the weightiness of life events and relationship circumstances came upon me with full force. Joel and I had developed a strained relationship; he broke my request that he not put my son out of our house.

Joel and I had a major disagreement, and I left the house to get some fresh air. During the two hours I had gone, Joel turned his anger onto my son by demanding that he clean up his area in the basement. Included in his demand was the alternative for him to leave the house if he did not want to keep his room clean. My son left. When I returned home and discovered Ozell had left, as Joel informed me in a matter-of-fact tone of voice, my eyes welled with tears as I became increasingly angry. My resolve was to not address this issue but to call to see where my son was staying. He was fine and safe but refused to return home after what occurred between him and Joel. My son left home because of this confrontation. At nineteen years old, this was the last time Ozell ever lived with me. Joel had broken trust in the one thing I had asked him to not do, kicking my children out of the house.

Over the next few days I experienced aches and spasms in my upper back. I ached morning and night. I ached during church services and found myself massaging my shoulders often during worship. I remember attending a revival service at my church and massaging my shoulder area as usual when someone sitting behind me began rubbing my shoulders for me. I sat back and relaxed and was grateful for the relief. By this time, I was assured that, although functional, I was deeply depressed. The pain of my life and my life story left me feeling as if I needed another escape plan.

Reflecting on my life every time I remember the pain I felt in my mind, body, and spirit, I ended up crying a river. I would be in my bedroom with the doors closed and I would just cry. Then when it was time for me to function outside of the house, I would fix myself up and perform whatever duties I was assigned by others or assigned to myself.

Upon returning home, I would repeat the crying, remembering, and lamenting. This went on for weeks. I wanted it to stop but did not know how. Killing myself was not an option. Suicide would send me to hell. I was afraid to make any attempts on my life, and this was the only viable method I could think of at the time. However, in my brilliance of mind, I discovered a way to end the pain of remembering these life events and struggles: I would go crazy.

One day when I was at home alone, I decided this was the perfect day to go crazy. My daughter was away at school, my son was in his own apartment, and Joel was at work. I took a shower so that I would be clean when I had to go to the mental ward of the hospital and then initiated my plan. Oh wait! I did not have a plan. I had no idea how to go crazy and there was no book that described how to go crazy. I just knew that going crazy was my desired pathway of escaping the reality and insanity of my life. Going crazy would free me of memories, and everything inside of me would be free to be, without normalcy getting in the way. All of a sudden, it dawned on me that my pathway to crazy was the mirror. My plan was to get in front of the mirror and simply scream until I went crazy. This sounded like a brilliant plan to me. I began screaming to the top of my lungs. I screamed for so long that I lost my voice and my throat was sore. All of the screaming I could muster ended and I was still not crazy. I cried and cried. So much for my brilliance. Nothing changed. I was melancholy, irritated, unhappy, and physically in pain.

I was depressed. My body was depressed. My spirit was depressed. And my house was depressed. My laughter stopped and my joy, if I ever really had joy, was gone. It was amazing I could still function. I knew I was in bad shape. I managed to engage my daughter and son and always made them feel loved. This took all of the energy I could muster, yet I did it. I basically ignored my husband and he ignored me. We were cordial, not affectionate. I placed more attention in my church and the department. I began to focus on more avenues to insert myself that brought me joy. One of my joys was conducting retreats for women police officers. I invited my best friend, Marsha, who was also in seminary, to attend the retreat as a facilitator.

By the time I began facilitating police women's retreats, my three best friends, Rhonda, Delores, and Marsha (each of whom I met at various times), knew each other, and we all had connections among ourselves. Each of these women has been a source of inspiration in my life and has supported me on this journey. Our relationships blossomed and we continue to be friends today. However, it was Marsha who I invited to attend the retreats for female police officers and serve as a leader for the retreats.

The women in the department were an exciting bunch to be around. They were loud and rebellious to any schedule I attempted to impose on them. They played cards when I had planned other activities on the agenda and would not sleep in the beds I had assigned. They taught me about my own control issues. That was my first and last retreat offered where I had a strict agenda. We had a great time during these retreats, which lasted from Friday evening until Sunday after sunrise service. We would all part by sharing hugs, kisses, and tears. However, when I got within a mile of arriving home, the depression would begin again. The lonely feelings would return. The tears would have already begun in the first mile. My house lost its light and energy. It seemed like everything in my home environment was miserable. The pain in my back began to worsen even more. This time, the pain was so bad that my entire body was tightening up and my mobility became affected.

My spirit was low! I had no happiness or joy! And now my body was in agony. While awake, my back was very sore and movement was slow and limited. However, when I went to bed, my back tightened up and I was not even able to turn over. I literally had to slide out of the bed just to change my sleeping position. The pain was comparably horrible in my body and in my mind. I thought, "I am going to die." But dying was not my main concern. My lament was that I was going to die without ever knowing what it meant to have joy in my life. This turned out to be my biggest fear. I was so fearful that on this particular night I prayed to God and gave God an alternative. I asked God to take this pain away from my body and my mind; and I asked God that if that could not happen to just let me die. The next morning I awoke pain free.

Yes! I woke up pain free. My back was totally relaxed and all the soreness was gone. And, to my delight, my mind felt free. I felt no sadness, depression, or hurt. My overall feeling was that of joy. This joy felt like internal peace and contentment in the midst of the sadness I was still experiencing. Everything was not right in my life or marriage; however, I had a peace I had never experienced before. I knew that something miraculous had occurred within me. I was not satisfied with what was going on in my life, but I was assured of one thing: I had joy.

This was my unspoken fear. I kept this secret from everyone except God. I had asked God to relieve me of this pain I was feeling on both the inside and outside of my body. On the inside, I felt the pain of the absence of joy. On the outside, I was living the pain and suffering that was literally choking the life out of me. And now, I was transformed both on the inside and the outside. Of all the gifts God could have offered me, I received joy. I was determined that I would never hand over my joy to anyone. It was brand new. It did not make me jump up and down with glee. It gave me peace, which is the only way I can describe what I experienced. I woke up determined that I would leave my husband.

During this period of reflection, I made some very important connections. I had never married out of love. I married out of survival, guilt, shame, and urgency. When I married my first husband, Buck, at eighteen years old, I was escaping from my father's physical and sexual abuse and my resentment of not being loved by him in the ways I needed to be loved. When I married my second husband, Greg, I was feeling shame and the weight of sin and damnation by God for dating Wallace, my daughter's father, and guilt of his early death at thirty-seven years old. Marrying Greg was my act of repentance. Finally, when I married my third husband, Joel, I was running from my abusive husband and ended up living with him for safety, protection, and as a witness that I was not crazy due to the false accusations against me by my abuser, Greg.

Even though I truly believed I loved Joel, I was only kidding myself and hoping I did. This was my second revelation regarding my wedding day blues: I did not love Joel. The third revelation came just after the revelation regarding my wedding day blues: I made a mistake. I am not certain what Joel was feeling that day. Perhaps he was just tired and being himself. Perhaps I was projecting my feelings onto him. I am not certain what he might have been thinking on that day. Yet, I took full responsibility for what I was feeling and could not then come to terms with. Hindsight is 20/20. My wedding day blues were real.

I made the decision to leave my husband. However, there was one barrier to leaving. I was now an ordained minister. I was a full-time police chaplain. And my husband Joel was an active member of Trinity UCC. Joel was just as loved and respected in the church as we both pretended more and more we were a happily faith-filled married couple. In addition to all of this, divorce was a sin. The Bible stated God hated divorce. My status as an ordained clergy was solid, and a divorce would make me look hypocritical. How could I possibly disappoint my church as well as God? The only way the Bible spoke of divorcing your spouse was if they committed adultery. The Bible speaks of divorce only as it relates to a man divorcing a woman. However, I knew divorce under the grounds of adultery was an acceptable way to divorce. And praise the Lord, that opportunity came.

I came home from work, and Sharell caught me alone in the house and began asking me questions. She asked me if Joel had ever bought me an expensive coat; I said no. She asked if Joel had given me money to buy a particular gift; again I said no. Then I looked at her as if to ask, "What are you attempting to say to me?" She begins telling me the things she overheard Joel saying to some woman over the phone. "Really?" I responded, wanting to know more. My opportunity had come—he was having an affair. This could be my excuse for divorcing him without God, my pastor, or the saints judging my motives.

I immediately went out to get some recording devices. My son Ozell worked for Radio Shack, which sold recording equipment, and he helped me to purchase what I needed. I went home and plugged these devices into the outlet in the room where I slept, as we slept in separate bedrooms that were separated by a bathroom. I warned Sharell that I was recording all calls and not to say anything over the phone she did not want me to hear. It did not take long to discover that Joel was not only talking to one woman, but he was also talking to another woman. What was said on these calls will not be repeated. Suffice to say that the first person indicated within the conversation that the relationship was sexual and the second woman did also. I had not been this excited in a long while. I finally had the proof I needed to leave Joel without guilt and file for my divorce. I was not sad, nor hurt, nor was I disappointed. I really did not care enough to be angry about his affairs. I just wanted my ticket out of the relationship.

That evening, I set the recorder on the bathroom counter, which separated our two sleeping areas, while he was in the bedroom lying down. I pushed the play button and turned the volume up so that Joel could hear himself in conversation with these women. The silence coming from his room was deafening. By the time Joel was able to allow his legs to dangle on the side of the bed and push his way up to a standing position to come towards me, I had already mustered up tears in my eyes and was in full victim/hurt mode. There was nothing he really could say. The facts were already on the recording, and I immediately went into acting mode. I expressed, through tears and a runny nose, how I felt betrayed. I expressed my disappointment and hurt, stating I could not believe he did this to me. I cried and mocked the fact that he had not just one girlfriend but two and one of them was married. The married woman belongs to a local church, and we knew some of their members. Still crying, I asked Joel, "Does her husband know that you are sleeping with his wife? Perhaps," I ranted, "I should send this tape to him?" In addition to all of this, I asked him if the first woman he spoke to knew that ten seconds after hanging up the phone, he had called the married woman. Certainly, my drama wheels were turning. For the next couple of days, I was so wrapped up in my hurt and sorrow that I felt as if my feelings were real. I finally had to tell myself to stop! I had to remind myself this was all just an act. But it was an act that would set me free.

With a sad face, I finally told Joel that I was leaving him. He wanted me to stay and work things out. I insisted that I needed to leave. Joel asked me if I was going to divorce him. "I don't know," I replied. "I know I need to leave. And if I feel as if I can come back to you, I will." He was afraid for me to leave and told me that if I left, I might not come back. My final response was, "And that might be the truth."

I went apartment hunting within the neighborhood to look for a two- or three-flat building. My best friend, Rhonda from the department, advised me to live in a high-rise building, that it would be better for me as a single person. I took her advice and I placed my down payment on a three-bedroom high rise apartment on the twelfth floor. It was 1993 and I had reserved my apartment to move in by July 1, although I was not going to move in until after my daughter, Sharell, graduated in June and went off to college in the fall. I was able to take her by the apartment to show her where she would be living in addition to her college dorm. And I assured her I would be fine. I continued to live in our home. Those two months I waited to move felt weird and a bit scary. My mind went back to my experience of domestic violence and leaving became a frightening move to make. I had not informed Joel that I had found an apartment and that I would leave very soon.

One lesson I learned in an abusive relationship is that leaving can be dangerous. Joel knew that I would move one day; however, out of fear, I would never tell him the specifics of when or where. Although I did not see myself as abused as in the past, I followed the same precautionary steps. I would leave first and then inform him I was gone. I visited the apartment often, bought objects to put in the house, and just sat alone in the apartment not really believing I was about to do this.

My main focus was getting Sharell all she needed for her graduation. On the day of her graduation, I struggled to get her ready to arrive early for graduation practice. My energy was low and I felt overwhelmingly exhausted. I was able to facilitate her needs and take her to her graduation early for their rehearsal. I returned home to get myself dressed and barely had the energy to do so. I managed to put on a loose-fitting, homely looking dress and a straw hat. After the graduation, Sharell met Joel and me outside, anticipating celebrating her on this big day. When Sharell saw me, she was amazed at how awful I looked. I laughed and told her to not mess with me as that was the best I could do—"But I am here." We both laughed as we took pictures together. Sharell still has this picture today, which always brings me to laughing and remembering that day when I had reached my bottom.

Joel and I took Sharell away to her new college, and a week later I moved from my home to my new apartment. I did not take any furniture and just moved objects that were mine specifically. I did not want to carry any of those negative energies into my space. My house was also depressed. I only took the essentials. Everything was bought new. I cannot begin to express how happy, excited, and joyful I felt having my own place. I loved it! I felt like a changed person. I felt free. The only words to describe my feelings living in my new place was, ironically, the song "Love Ballad." I believed years back this song was connected to my feelings of love for Joel. Instead, I learned it was the new feeling that was emerging, my love of self. The song "Love Ballad" played during the marriage really was a prophetic voice of things to come, which was my newfound freedom and beginning of a relationship of loving myself, "Though it's not the feeling I had before, it's much much more!" And this time I meant it!

> *"i found god in myself & i loved her/i loved her fiercely."*
> —NTOZAKE SHANGE[2]

---

2. Shange, *For Colored Girls Who Have Considered Suicide/When the Rainbow Is Enuf*, 27.

Reflection: How Do We Navigate Self-Care in Mind, Body, and Spirit in Times of Trauma, Crisis, and #BlackLivesMatter?

Over the years, I am blessed to have achieved academic success having received five degrees. At the same time, I have found myself working two or three jobs at the same time and taking on projects, volunteering for special events, etc. Actually, I don't remember a time when I did not have at least three projects or activities going on at the same time. During the years when I was actively suffering through sexual assault and other forms of interpersonal violence, I remember being busiest. As a child, I spent quite a bit of time outside. I loved sports and was actively involved in programs with the WMCA, going to the gospel center for Bible study, walking the streets and participating when I needed to say no. I earned my associate's, bachelor's, master of divinity, doctor of ministry, and my doctor of philosophy degrees while working full-time. I graduated on time because of the option of attending school part-time. I am certain I have not called the complete roll on my busyness. Many people were in awe of my achievements as a full-time employed person. Some would affirm my ability to navigate and refer to me as strong. Others referred to me as a go-getter. And others challenged me on the busyness.

I had several conversations with my best friend, Marsha, regarding my busyness. I knew she was correct in her assumptions that my busyness was me avoiding getting the psychological help I needed to properly handle the stress I had and was enduring. One time, I just came right out and asked her, what did she propose I do to replace the void I feel when I am not busy? She remained silent as if to admit she had no replacement. Being busy was my pathology. My busyness was avoidance and overwhelming. Yet, it was my saving grace, my distraction from my problems and sadness, and my way of at least doing something positive. I was aware my solution did not leave time for taking care of myself and doing what I needed to do to recover. Since this time, Marsha never questioned me about my busyness in that way again.

Yet there came a time when I loved being busy. I loved doing the work I was called to do. My best friend Marsha was an introvert. She found solace in her private spaces and places. I was an extrovert, and quiet was just not my thing. I loved being among the people and I was fiercely committed to the jobs, duties, and responsibilities I signed on to. I was committed to works of justice, and having retired from the department in 2010, I was ready to lean into my new profession as a professor and develop myself to be what I referred to as an academic activist—teaching in seminary, mentoring, and providing training with the two organizations I had become active in. The FaithTrust Institute and the African American Peace Project afforded me the opportunity to provide needed clergy boundaries training to clergy and safe and healthy church training and sexual and domestic violence awareness training to congregations and other agencies outside the congregation. The celebration of my retirement from pastoring was titled "My Next." This title automatically inferred I was not finished yet. There was more in ministry and in life. I desired to do it, and it was my intention to do it.

I chuckled when I happened to look at my Twitter feed and in front of me was a tweet from Rev. Renita Weems: "I've decided to keep going till I'm 80 like Maxine and Nancy" (meaning Maxine Waters and Nancy Pelosi). Weems continued, "I'll keep fighting the patriarchy and everyone who thinks women in their 80s shouldn't be seen or heard from. After that I'm going to see Jesus or sit my arse down and do nothing for nobody but myself! #wisewomen."[3] Reading this post was an act of self-care. Moments of laughter have always brought me release and allowed me moments to regroup from whatever I was attempting to get done. However, I connected with this tweet because it causes me distress and I become irritated when people individually decide for any reason that it is time for me to stop doing anything, especially because of my age.

I am certain that at the time my busyness began, it was an act of avoiding my feelings and replacing it with busyness. Yet in many ways it was an act of self-care. Going home was depressing, and I cried silently every time I approached and entered my house. I am not certain how my busyness later in life was impacted by my past. Or was it because of my urge to be involved or my call to make a difference in this world before I die? I would like to believe it is the latter. But whatever my reasons may be, the choice is always mine, as when a victim of abuse will leave a violent domestic relationship. And I own the consequences with my choices.

Yet as I think of the title of this reflection, "How Do We Navigate Self-Care in Mind, Body, and Spirit in Times of Trauma, Crisis, and #BlackLivesMatter," the answer must be through our individually discerned decision about how the load and limit should be balanced. More than simply my individual trauma, I recognized that we are all, especially within communities of color, experiencing trauma and a great deal of

---

3. Renita Weems, Twitter post, April 29, 2021, 11:07 p.m. @somethingwithin.

stress. We are in a fight for our life and our humanity. It requires us in these times to go to battle. We owe it to our children and our future generations to do whatever is necessary to change the tides of racism, sexism, gender oppression, the killing of Black and Brown bodies by the police, structural racism, violence in our own communities, the COVID crisis where we are forced in isolation from one another, death of our loved ones, killing of transwomen of color, gender violence, crises within our church communities, gang violence, the health crisis in the midst of an economic crisis, as well as dealing with principalities and powers we cannot see with the naked eye but we know are active among us. Everybody who roams is not lost.

In 1 Pet 5:8, believers are instructed, "Stay alert! Watch out for your great enemy, the devil. He prowls around like a roaring lion, looking for someone to devour." We are busy doing the work of justice not simply as activists demonstrate. We are doing it while we are wondering when we will be devoured by the faceless enemy seeking in every corner to run us out of existence. We are called to face this enemy as our ancestors did in the midst of enslavement, Jim Crow, and the civil rights movement, and many gave their lives in the process. And there is not a lot of time for rest when we are faced with evil. Yet, our ancestors died way too early fighting tirelessly, grew old fast, suffered diseases untold, and some suffered from mental illness because of their choice.

I believe we must practice self-care in mind, body, and spirit because we are called to love ourselves. I also believe that in the midst of our individual and collective commitment and call to the work self-care in mind, body, and spirit may look different. Sometimes we may have only moments. And we must refrain from our self-righteous attempts to decide when or how others should take care of themselves and we must refrain from judgment, which is a form of abuse itself. We must do the work through prayer and discernment guided by the Holy Spirit, no matter how great or how small.

Discussion

1. What is the work you believe God is calling you to in the places and spaces you find yourself and in this world today?
2. Is God calling you to do more? What does this mean for you?
3. How will you find time for preparation?

Activity: Self-Care

- Have you discerned the ways you will care for yourself—mind, body, and spirit—in the midst of your call?
- List all of the things you like to do that, for you, feel like self-care?
- Keep this list close to you at all times!

"Synchronize—may your mind, body, and spirit be synchronized, and work as one today."

—THOMAS HONG[4]

---

4. Thomas Hong, remarks at the Pacific Health Ministry, Queen's Medical Center, West O'ahu in Ewa Beach, Hawai'i, June 17, 2019.

Chapter 8

Concluding Thoughts: Reflections and Lessons—Blessings, Trauma, and Resilience

THE NEXT EIGHT YEARS or so were filled with lessons, blessings, and opportunities for growth along with new beginnings. I was happy as a single woman living in an ideal location that did not isolate me, thanks to the encouragement from and recommendation of my friend, Rhonda. Originally, I was going to move into a residential neighborhood with older three-flat and courtway buildings that were large enough to house multiple families and individuals.

However, Rhonda got to me just in time and was able to change my mind about moving there. Alternatively, she suggested that I not move into a close residential area such as described, but rather into the high-rise buildings located from south to north along Chicago's Lake Shore Drive, which was bright, wide, and had more open space. It was also, she asserted, filled with healing energy, being next to the lakefront that moved along the shores, beginning at 32nd Street and stretches all the way north to downtown and beyond.

The lakefront was located in the same space just east of Lake Shore Drive. The lakefront area housed small recreational areas with trees, gardens, a roller blade area, bike and walking paths, and various large pieces of colorful artwork. This is the area she suggested I live in. And, for the life of me, I have difficulty understanding why I did not make that decision in the first place. Yet, moving into my twelfth floor lakefront high-rise apartment was the best decision I had made thus far.

Living in the high-rise building along the lakefront was all it was hyped up to be. Meeting people every day and sitting down in our vestibule, just spending time outside the apartment talking with whomever came down at that time, was a welcome relief, as opposed to sitting alone in my apartment, which I loved, but I also craved company from time to time.

Christmas was a joyful time as the volunteers, self-chosen and self-described, assisted the maintenance crew in finding and setting up our live Christmas tree for the lobby. Together, we decorated both the tree and the lobby while we hung around the vestibule admiring our handiwork and enjoying each other's company. It was delightful taking walks in the park alongside the waterfront, meditating while walking, speaking to our neighbors, and meeting others as we walked toward one another. Seeing the sunrise and sunset from my apartment as well as the fireworks coming from the White Sox ballpark just a few blocks west and south of our apartment complex brought me overwhelming joy. And I simply loved the spaciousness of my three-bedroom apartment with multiple windows, which kept my apartment bright and sunny in the day and beautiful calming lights at night with fireworks that lit up the sky during baseball season.

This was mine, all mine. I felt less stressed! And I felt a peace and sense of belonging that I had never felt before. I felt freed of anger and any desire for the type of revenge I had acted out over the years. With this newfound freedom, singleness, and change of scenery, I was ready for the healing and transformation to begin. Yet, I quickly discovered this healing journey would be a marathon and not a sprint. Sprints were more my style. When I saw something I desired to purchase or had a particular goal I wanted to reach, I would immediately place my plans into action and take the steps necessary to achieve the goals. Then I would bask in my accomplishments and prepare for my next goal. Sometimes I would work successfully to reach multiple goals at a time.

My personality is a get-it-done type, and it bothers me when others attempt to stifle me in reaching my goals or make excuses as to why they cannot reach theirs. So, to discover that this healing journey and transformation was not going to be easy nor quick was quite disappointing. To recognize that my anger had subsided, but it was not completely gone, troubled my spirit. I wanted a *right-now* type of healing and that was not going to be.

CONCLUDING THOUGHTS: REFLECTIONS AND LESSONS

In spite of this newfound happiness and joy, and in spite of my new and beautiful surroundings and social setting, the walls were still there, the fear of being hurt again remained, as well as the guilt, shame, and trauma, which were never fully resolved. These, all couched in the anger I believed was gone, were at the least still smoldering inside me. Yes, this journey would not be a sprint, rather a marathon. The word *smolder*, as used by firefighters when fighting a fire, best fits the places that I attempted to mask with claims of being free. Yet, smoldering anger is not freedom.

When fighting a fire, the firefighters are usually capable of putting the fire out. However, they still must hang around the fire to watch for smoke that may be smoldering. Smoldering indicates the eventual return of the fire, which can be even more destructive than the original fire. The goal of fire fighting is to ensure the fire is completely extinguished. This includes the smoldering. Coming to terms with this reality was the real beginning of the healing journey. And on this journey, I needed to always be on guard for flare ups. One experience I had that helped to assuage my anger was through my friend Marsha, who is an ordained clergywoman and mindfulness coach who practices and engages in a diversity of spiritual practices.

Marsha introduced me to *A Course in Miracles,* practiced by Marianne Williamson. Williamson is an author of several books, a spiritual leader, politician, and activist, who also ran for president of the United States in 2020. It was in her book *A Return to Love: Reflections on the Principles of a Course in Miracles,* where the course in miracles practiced and examined by Williamson positions love as the reality toward self-healing and thus healing the world. She teaches, "Love is what we were born with. Fear is what we learned here. The spiritual journey is the relinquishment or unlearning of fear and the acceptance of love back into our hearts."[1] In this practice Williamson, as in her book title, invites us to return to the innocence of our childhood where we were "connected to our softness, our innocence, our spirit."[2] Returning to love is extinguishing the fear, which is not our reality, and returning to knowing who we are and are intended to be, absent of fear and replete with love, as exemplified in Williamson's statement:

---

1. Williamson, *A Return to Love,* 21.
2. Williamson, *A Return to Love,* dust jacket flap.

> Our deepest fear is not that we are inadequate. Our deepest fear is that we are powerful beyond measure. It is our light, not our darkness, that most frightens us. We ask ourselves, who am I to be brilliant, gorgeous, talented, fabulous? Actually, who are you not to be? You are a child of God. Your playing small doesn't serve the world.[3]

Williamson's book is the only written knowledge of the course in miracles I had, with the exception of the information Marsha and I discussed.

Reading Williamson's book and listening to her gentle yet firm wisdom and philosophy became a source of strength for me in this journey toward healing. Between reading her book, *A Return to Love*, and talking with Marsha, I learned at least one practice that helped me keep my anger, and its subsequent unhealthy behavioral reactions, in check. Marsha especially taught me about the principle of *volunteerism*. Instead of being angry and or seeking revenge on those who harmed you, she taught, we must think of them as volunteers who came into our lives to help us achieve the character we have already prayed to God to produce in us. The practice of referring to people who harmed me as volunteers was helpful in changing my attitude, as I began to name those who harmed me as my volunteer instead of seeing them as an enemy. It was during this time when I began the reframing process of not calling the men who hurt me as *assholes* and instead chose the word *volunteer*. When I recalled them, I saw them as my volunteers who helped me become the woman I am today. This change in attitude alone helped me to refrain from my thoughts of my abusers and users, consequently lessening my anger or my desire for revenge.

I did not stay with the course in miracles as an exclusive practice because I recalled reading on the internet how practicing the course in miracles required exclusive dedication to its spiritual practices and philosophy. This was certainly a problem, having come from a denomination that required the same even when those practices were harmful, triggering, and resulted in re-traumatization. I, in the places I found myself, abhorred any faith practices whose leaders hold onto absolutes and rules so tight that there is no room for including other healing modalities except those named in their specific practices. New age practices, through the *Course in Miracles*, was one such example.

---

3. Williamson, *A Return to Love*, 165.

Yet, in many of these spiritual/religious communities, just as in practicing the *Course in Miracles*, there is limited space for diversity, critique, or receiving wisdom from multiple sources—just absolutes. My tendencies are to shy away from spaces where I feel stifled in how I practiced my faith. I understand in many of the Christian traditions, of which I was reared, my thoughts may be seen as the antithesis of what our faith teaches and what the people believe, in the traditional sense. Yet, I see them as not disconnected from my faith. As a professed Christian, I reserve the right to accept other interfaith practices, philosophies, etc., if it makes me a better person. Giving myself the freedom to pick and choose, without feeling as if I disappointed or betrayed Jesus and Christianity, was not only healing, but freeing. And, even today, if I am challenged regarding how I practice within my community and not accepted, this may mean mourning the loss of my community of practice and moving on.

Yet, my Christianity follows me, and I am the better for learning and holding on to those practices. One of them was this newfound notion of *volunteers*. Another practice that helped to curb my anger was assessing the gifts of psychological therapy. Ironically, this is often rejected by some church leaders who see God as the only healer and reject medical intervention. Although, admittingly, I resisted therapy early on for various reasons, I did learn a few things regarding my issues with anger and why they continued to smolder over a period of time and why I avoided, in the past, addressing many underlying issues driven by my anger.

My refusal and fear of being vulnerable and the harm vulnerability could cause stopped me from receiving what I needed most during those particular times—therapy. One therapist I visited induced fear as I recalled accusations of past infidelity and negative relationships with women. He was both a clergyperson and a therapist, and I had heard through the grapevine of women's circles that his history included predatory behavior. I was not certain if these rumors were true, and I knew all of this before I made an appointment with the therapist. However, I believed as a Black man he would have the skills, abilities, and cultural knowledge that would aid in my healing process. However, I became internally shaken when I walked into his office. And when he sat near me, I was even more anxious.

The moment I walked into his office and sat next to him, I knew I could not allow myself to be vulnerable with him out of fear he would take advantage of my vulnerability and pain and make attempts at sexualized behavior. And given my history, I feared I would allow this to occur as I had done in the past. When I left that day, I never called for an appointment or returned to that location. Later, my refusal to be vulnerable played out in other surprising ways. I had developed the gift of bullshitting people into thinking I really had it together mentally and did not need therapy. By this time, I was smart enough and had access to the psychological and manipulative language necessary to convince individuals that I knew what I was talking about.

This is exactly what occurred on another visit to a therapist. She was a Black woman, and I was happy to find her. However, after a couple of visits, I did not think she had the skill set nor the sternness I believed she needed in order to be effective with the personality I had developed and come to know. This particular therapist, although I liked her, because of her seeming incompetence, triggered my inner resistance to deeper conversations with her. Consequently, I went into what is known as bullshit mode. When she would ask any of her various questions, I would put into motion all the correct language that I knew would allow her to believe I was okay. I had gotten what I desired. On future visits, we were more like friends, and she shared more of her personal stories with me than I did with her.

I finally ended my sessions feeling as if they were a waste of time. I believe, subconsciously, I wanted someone professionally to break through the wall of self-protection I had built. I am not certain if this failure was a result of my actions or the ineptitude of the therapist. What I did know at the time was that I was not pleased and continued to desire progress in my healing journey toward total freedom and empowerment, which for me meant I would no longer feel the sting, burdens, and shame of my past. I had almost given up on therapy until I realized that for therapy to be effective, I had to lose the fear of vulnerability and bring my whole self to the table.

Until I was able to talk about the anger and other issues that smoldered inside of me with threats of igniting, therapy would never be effective. I also realized it was in my own self-interest that I commit to engaging in therapy. Although my third contact with a therapist lasted only about six weeks, I did learn some things about my need to grow and commit myself to truth-telling regarding the process of making the choice to leave my ex-husband, Joel. Second, I needed further discussions with my daughter, Sharell, about the possible identity of her father. And third, I needed to understand more about the positive nature and possibilities that stem from anger. Thus, the truth-telling began.

CONCLUDING THOUGHTS: REFLECTIONS AND LESSONS

I started with my ex-husband, Joel. I committed myself to meeting with him and having honest conversations regarding the ways I set him up for failure after discovering he was having multiple affairs with women. I contacted Joel by telephone and asked him if he would come by my home because I needed to share something with him. He accommodated my request and we soon met. After some small talk, I began this process of truth-telling. I told Joel that I did not love or ever loved him and offered my apologies for whatever impact my actions and decisions had on his well-being or ability to move forward in another relationship.

I explained to Joel, as I had before and mentioned in a previous chapter, that after three marriages, I had come to recognize that I had married everyone for the wrong reasons. My first marriage was my get-away-ticket from my father and an abusive household. My second marriage was a form of repentance from dating a married man who had suddenly died. And my third marriage to him, I explained to Joel, was to provide me with protection from the second spouse who was physically and emotionally abusive. I further declared that living with him, from my previous faith teaching, was a sin. Consequently, marriage was the only alternative to living together. I never thought about simply leaving him and renting my own apartment. However, upon personal reflection, I suddenly realized how closely my reason for marrying Joel was connected to my finding a reason to divorce him—my deep connections to the doctrines of the church, which at first taught living together was a sin but also taught that the only case for divorce was adultery.

I described to Joel how I overheard him on the phone with a woman talking to her in ways that sounded like more of a relationship than of friendship. I lied about this part so as not to reveal the involvement of my daughter. I also did not tell him the part where I got my son to purchase from his workspace some eavesdropping equipment. I did not want to unnecessarily cause harm between the two of them and Joel. I simply told him I taped him after that and played the recording for him to hear. I confessed to him that I did not love him then and that finding out he was having affairs was not a big deal. What was a big deal was my being biblically correct with my grounds for divorce, which was adultery, which freed me up to file divorce papers without the guilt and shame. My apology to Joel was my attempt in truth-telling, but mostly, it was an attempt to release him from any of the guilt and shame of having these and other affairs. As a person with little skills in having relationship conversations and not much of a talker, especially about relationships, Joel simply shook his head, indicating he heard me and was grateful for my sharing with him. We talked for a little bit more and then he left. Now it was time to speak with my daughter.

After Sharell's eighteenth birthday, she developed an interest in finding her siblings on her father's side of the family and began asking more about them and her father, Wallace. She was only four years old when Wallace died. I kept an album to present to her when she was older or on her eighteenth birthday. Those albums carried pictures of her and her father. However, those pictures were not enough, she wanted to know more about her father and his children, her half siblings. After Sharell reached her eighteenth birthday, we began talking more candidly about her father. I was always honest with her regarding my relationship with Wallace and about his wife and children, once she was old enough to understand. She had pictures of him, and I was able to tell her stories of our relationship and his relationship with her.

It was no surprise to me to discover by the late 90s that Sharell had located her half-siblings. Meeting them was another situation. I had already warned her that if she ever located her siblings, it may not turn out as the happy gathering she may have been imagining. However, she would not give in. Sharell thrived from the closeness of family and desired the same for her relationship with Wallace's children, so she arranged a visit with them, herself, and me. Two of the three children, the older and the middle, showed up at our home.

The eldest of Wallace's children was a female. The two younger children were males. The one thing Wallace's daughter wanted to know from me was if I regretted having the relationship with her father. My answer was truthful but could have been followed by an explanation. I simply said no, I didn't regret the relationship. There were many other questions asked and pictures presented to Wallace's children to show the extent of my and Sharell's relationship with Wallace. After a while, they thanked us for the visit and left. After a few days, Sharell had the opportunity to speak with Wallace's daughter by telephone and learned she was greatly disturbed by a couple of things.

One of the things she was disturbed by was the number of pictures we had of her father and us as a family, stating they hardly had any pictures of their father or them together. I am certain this must have been painful. However, her other disappointment was surrounding my lack of remorse for being in a relationship with her father. She made special references to this point, emphasizing it: I was a clergywoman. Sharell was left trying to explain to her I didn't mean it the way I sounded and that she was certain there were no regrets because the relationship resulted in me having her. I had previously learned, during our many conversations, that to regret my relationship with Wallace, who I loved, was to also regret having her, and I did not regret having her. What I deeply regretted was not saying this to Wallace's children while I had the opportunity and leaving my already vulnerable daughter to make explanations for my remarks that night.

In time, the two brothers cordially accepted Sharell, and there were more conversations with them along her journey than with their older sister, who seemed more distant in her acceptance. Sadly, both brothers died of illnesses, and their passing added to the loneliness and wounds Sharell already carried. With her brothers gone and no real relationship with her eldest sisters, she felt intense loss and sorrow. This pain was compounded by the fact that her last name was that of my first husband, Buck, since I was separated but had not divorced him at that time. All of these matters had caused identity issues spurred by her father's death in 1984 and the loss of what little connection she had with her siblings. And my love was not enough to compensate for this loss.

This really concerned me as I understood my daughter's need for this type of closeness with family as our nuclear and extended family exemplified in many ways this closeness and commitment to family. And, where she loved me and her brother, it was not enough to fill the hole in her soul. Our love could not compensate for the inner pain she had longed to suffer. We knew our fathers, but she did not know hers. For these reasons and more, I broached the subject, once again, that it was a remote chance that Judge could be her father and not Wallace, given his unavailability to me in the ways I had longed for. Judge made me feel as if I was fully chosen by someone who was actually single and available to be in a relationship. We continued in relationship with each other during the same time that Wallace, the man I loved, and I were still together. The possibility of Judge being her father is what I wanted to revisit with Sharell in ways that really stressed that, even though I had doubts, there remained the possibility that Greg could be her father, and I believed she should sincerely investigate this possibility.

We both engaged this subject before we simply shrugged it off. Sharell was convinced that I was convinced that Wallace was her father and there was no way it could be Greg. But now, with Sharell experiencing this lack of belonging, I also knew that I owed her this information, just in case Judge was her father. Sharell lit up with the possibility of actually having a father who was alive, as Wallace died when she was four. And, again without my knowledge, she began the search of discovery.

Quietly, she began researching this possibility and eventually, by getting a DNA test through Ancestry DNA, discovered in the 2000s that she was indeed the daughter of Judge and not Wallace. This sparked the journey toward her contacting loved ones to locate him, but ended in disappointment. The joy of finding out she had a father was met equally with intense sadness that he had died three months prior to this discovery. I regret today that I had not emphasized this possibility years ago. The relief that I had finally relayed this information to her, continues to be masked by the pain I felt for her, that Judge had also died. Sharell and I had intense conversations about this, and I gave her permission to feel and say anything she needed to say regarding her thoughts and feelings toward me. And even today, I believe she is still processing those and other feelings, and the wounds continue to exist. I have some joy knowing that she is connected to a family who has truly received and accepted her, and I sense she is much better for having her other family in spite of the loss of two fathers in the process.

Having these conversations with both Joel and my daughter was freeing for me, and I was thankful for the professional help I received which enabled me to continue on the journey toward healing. Until Joel's recent death, we continued to be in contact with him on some level, especially my son Ozell, who seemed not to carry the same anger as me, when he demanded that Ozell leave our family home. Joel eventually remarried and recently died of lung cancer. My son attended his funeral services, and Joel's surviving widow, who also attended Trinity United Church of Christ, was gracious enough to include my children in his obituary. During the funeral, Ozell got back in touch with Joel's daughter, Karen. It is a joy to have her back in our lives. Though the relationships have changed between us, it is probably better. The love, memories, care, and connections remain. We continue to communicate with her today. Sharell is basking in her new identity and last name. I cannot wait to read her story from her own lens. I am both excited and grateful for her having these opportunities for growth and healing.

With these tasks completed, I spent valuable time, in my newfound singleness, reflecting on the conversation I had with my new desire to connect with a therapist that continues off and on to this day. Specifically, I was challenged to think more on how I made positive steps in my life before, during, and after my abuse as a way to appreciate how I had survived and even thrived in the midst of the behaviors I consistently named as negative, which produce feelings of guilt, shame, and self-blame. This is what it means to remember resiliency and its importance in the healing journey. There were challenges in both my personal and professional life, especially in my personal relationships. Yet, I have, with intention, excelled in my professional life.

By the time I moved into Lake Meadows, I had already completed and earned my associate's degree in applied science in law enforcement, my bachelor of arts degree, and my master of divinity degree, which ended with my being ordained to the Christian ministry at my home church, Trinity United Church of Christ, in 1988. By 1995, I had been appointed by the superintendent of police as one of the full-time police chaplains and held the distinction of being the department's first African American female police chaplain. I had graduated with my doctor of ministry degree in pastoral care and served as an associate pastor on the north side of Chicago. In addition, I had two grown children, one who joined the military and one who was attending college.

All of this occurred during the most turbulent seasons of my life, which negatively impacted my mental, physical, and spiritual well-being. It was nothing short of a miracle that I was able to achieve these goals given the level of brokenness I was experiencing. Yet, the burden of my personal life, including three failed marriages, some poor life choices, and engaging in other pathological relationships with men, blinded me from seeing the ways I had become resilient. By the time I moved to my new apartment, I was thinking with more clarity. I no longer felt the push of my anger, which had previously led me into developing unhealthy relationships that only fed into my self-sabotaging and destructive behaviors.

Yet, in spite of this new mindset, my past continued to follow me when it came to my personal relationships. I actually dated men who were kind, great conversationalists, and fun to be around. Most of the time, however, I sought friendships versus relationships and the level of intimacy varied. Yet, my survival patterns continued. The wall I built for self-protection still remained. I claimed love not knowing what love meant or should feel like. I continued my attraction toward men who were not emotionally available to me. And I continued to deny any desire for a long-term committed relationship. "Why should I?" I continued to believe they would be unfaithful anyway. Consequently, men came in and out of my life in a period of seven years, and I continued to accept many of the conditions of our relationship without reflection, acknowledgment, or demand. These things certainly became barriers for me in appreciating my journey and all I had accomplished and in developing healthy relationships. This burdened me so much that I made an appointment to talk about these feelings with my pastor.

Pastor Wright and I did meet, and we spoke about my life, abuse, being sexually abused as a child, and where my mindset was now that I had left my marital home and was living in my own apartment. Out of all we discussed, the most important subject I wanted to engage came when I lamented to him about how it seemed as if I excelled in areas of education and career but couldn't seem to do the same in my intimate relationships. I also mentioned that it seemed like my children were having some of those same relationship issues I had and how frustrating this was for me, as I did not want them to go through anything I had experienced. Pastor Wright affirmed that many clergy and others seem to do better in their professional life than in their personal life. However, hearing some of my personal journeys, he gently reminded me how my children would most likely repeat some of the same patterns I experienced in my own life.

I left our conversation feeling a greater appreciation for my professional accomplishments and understanding the resiliency and strength it took for me to accomplish these varying levels of achievement. Yet, I felt a bit hopeless about ever having a healthy and meaningful relationship and a spouse with whom I could share my life. And I felt fearful for my children, not desiring them to repeat any of my patterns. Regardless, speaking with my pastor, as in my therapy sessions, helped me to again realize I needed to focus less on my failures and more on the strengths of resiliency and empowerment that has brought me this far along the way.

Although I felt, at times, like a failure in the relationship field, I began to remember and reflect on how I had survived. I reflected on the pain and trauma of experiencing sexual abuse, interpersonal violence, sexual and domestic violence, and the many ways my body was damaged through the exploitation I experienced as both a child and adult, and how my self-protection served its purpose and my strength to resist was ever present. I was stronger than I imagined. And as I reflected on those things, I began to understand and believe, just as my professional life was birthed, likewise healing would take in the area of relationships that would allow me to birth healthy relationships into my life.

In this healing journey, I learned even more! I learned the relationship part of my life would be a life-time journey of ebbs and flows, ups and downs, joys and sadnesses, and laughter and tears all intermixed with this wonderful life I was ready to live. I knew by now the journey toward wholeness would not be easy, but it would be possible. Continuing in therapy, learning more about myself and how to love me would be important tools to have with me on the journey. For me, being aware of my triggers and my trauma and the impact they can have on my life, and then learning how to avoid them or respond differently to them, are the main tools. I learned the walls I have built are not to be torn down. They are not a weakness; rather, they are strengths. They serve as protection for anyone who may attempt to cross the established boundaries for my safety, and they can be let down when I recognize I am safe. And I learned the difficulty of loving again can be revived in circumstances where I feel loved, valued, and safe.

I am so afraid of disappointing the people I love that I sometimes forget I have to love myself also. And in some cases, loving me often involves making others uncomfortable hearing my truth from my lens. This saying mentioned previously, *it is not a sprint, it is a marathon*, used to describe the process of healing and recovering from childhood sexual abuse, sexual violence, and domestic violence (a.k.a. interpersonal violence), only serves as an indicator of the length of time it takes to recover and a warning not to rush the recovery.

Any attempt to accurately paint a complete picture of the impact of violence on my life covering a span of fifty years (1952–2020) only represents the tip of the iceberg. I say this to verify that any story one hears from a victim/survivor is only the tip of the iceberg of their actual experience. The majority of an iceberg is under the water, unseen by the natural eye. Like the metaphor of the iceberg, the stories of the suffering, shame, and blame that are both hidden and lost to the conscious mind represent what is untapped, undiscovered, and often unrecognized by others, including myself; nevertheless, the body remembers the trauma, and its impact can last a lifetime. The entire picture of the iceberg, for survivors of sexual and interpersonal violence, is what I now describe as *post-trauma* stemming from traumatic events that occur in a person's life. Understanding trauma and its impact helped me to understand how, in order to truly heal, we have to go beneath the surface, which often means we must face the fact that healing is an investment of a lifetime.

It is not a quick fix. In fact, any attempts to heal quickly will only scratch the surface of the iceberg but will not reach the underbelly, and the pain will remain. In the midst of periods of engaging in negative and self-destructive behaviors, self-discovery, and therapy sessions, I had not heard of the words post-trauma or trauma as they relate to mental health. And these words were not introduced to me as something I may have been experiencing throughout my life span as a result of my abuse tracing back to childhood sexual abuse and its subsequent triggered reactions. What I did know about trauma occurred when I was a nursing student.

The term was used to describe physical or bodily injury. Thus, there were designated spaces within hospital settings known as trauma units. Persons who were severely injured were placed in these units for specialized care to heal the wounded body. I had even heard of post-traumatic stress disorder (PTSD). However, PTSD, in my memory, was for those returning from military service, who were suffering psychologically and were triggered by sounds, motions, or other sudden actions. In this state, they could be dangerous to themselves as well as others.

Until 2000, these were my basic understandings of trauma. And, when these terms were used, it mostly referenced men. It was only through my work on the PhD level, serving as a professor and mentor at various seminaries, working as a trainer for faith communities, and speaking with friends and colleagues and engaging in therapy, that I was able to discover that past traumatic events can have long-lasting effects on women survivors of sexual and interpersonal violence and its long-lasting impact, throughout our life span, physically, psychologically, and spiritually. These impacts are best known as post-trauma, meaning their impact can occur way past the event itself. I am now privileged to share this information and its impacts with my seminary students when I teach the class "Sexual and Domestic Violence."

One key factor in understanding trauma as it relates to various triggers is that it is not the victim's fault, and there was nothing, at that moment, I could have done to prevent my actions. This explained quite a bit to me regarding my behavior, although it was the hardest pill to swallow since I believed I always had the control to act or not react. This is the complex nature of trauma and its impact. Trauma is a natural reaction, and it impacts individuals, communities, and families in a multiplicity of ways. It impacts our own mental/emotional and physical health, our relationship with others, and our behaviors. And it has spiritual ramifications. This includes the possibility of divorce, losing friendships, driving away family, and questioning our faith. No part of us (mind, body, or spirit) is exempt from the impact of trauma. And neither are those who surround us, including our children. The impact is wide and deep. And this is why from our early years through our senior adult years, we can still be attempting to figure out and rectify as best as we are able how to live a healthy lifestyle in spite of trauma that replicates itself in us and in our loved ones.

I cannot help but wonder how my life might have been different if I had known then what I know now. I cannot help but wonder if my cancer and other health challenges had anything to do with my childhood trauma, sexual exploitation, and interpersonal violence. Today, there are studies that show there are connections to physical disease and childhood trauma. However, that would have been an exercise in futility. What I understand now is that it can take a lifetime to figure all of this out. Now, however, I also understand that in this lifetime, we can learn, grow, become more and more healthy, learn to forgive, learn to thrive, and find both joy and happiness in our lives in spite of our trauma. Oftentimes, this joy lives together with the sadness and anger within our lives as our new normal. And many of our hopes for total healing will not feel the same as the change we believe we desire, an absence from the impact of life's trauma.

This, for me, is the good news. Healing happens when we decide we want to be healthier. It happens when we have friends and family who travel this journey to wellness with us and we both learn from one another. It happens when we recognize we are more than the sum of our trauma. It happens when we learn how unique and wonderful we really are. It happens when we place ourselves as our priority rather than wait for someone else to fill that role. And it happens when we learn we do not have to navigate these systems on our own.

Just recently, a former student of mine graduated with his doctorate degree. They wrote me a note of thanks and thereafter gave me permission to share in this writing. I have changed some of the words to help maintain anonymity. The note said (and I paraphrase):

> Dr. Davis, you are a blessing to me. When I first met you, I explained to you some of my handicaps and learning issues and expressed fears. I would not complete the program because of these handicaps. You immediately gave me the look which said, *I got you.* From that moment forward you demonstrated to me through every turn and transitional moment your commitment toward my positive and affirming learning experience. You helped me to navigate my way through the program.

This is the call for us all within the faith community, in our capacities as survivors, activists, allies, clergy, professors, chaplains, etc. We must never let victim survivors feel they are alone. We must let them know that although we cannot experience your journey, we can accompany you on the journey, helping you to navigate the systems, powers, and principalities that seek to kill, steal, and destroy. To those who showed up, seen and unseen, in various points of my navigation through the trauma of sexual and domestic violence: Thank you! *Life is a marathon and not a sprint!*

Reflection: I Continue to Learn and Grow

On My Relationship with the Church of My Formative Years

There are several doctrinal tenets I struggled with, and on some level continue to do so, for many years as a result of being a part of the Pentecostal church of my childhood. In my formative years, I was introduced to a God who was unforgiving and a doctrine and theology that left no grace and mercy. In the midst of the many negative choices I made as a result of my traumatic experiences, the doctrinal nuances and spiritual resources available to me were those from my past teachings, which left me shamed, eternally a sinner, and doomed for destruction. Although by the time I was in my late twenties, I was already receiving a more liberating presentation of God through Jesus Christ, I was unable to hear the news because the old had me bound. And I was too busy judging everyone else in my new surroundings by those same damaging measures. This combined with my childhood sexual abuse by my father as well as the hypocrisy of the church leaders who dished the harsh words of God out but did not live their lives by their preaching, while being seemingly exempt from any punishment by God, influenced my desire to simply cut ties with the church.

As I am aware of today, this behavior is not a Pentecostal church issue; it's a church issue. In my mind, it was the Holiness, Jesus Only, fire-baptized church to blame. I had resigned that I would never set foot in the Pentecostal church again and had joined Trinity United Church of Christ, which is part of the United Church of Christ denomination where, in spite of the damages of my early rearing. I was beginning to flourish and did not want to be anywhere that would reverse my course. I had grown both leery and weary of the church and hearing over and over quotes such as, "God said it, I believe it, and that settles it," which for me was the epitome of people being incapable of interpretation, simply comfortable with reading it and reinforcing the words or making up an interpretation that benefited the preacher and not the membership. This is the position I had taken, and were it not for my mother and my pastor, Dr. Jeremiah A. Wright Jr., I might have disavowed the church entirely.

My mother knew how I felt and strongly advised me not to give up on the church, which had the possibility of also cutting out most of my family that continues to be Pentecostal. And Mother knew, for several reasons, that possibility was fine with me. In spite of my anger and determination to cut these ties, my mother's words stayed with me. Her voice, combined with my pastor's voice, offered me the opportunity to release some of the anger and think more about what I was proposing to myself to do. Pastor Wright had many familiar sayings, which I believe were his original thoughts and were recurring words in many of his lectures and preaching moments. One of these thoughts was, "They may be sincere, but they were sincerely wrong." I continue to use this reference in my professional life as a lecturer and seminary professor. Those who I wanted to cut ties with might have been sincere. Yet, they were sincerely wrong.

The wisdom of my mother and pastor was the glue that allowed me to never give up on the church of my origin. How could I? It was the church of my ancestors who, when they did not know how to read or write, understood the Bible as a liberating gospel that demanded justice. It was the church of my childhood that brought me more than pain; she brought me Jesus. It was the church where I fell in love with Jesus. I often tell congregations to stay awake during the first part of my sermon and if they need to sleep, sleep during the last part, because it will always be about Jesus. This is the gift I was given in my early church experience and it is the gift that keeps on giving. I can now claim, praise, and rejoice when I speak of my Pentecostal roots. Yes, I was wounded and its impact was devastating as it related to my ability to heal. I now realize the possibility that those pastors and saints may themselves be sincere in their faith but sincerely wrong. In reality, this is who we are as the church universal.

When I think about it, I have had the best of two worlds. I do not speak these words because of its perfection; I speak these words because of the love I have for Jesus and the love my family and those saints had for Jesus and how this love carried them through dangers seen and unseen. I love me some Jesus. However, what was missing is that I did not know that Jesus loved me. Thanks be to God, I discovered Jesus in new ways after I joined Trinity United Church of Christ. I met Black Jesus. I met the radical Jesus, the priestly Jesus, and the justice-making Jesus. And even more importantly, I met Jesus who loved me unconditionally. The best of two imperfect worlds within the Christian community. I am grateful that I never gave up on the church because it is the solid rock on which I stand today.

On My Relationship with the Church Currently

After serving as co-founder and senior pastor of God Can Ministries for fourteen years, I am now pastor emeritus. Pastor Jeremiah A. Wright Jr. is now pastor emeritus of Trinity United Church of Christ. I recommitted myself as a member of Trinity United Church of Christ, Chicago, even though I currently live out of state. The current pastor is Rev. Dr. Otis Moss III, who is self-described as a jazz-influenced pastor with a hip-hop vibe and is also known as OM3. He is a teacher, preacher, community minded, socially engaged, and justice-oriented pastor who brings his whole self to serving God's people with an ecumenical- and global-minded presence in the world. This is the base where I choose to connect until God calls me home. I am committed to being connected with the United Church of Christ as a denomination because of its commitment to justice, ending systemic racism, gender bias, and inclusivity.

The United Church of Christ represents more of who I am, and I believe in denominational affiliation among congregations. Yet who I am and who God calls me to be to cannot be captured in a denomination nor in a particular congregational setting, just as God cannot fit into a box created by imperfect humans. I am a box breaker, a justice-minded speaker of truth to power, and a Jesus lover who is not afraid of the gospel of Jesus Christ because it is the power from which I receive power, salvation, and liberation. I am respectful of other faith practices. My heart is within the Christian tradition. My home to express and live out my faith is within the United Church of Christ.

On My Escape-Plan Husband Number 1, Buck

Buck and I were married only a few years. We were young! He is doing well in the places he finds himself. He has had his own share of trauma and I wish him well. His extended family and my extended family connections run deep, and on several levels our family continues to see them as family. I still refer to Buck's sister as sister-in-law. I have no malice against him and wish him well.

On My Abusive Husband Number 2, Greg

My marriage to Greg was a short two years, but with two more years of continuing abuse, etc. I never felt safe around him. The trauma is lasting and the impact is decreasing. Trust me, it will. I have forgiven him but will never forget. God does not call us to forget! I conducted his funeral just before I married my current husband. It was a liberating moment. There is some good in everyone. Sometimes, you have to dig really deep to discover the good. And it was the first time I felt safe in twenty-four years. Greg's mother, whom I saw for the first time since our break-up, attended the funeral for Greg. She contacted me after the funeral and asked me to come over to her house because she had something to give me. When I arrived, she gave me all of the belongings my husband had stolen from our home (pictures, my police uniforms, etc.). She said to me Greg that had given her these things and told her to keep them. Then she apologized. She had held on to my possessions for twenty-three years.

On My I-Married-Him-for-Protection Husband Number 3, Joel

Joel and I remained married for ten years. After our separation and divorce, I kept up with Joel on and off over the years. My eldest, Ozell, kept up with him consistently and would often visit him. My daughter, Sharell, not as much. Joel, for better or worse, helped to raise my two children and my son Ozell, as an adult and in spite of my anger over Joel's methods of raising children, appreciated his style of discipline in part because he believed it saved him from getting in trouble in the streets. My gratitude for Joel was that he married again and seemed to have acquired the love I could not give him. Joel passed away a couple of years ago before the COVID pandemic hit. I am grateful for his life. I have continued a relationship with his daughter since our reconnection through my son, Ozell, attending Joel's funeral. Although we don't speak in mother-daughter terms to one another, the feeling of love and the memories of our time together remain.

On the Importance of Friendship

I cringe when I hear Black women speak about not trusting other Black women or declaring they do not have nor desire women friends. Generally, when these words are spoken, I never hear women articulate a context where this trust was lost. I certainly understand that both women and men can break our hearts, betray us, and cause us real pain. I know there are some exceptions that all come with painful stories. However, I believe much of these attitudes are a subconscious response to our history of generational trauma, which originated in this country through the enslavement and Jim Crow periods and continues until this day. During these times of colonization of our minds, bodies, and spirit, we were offered a Westernized religion that sought to keep Blacks oppressed through tactics that kept us from trusting one another. There were tactics to separate families, knowing that strong families will resist oppression and demand justice. And in that same offering, women were taught to not love themselves, their bodies, or each other.

There were always efforts to move Black communities from an atmosphere of interdependence to the Westernized notion of individualism and competition versus collective works and responsibilities. And as a result of this consistent oppression, known today as generational trauma, both women and men have developed what is now known as internal oppression or internal racism toward our Blackness and each other. Unfortunately, far too many women have bought into this myth that we cannot trust and love one another. I am so grateful for the women in my life.

I am thankful for the women who over the years have provided arms to cry in, financial support, a listening ear, as well as a challenging voice. Some have come and gone and I have met new sisters. And I'm still connected to some whom I have known over forty years. Women were always there in every sector of my life, beginning with my mother who loved me unconditionally and nurtured away my physical pain.

My siblings were there in particular ways. There was Gloria, who bought me my first bra. There was Peggy, who, when I was depressed, bought my clothes and declared, "No matter how bad you feel, never look bad." There was my sister Linda, when we were younger, who was my role model, as we were two years apart. From her I learned how I wanted to dress, comb my hair, and catch boyfriends, which she did well. And all of these women, later on in life, allowed me to be their pastor. I am thankful today for my three seasoned friends, Rhonda, Delores, and Marsha, and how we have traveled this road called life together for over a collective one-hundred years' worth of fun times, sad times, and challenging times.

There were times when we offered informal counseling to one another as well as times that we challenged each other toward personal growth. We have supported each other through our grief and loss and our joys and pain. We celebrate each other's victories and cheer each other on in all of our undertakings. Until we moved to different states, we gathered together regularly just to see each other face to face and catch up on the latest anything. Since this time of COVID, we now gather together on the Zoom platform.

During one of our girlfriends' Zoom talks, Rhonda, who I have known, as she reminded me, for over forty years, exclaimed that true friendship was a gift from God. Then she continued, "It's knowing you're in a safe space to share the love, laughter, and sorrows of life. I love you, my dear friend!" Listening to and reflecting on these recent words brought a sense of gratitude for the women who have constantly encircled me, and I them, in life. I often say to my *besties* jokingly, "You know so many secrets about me that if our friendship ended, I would have to kill you." Them betraying my secrets and me betraying theirs is never a concern we even entertain. No matter how far apart we are or how distant we become, we trust each other completely to cherish all the confidentialities we shared together.

Last, but not least, to my beautiful daughter of my womb, Sharell, and my two beautiful bonus daughters, Bianca and Ashley. I love you all to infinity. All three are my children I consider both as daughters and friends. They have blessed my life and have become sisters-friends to one another. They are a force to be reckoned with and a joy in my life. This is what I wish for every woman, but especially those who are or have ever been victims/survivors of sexual and interpersonal trauma. Please do not believe the hype. Find and cherish the women who came into your life briefly as well as those who came and stayed. If it were not for the women in my life, I do not know where or who I would be. Although I do not refer to every woman in my life as my best friend, there are many who I cherish and love like sisters. Girl power is a thing! I am blessed! Quoting our late sister, womanist theologian Katie Geneva Cannon, I leave you with her signature quote, which continues to be prominent in the work of the now Katie Cannon Womanist Center and popularized by her students and mentees, I say to all women: continue "doing the work your soul must have."[4]

On My Thoughts about My Father

Marsha's reflection helped me also to come to terms with my feelings about Daddy. I love my father and I will love him on my terms and in my own way.

I no longer need confirmation of Daddy's goodness. I have begun the process of posting very little or nothing at all on Facebook about him. I know he was a good man. His joining the masonic organization and becoming an associate pastor at our home church gave him the mental, spiritual, and emotional boost to spend the last years of his life happy and free to worship God, preach the gospel, and visit the sick. He was able to boast to Mother how he had changed. Even though I experienced his mood swings, it was not in a violent way. When my children were younger, I always stood ready when visiting my parents for the Thanksgiving and Christmas season to collect my children and leave if I believed his mood was changing for the worst, and I thought he would take it out on my children as a disciplinarian. There was one time when I saw this beginning to occur.

Daddy observed my son Ozell grab something off the dining-room table, and began to move toward him with the intentionality of disciplining him physically. I immediately grabbed my son, collected my daughter, gathered my belongings, and left the house. I set this as my boundary for anytime I believed or felt them in danger of being harmed by Daddy. I never understood those mood behaviors and, of course, I now understand them as part of a wider range of mental illnesses. On the other hand, while at my home church with Ozell one Sunday, I was placed in a position where my son would face danger and there was nothing I could do to avoid this encounter.

It was a Sunday after worship. Daddy was in the office space of Dr. Wright, engaging him in a conversation. The office door was open and before I could notice it, my young son had run into the office to greet his grandfather, who I assumed either saw him go into Pastor Wright's office or happened to see him sitting in there. This happened so quickly I did not have time to grab Ozell and stop him from entering this space.

---

4. Katie Geneva Cannon, quoted in Spong, *The Words of Her Mouth*, 83.

CONCLUDING THOUGHTS: REFLECTIONS AND LESSONS

As I saw Ozell entering the office, I began remembering when I was at our family church and how Daddy knocked me down the stairs because I was on the stairway where he was lifting his mother in a wheelchair up the stairs. Apparently, I was interfering with the success of this process and in his way. I began to shake and broke out in a sweat while trying to figure out how to rescue my son from the office or at least calm myself so I would not act a fool in the pastor's office. All of a sudden within a minute, Daddy came out of his office with Ozell in his arms, laughing and talking with Pastor Wright. He put Ozell down and Ozell ran right over to me, excited to have been with Grandaddy in the office. What a relief and joy to discover Ozell had been treated well and that he had experienced something with my father I never had—total acceptance.

Daddy wrote Ozell a letter just before his untimely death and before Ozell's thirteenth birthday. It was an emotional letter basically sharing his love and admonishing him to not grow up like him. Daddy then named some of the hardships he had to endure because of choices he made and he pleaded with my son not to travel that same path. My son loved Daddy then and he continues to love him now. Even when I am joking about Daddy negatively and laughing, Ozell will always say, "Leave my grandaddy alone."

Yes, there were some changes in Daddy's countenance, and I am happy he died experiencing this type of joy while at the same time able to offer this part of himself to others. He would say to Mother, "And they pay me for this." Yet, I will never lose sight of the sexual abuse, physical violence as a disciplinary tactic, and being kicked down the stairs. I will always wonder and I will always mourn the father I could not have. To be honest, I love him more in death than I had the capacity to do in life. I am even a little jealous when I see other fathers with their children and sharing the type of love together that was impossible for me to give, let alone to receive.

There is no excuse for the harm that was done to me and the emotional toll it cost me throughout my lifetime. I refuse to explain his behavior away as Mother, out of her love for and commitment to Daddy, did. She always wanted the best for him, and it was a great joy for her to witness this changed behavior. As for me, I believe Daddy's accountability is now with God and not with me. I am a survivor. I am victorious. And I am more than a conqueror. I am reminded of the ways I have grown, advocated for others, and continued to fight for justice especially on behalf of Black women and girls.

I will continue because God has called me to this task. I did not choose this path. It chose me. I was called to respond. I must speak for those whose voices have been silenced through society's refusal to listen, hear, and act. I must and will continue to speak truth to power and engage in biblical and ethical critical analysis of the text and interpretations that seek to oppress women. In the community, I will continue the process of deconstructing and reconstructing the text and committing myself to sharing the unconditional love of God, who sees us even when others shun us. I realize now how knowing how much God loved me became the catalyst for me desiring to be in a right relationship with God, not the scare tactics of church and society.

This was not an easy journey to make it to this day. And the journey continues. Yet, I am in a much better place than I used to be as I now live with love, justice, and purpose in fulfilling my call until God calls me by name. When I think of my journey and the journey of many Black women who I have encountered or heard stories from, Lucille Clifton's poem, "Won't You Celebrate With Me," expresses my inner thoughts in this current phase of my healing, which ends with these words, "come celebrate with me that everyday something has tried to kill me and has failed."[5]

On My Current Husband, Rev. Dr. Edward Smith Davis

Edward and I have maintained a twenty-year relationship. For eighteen of those years, we have been married. I, for so many years, wanted someone to choose me. I ended up choosing myself and that was the best choice I ever made. Edward and I chose one another. Edward is the first person I developed a relationship with where I was not running from an abusive household, running from an abusive marriage, and marrying for protection. I made the choice free and clear and in my right mind, or at least what was left of it. Marriage is not easy and it's even more difficult after the experiences of trauma.

There were mountains, valleys, and difficulties, as in any marriage. There were times I wanted to do the familiar thing I learned at eighteen: run. And there were times I wanted to do what I learned to do later in my adulthood: fight. Edward would say that *I would bring a shotgun to a water pistol fight*. And yes, there were times I wanted to revert back to the

---

5. Clifton, "Won't You Celebrate with Me," 25.

old pattern of behavior with men. But that was not me anymore. I knew how to do quite a number of things, but being in a committed marriage relationship was not one of them. I brought my trauma and triggers to the relationship and had to work through them. Thank God for therapy.

I had earlier in life created a narrative of what I would never let a man do to me ever again. I learned to watch for triggers and put them in perspective. As my sister-friend, Rev. Dr. Delores Johnson, founder of the organization Women Empowered, determined, "I have learned to never accept and compromise myself in any situation that abuses me physically, emotionally, or mentally." This is why I have always been a proponent of premarital counseling. My husband knew of my abusive past and he knew of my prior three marriages. I remember saying something like, "I have been married three times and you should be concerned about this and have the right to ask me about this." We had extensive conversations about both of our histories. This is the reason why I believe in premarital counseling for everyone, but especially for those who have experienced sexual and domestic violence.

As my best friend Delores and I continued our conversation about not allowing herself to be abused again, she said, "We need to choose our mate with God's guidance and carefully." Premarital counseling, although not proven to prevent divorce, is a useful tool to flush out past issues, present states of mind, value systems, and other behaviors and beliefs that might work against the marriage. As my current husband constantly advises our family and others who have been previously married, "Take a year out of your life to know who you are before considering any temporary or permanent relationship."

Edward taught me more about married life than I knew, and I taught him from my own experiences and the gifts of my learning from the past. In this marriage, I have experienced more times of feeling loved, valued, needed, affirmed, and safe than I ever experienced before. When we reached ten years of marriage, I literally got afraid. And in a joking way, I said to my husband, "I never stayed with anyone past ten years." I felt insecure about my ability to be in a marriage that long knowing I have been running away from things. I love Edward and I know he loves me. He is a valued asset in my life. He has been my confidant, adviser, and constant companion. I never had to fear harm from him or that he would leave the marriage at the first sign of distress. Edward is smart, intelligent, and a smooth operator in life and in love. I have learned, kicking and screaming, from him and, for the most part, in our debates, he was right.

I value all the gifts he brings to our relationship, and his strength and willingness to travel light with me is a main reason I was able to navigate my marriage.

I am faithful, committed to our marriage, and refuse to run when I am triggered. I have also learned to set boundaries well. Sometimes setting clear boundaries may trigger things in our partners. I have learned to be true to myself and understand when it's me and when it is not. And I have learned to love myself. These are important to maintaining a healthy marriage. We enjoy our blended families and have weathered the storm of losing our son, Andrew, Edward's son who was a twin to Ashley. I am committed to us for our lifetime and he feels the same. We are well together and have learned to heal each other. I look forward to our continued journey as we grow in love.

On My Relationship with Myself

I am good enough! I am loved by God unconditionally! I am perfectly imperfect and fearfully and wonderfully made. All of the processes I have engaged in thus far have enabled me to grow into the person I am today. I am closer to God than I have ever been in life. I could not always affirm who I was in positive ways, but today I can. I have done and will continue the work to become a better version of myself today than I was yesterday. I love me. I embrace my past. I chose me. The noise of unworthiness is quietly going away. Recently, while having a conversation with my best friend Marsha, who is my unofficial mindfulness coach and teacher of compassion, we brought up the topic of forgiveness as it relates to myself and to my father. We had such a dynamic conversation that I asked her to provide me a write-up which captured what we discussed via telephone to be included in this book. The following powerful statement is what she wrote.

> Having empathy for ourselves as we live with the effects of trauma we have endured in the past, or even in the present, is a most important step in practicing self-compassion. Once we acknowledge and allow ourselves to sit with our painful truths about a challenging and traumatic occurrence or situation, we can move from empathy to self-compassion, where we begin to actively care for ourselves in healthy and meaningful ways. Some may benefit from positive affirmations, others by creating and sustaining supportive and positive relationships; still others

by simply having the courage to say no! Discovering ways of showing love and compassion for oneself is an inward journey well worth the time and effort.

Reflecting back over this journey through childhood abuse, sexual abuse, and interpersonal violence, this is what stood out for me while reading this powerful quote. This statement represents what started my capacity to love and forgive myself, especially for the ways I reacted to the trauma and triggers of life that began in childhood and led me into the trajectory of unrelenting anger, unforgiveness, and unworthiness. How could this have happened to me? Why me?

How does a young child unpack familial childhood sexual abuse to make sense of how it happened, why it happened, and most importantly, was what happened her fault? How as a child do I unpack and come to terms with a father who kicked his child down four stairs at our church entry simply because she was in his way doing a good deed for someone else? How do I overcome these feelings of unworthiness and my lack of self-love already unconsciously present in my childhood before I was old enough to know I did not like myself? When does forgiveness come *for* me?

Although my head knew the answers to these questions, my heart did not always receive this truth. I have reviewed these questions over and over in my head for years and years. While writing this book, it provided me the opportunity to ask again. Marsha's revelation, although not unfamiliar, seemed to ring at the right tone and at the right time, "Once we acknowledge and allow ourselves to sit with our painful truths about a challenging and traumatic occurrence or situation, we can move from empathy to self-compassion where we begin to actively care for ourselves in healthy and meaningful ways." The process of sitting with myself is less than ten years old. Most of the 80s through early 2000 found me engulfed in business that distracted me from having to sit with myself. I am more and more assured that even as the questions remain, the voices that speak are becoming quieter and quieter. I continue to learn from my past as I embrace my future with anticipation of cultivating a softer and more loving me to emerge.

I am excited about the continued journey of discovering the goodness and goddess inside of me which will allow me to love more, trust more, and allow my vulnerability to emerge. Yes, the walls remain. Walls are built for reasons of protection. However, I am trusting myself to allow them to come down when I feel safe, but not broken down. I am trusting myself to know when these walls should return. I am good enough! I am loved by God unconditionally! God's love produces freedom from any bondage. Or, as my friend and colleague states in her poem, titled "Broken": "when those shackles break and I am b-r-o-k-e-n—loosened from all that was. I breathe differently. Air has a new and peculiar taste. I smell it for the first time. It's sweet-freedom and my taste buds' delight. I inhale. I exhale. I hear her calling my name. Her Freedom. She's soothing. And just like that I understand, all things are possible."[6] I am perfectly imperfect, fearfully, and wonderfully made.

---

6. Serene Bridgett, "Broken," unpublished from the author's personal collection, *Writeous Life* (2019). Used with permission from the author.

Afterword

I BEGAN THIS WRITING journey with a preface discussing two recent events, both of which concern themselves with the survival and thriving of Black women. One was the murder of Breonna Taylor, and the other is #GirlTrek[1], an organization concerned with the health of Black women and girls. Both encounters inform my thoughts around prioritizing Black women's safety and physical, spiritual, and mental well-being. Further, both forge my path of facing sexual trauma and domestic violence issues, which create the triple jeopardy of race, class, and gender in a Black woman's survival.

The first event was the news reports of Breonna Taylor, a Black woman who was shot and murdered in her own home by police officers attempting to enter her apartment on a no-knock warrant. The warrant was for a person who was already in custody due to drug possession. While the police officers were never charged with Breonna's murder, her family received a substantial amount of money, begging the question, what is the worth of Black women's lives? And this event with Breonna continues the suspicion that #BlackLivesMatter only focuses on Black men. This position diminishes and ignores the historical and present-day realities of violence against Black women, including Black transwomen. Black women have long been victims of violence. Thus, now another hashtag, #SayHerName, challenges the notion that simply writing "sayHISname" would not be sufficient to remind Black men to value the harm done to Black women and Black transwomen.

In my preface, I mentioned George Floyd among several Black men and women murdered by police. Floyd was murdered by police officer Derek Chauvin, who knelt on his neck for nine minutes and twenty-nine seconds. Floyd died an agonizing death at the hand, or the knee, of the

---

1. See the website: www.girltrek.org.

police as other police watched with wanton disregard for Floyd's humanity. Citizen bystanders pleaded for the public execution to stop. At the time I am writing this book, the officer involved has been tried and convicted on all counts and is in police custody awaiting sentencing. A large community gathered for days awaiting the trial results, and both police and citizens feared violence if the officer was acquitted. To the surprise and joy of the protestors and many others, the judgment of being found guilty turned the crowd's mood from a presence of tension to dancing, tears of relief, and joy. Although this guilty verdict could not bring George Floyd back, there was a sense that at least one officer faced fierce accountability in his death. Floyd's murder also brought about a sense of justice and a promise for reform within the police department, and an anticipation of an investigation by the Department of Justice (DOJ) for their practices within the Minneapolis Police Department. And, according to CNN reports, chokeholds are banned and police kneeling on the backs of citizens are banned. Police will not respond to non-criminal charges. Yet, as it relates to Breonna Taylor, justice or accountability is still in waiting.

According to a recent *National Public Radio* (NPR) article, "America Reckons with Racial Injustice," although there was a $12 million settlement and three officers were fired, none of the thirty-two officers involved in the shooting have faced criminal charges relating directly to Breonna's killing. Recently, the Kentucky Senate passed a law that would restrict no-knock warrants but not eliminate them. In this article, Representative Attica Scott, who sponsored the legislation, was quoted as saying, during one of their NPR "All Things Considered" broadcasts, *"Justice has not been served"*—activists still want accountability for the officers involved in Breonna Taylor's murder.[2] They want all of the officers fired, arrested, and charged. To date, one of the three officers has been indicted by the grand jury. The pain and trauma still exist for their family as the families and loved ones of other women who have been injured or killed while in police custody.[3] The trauma in the lives of Black women continues. And the question of who cares about the life of Black women resounds still.

In the midst of the increasing trauma, women carried burdens that are often too heavy of a yoke to bear. The founders of this organization,

---

2. Representative Scott, quoted in Booker and Treisman, "A Year After Breonna Taylor's Killing," para. 15.

3. Grisales et al., "Democrats Unveil Police Reform Legislation Amid Protests Nationwide."

Morgan Dixon and Vanessa Garrison, discerned they needed to provide an atmosphere where women can do self-care, meditate, and increase their chances for the survival of both women and girls. Together they created the twenty-one-day walk discussed in the Foreword which boasts over 800,000 members and today brags of one million followers. The concern for and actions toward Black women's health and survival are unmatched by any organization I have encountered thus far. I had the opportunity to attend two of these walks.

Recently, however, it was my latest encounter with the newly initiated walk beginning March 1, 2021, that energized me the most and left me determined to continue the legacy of fighting for the freedom of my people as well as taking the necessary time out for healing, rest, and recovery. March is women's history month, and the founders decided to feature Black women for the entire thirty-one days. The speakers consisted of living legends as well as the wisdom and legacy of our ancestors.

During this time, two of our foremothers who stood out to me were Nina Simone, and the other was my long-time *she*ro, and well-known for her involvement in freeing slaves, Harriet Tubman. I was familiar with Nina Simone as a singer but past that, I did not know much about her. Walking and listening to the founders introduce Nina Simone and her life story intrigued me to the point that I had to view the documentary/movie on Netflix, titled *What Happened, Miss Simone?* The following captures are what my takeaways and thoughts are about both Simone and Tubman's, based heavily on the stories told during my daily walk with GirlTrek, and secondary the movie.

Nina Simone's experiences of rejection and dislike within her community due to her race, class, and gender, coupled with the emotional and physical violence by her husband due to his hatred of her and her boldness outside and inside their homes, was in many ways a familiar story. Yet, there was no time to bow down; instead, she had to lift herself up. There was too much work to do, not simply for herself but for others. When interviewed about what freedom meant to her, it only fitted that her definition of freedom was described as *free from fear*. When I look back over my life, I realize that even before I knew the term "speaking truth to power" or reflected on what it meant to be free, I was already doing the work of justice-making, advocacy, and using my voice toward my liberation and the liberation of others during and after my abusive episodes. For this to occur, one has to be free from fear because that is, for me, the ultimate meaning of freedom, as it was for Nina Simone. Yet, for me, the absence of fear does not mean you are not fearful. However, it is that you dare to move and forge ahead in spite.

Being fearful is an act of survival. Fear keeps you watchful and helps one to be cautious. Being free from fear means that I am emboldened and empowered to speak, act, persist, and resist despite the fear. This knowledge is what makes me genuinely free, not succumbing to the powers and principalities that seek to hold me in captivity. Often we focus on our pain, which is real, rather than understanding our resiliency and recalling and remembering we are already survivors and were even before we were born. I am a daughter of African descent and exist today because my ancestors survived the middle passage and the tortures of being enslaved. Despite the separation of families, the seeds of their existence are why I am here today. I am because they were. I also survived the egg race toward my mother's mature eggs that waited to be fertilized by the sperm swimming toward it. Men can ejaculate millions and possibly billions of sperm cells. And guess what? They all raced toward that unfertilized egg. I exist today because that one cell out of millions won that race and produced me.

Having a child can be a deadly experience for the parent and child. My mother and I survived the nine months of pregnancy and my ultimate birth. I am here because I survived through the odds and continue to be here because I survived despite the odds. So, what do I need to fear? I am free! Nina Simone eventually died after living through physical and mental illness and having minimal financial or emotional resources. She divorced her husband and was estranged but never stopped before her death to take care of herself. The movement was her life.

During this work, the lesson is not to become so immersed on the outside that we forget to take care of our insides and to love our families. In June 2020, I attended an online presentation that took place in Hawaii at the Queen's Medical Center, the only level 1 trauma center in Hawaii. My friend and colleague, Chaplain Miles, spoke about his work in the hospital during these troubling times. It was titled *Ministering in a Pandemic*. As usual, he spoke well, and they are doing great things at the Queen's Medical Center. Chaplain Miles invited one of his chaplains, Thomas Hong, to talk about the work he was also doing. One of the statements Chaplain Hong made toward the end of his comments continues to resonate with me, primarily as I reflect on the wellness of survivors, advocates, and activists who work tirelessly and sacrificially in efforts toward a just world. He stated as he ended his talk, "synchronize . . . may your mind, body, and spirit be synchronized, and work as one today." I offer these words as a gift to all of you. I am the daughter of Nina Simone. I carry the spirit of my ancestor Nina Simone inside of me.

Harriet Tubman has always been my person. I identified with her determination to free slaves. For me, she was a woman with a gun on a mission and was willing to use it. Tubman escaped slavery and then was called, in a mystic type of experience, to return to Africa to free slaves. And in this process, Tubman understood she could not leave anyone behind and would kill them rather than leave them there to spoil this mission. As a police officer for thirty-one years and a pastor for twenty years, I developed the name within the department and with colleagues and friends: *Pistol-Packing Preacher*. I considered Harriet Tubman to be a *pistol-packing preacher* herself. I would say this made-up phrase regarding Harriet, as I believed regarding the seriousness by which she took her work that had a *have gun will use it* mentality (a phrased modified from the 1957 western, *Have Gun Will Travel*). This is how I came to know, admire, and claim Harriet Tubman as my shero, only to find out later and especially during the second half of our twenty-one-day walk, her life was much more profound than my superficial *gun-toting* admiration of her.

Many writers describe Tubman as being mystical, and there is no denying this. I believe she did talk with God, and God talked back to her and gave her visions. I, as well as others, believe in listening for the voice of God in every situation. However, Tubman's claims were exceptionally described and detailed in the many stories regarding her and the Underground Railroad. She was born into slavery, and at some point in her life, she married a free Black man who was very comfortable with her not being free. Yet, Harriet wanted and demanded freedom and eventually, by herself, escaped from slavery. Tubman returned to reunite with her husband, a free man who chose to return to the plantation, only to discover he had married someone else. While engaged in our walk, the leaders encouraged us to think about Harriett, past her mysticism, and as a human being, and the pain and heartbreak she must have experienced finding out her husband had remarried.

Yes! Harriett Tubman was a mystic. But recognizing her humanness is a way, as in the stories of women survivors, to see us as more than just some type of shero or superwoman who made it, but as someone who had to struggle and suffer to survive. She was not just a mystic. She was not just someone who ran around aimlessly with a gun in the wild, freeing Black people. Tubman was a strategist toward practical and often dangerous solutions in challenging and deadly situations. In addition, this is often overlooked or disregarded in the characterization of Tubman and abused women today. The history of women who have survived violence demonstrates their abilities to organize, plan, and strategize their way into freedom. And as we think about words such as *resiliency*, we must remember strategizing was an important aspect of women's survival and their navigation through systemic evils that worked against them.

Tubman was a strategist. *The Boston Globe* once asked Tubman to come and serve as a spy providing covert information from navigating backwoods and rivers. She was also part of the strategic planning team that created the methods to do so. She was the first woman to lead a military raid as part of the strategy she helped to develop. Freeing slaves required intelligence, which is something society refuses to believe Black women are capable of possessing. Rather, Black women are seen by many acting out of their emotions with no thought, plan, and action toward solutions and interventions. Therefore, when history is told about us, as was of Harriett Tubman, the information becomes someone else's depiction of us rather than our truth. We must tell our own stories.

Some writers hold that Tubman freed seventy slaves. One of our walk leaders expressed anger when she heard this misinformation, immediately interrupted the speaker, and told her those numbers were incorrect. Morgan, in particular, asserted that as a covert operation, there was no way to have an accurate account of how many slaves were actually freed. Regardless, the number was certainly higher than seventy. On another occasion, Harriet Tubman had the occasion to correct the numbers as told to the group. One story told was that she said that she had freed 725 slaves, but she corrected the number and said it was 756. The speakers proclaimed that was because every person Tubman freed *mattered*. In this same spirit, the GirlTrek movement originators now claim Harriett Tubman as the Patron Saint of the GirlTrek movement.

Because *lives matter* is why both the Black Lives Matter and the GirlTrek movements became so crucial to this work and why I had to include these episodic moments in the twenty-one-day walk, they were so influential and instrumental in my ability to write. They offered what I believed we needed for our very own survival and thriving. The leaders at first told us to walk alone in our gaining health and wholeness, but also we were charged to go back and bring someone else along, as Harriet Tubman exemplified. Harriet Tubman is more than my shero; she has become my *Patron Saint of Revolutionary Acts*.

The call I have received through my GirlTrek experience is the clarion call to put one foot ahead of the other and walk toward our health while carrying our ancestors along with us. Why, because, as one of the GirlTrek leaders proclaimed, *"Living breathing Black folk, to great personal risk, put their lives on the line. Now we must get in the fight because we don't have a choice."* As God has gifted you, go and do likewise. This charge is our collective call.

CALLED TO MAKE JUSTICE

There's a woman who is silent as the blows begin to fall,
there's a child who is screaming as he's thrown against the wall;
And it's someone who you know, although we cannot know them all;
And their voices are around us if we only hear their call.
There's a memory she's hidden, yet it poisons each embrace;
there's a shame so overpowering he cannot show his face;
And they're told it never happened, they are kept within their place;
This crime, this wrong cannot belong within our human race.
And we are called to make justice called to make it right,
called to join the holy work of turning back the night;
Called to reach out into each shattered shaken soul;
Called to make their world and our world whole.
There's a strength that comes in telling the unspeakable we knew;
There's the tenderness that reaches out to pull another through;
But another generation will be lost if we ignore the ones in need,
and if we help, we'll get back so much more.
There are none so blind among us as those who will not see;
Our voices must be loud for those who cry out silently;
When some of us are still enslaved, then none of us are free;
the Word has come from God, and it is calling you and me.
And we are called to make justice called to make it right,
called to join the holy work of turning back the night;
Called to reach out into each shattered shaken soul;
Called to make our World, the home we all must share,
called to make our whole world whole.[4]

---

4. This reading was specifically gifted to Marie Fortune, Founder and Senior Analysist of FaithTrust Institute, Seattle, WA, and became the exclusive property of this organization who granted permission for this writing in its entirety to be included in this book.

Bibliography

"Adverse Childhood Experiences." *CDC-Kaiser*. https://www.cdc.gov/violence prevention/aces/fastfact.html.

Alexander, Michelle. *The New Jim Crow: Mass Incarceration in the Age of Colorblindness*. New York: New, 2010.

Bass, Ellen, and Laura Davis. *The Courage to Heal: A Guide for Women Survivors of Child Sexual Abuse*. New York: William Morrow, 2008.

Booker, Brakkton, and Rachel Treisman. "A Year After Breonna Taylor's Killing, Family Says There's 'No Accountability.'" *National Public Radio*, March 13, 2021. https://www.nwpb.org/2021/03/13/a-year-after-breonna-taylors-killing-family-says-theres-no-accountability/.

Bridgett, Serene. "Broken." Unpublished manuscript, 2019.

Catalano, Shannan, Erica Smith, Howard Snyder, and Michael Rand. "Female Victims of Violence." *US Department of Justice*, September 2009. https://www.bjs.gov/content/pub/pdf/fvv.pdf.

Clifton, Lucille. "Won't You Celebrate with Me?" In *The Book of Light*, 25. Port Townsand: Copper Canyon, 1992.

Cone, James H. *A Black Theology of Liberation*. Maryknoll: Orbis, 2004.

———. *The Cross and The Lynching Tree*. Maryknoll: Orbis, 2012.

Enright, Robert D., and Joanna North, eds. *Exploring Forgiveness*. Foreword by Archbishop Desmond Tutu. Madison: University of Wisconsin Press, 1998.

Forestiere, Annamarie. "America's War on Black Transwomen." *Harvard Civil Rights-Civil Liberties Law Review*, September 23, 2020. https://harvardcrcl.org/americas-war-on-black-trans-women/.

Fortune, Marie. *Keeping the Faith, Questions and Answers for the Abused Woman*. New York, Harper & Row, 1987.

———. *Sexual Violence: The Sin Revisited*. Cleveland: Pilgrim, 2005.

Goodmark, Leigh. *Decriminalizing Domestic Violence: A Balanced Policy Approach to Intimate Partner Violence*. Oakland: University of California Press, 2018.

Grisales, Claudia, Susan Davis, and Kelsey Snell. "Democrats Unveil Police Reform Legislation Amid Protests Nationwid." *National Public Radio*, June 8, 2020. https://www.npr.org/2020/06/08/871625856/in-wake-of-protests-democrats-to-unveil-police-reform-legislation.

Harding, Kate. *Asking for It: The Alarming Rise of Rape Culture and What We Can Do About It*. Lebanon: Da Capo Lifelong, 2015.

Hess, Lisa M. "Conscious Feminine Leadership." Lecture at United Theological Seminary Doctor of Ministry Intensive, Dayton, OH, January 29, 2019.

Johnson, James Weldon. "Lift Every Voice and Sing." *NAACP.* https://www.naacp.org/naacp-history-lift-evry-voice-and-sing/.

Karaban, Roslyn A. *Crisis Caring: A Guide for Ministering to People in Crisis.* San Jose: Liturgy Training, 2005.

L.T.D. "Love Ballad." Track 3 on *Love to the World.* A&M Records, 1976.

Miles, Al. *Violence in Families: What Every Christian Needs to Know.* Minneapolis: Augsburg, 2002.

Menkem, Resmaa. *My Grandmother's Hands: Racialized Trauma and the Pathway to Mending Our Hearts and Bodies.* Chicago: Central Recovery, 2017.

Powell, Bernice. "Sermon." Presented at the United Church of Christ Southern Conference Annual Meeting, Burlington, NC, April 17, 2021.

Rambo, Shelly. *Spirit and Trauma: A Theology of Remaining.* Louisville: Westminster John Knox, 2010.

Shange, Ntozake. *For Colored Girls Who Have Considered Suicide/When the Rainbow Is Enuf.* New York: Scribner, 1975.

Smith, Mitzi J. *Womanist Sass and Talk Back: Social Justice, Intersectionality, and Biblical Interpretation.* Eugene, OR: Cascade, 2018.

Spong, Martha, ed. *The Words of Her Mouth: Psalms for the Struggle.* Cleveland: Pilgrim, 2020.

"Statistics." *National Coalition Against Domestic Violence,* 2021. https://ncadv.org/statistics.

Terrell, JoAnne Marie. *Power in the Blood?: The Cross in the African American Experience.* Maryknoll: Orbis, 1998.

Van Der Kolk, Bessel. *The Body Keeps the Score: Brain, Mind, and Body in the Healing of Trauma.* New York: Penguin, 2014.

Wallace, Mike. "MLK: A Riot Is the Language of the Unheard." *CBS: 60 Minutes,* August 25, 2013. https://www.cbsnews.com/news/mlk-a-riot-is-the-language-of-the-unheard/.

Williams, Oliver J., ed. *Speaking of Faith: Domestic Violence Programs and the African American Church.* Minnesota: IDVAAC, 2011.

Williamson, Marianne. *A Return to Love: Reflections on the Principles of a Course in Miracles.* San Francisco: HarperOne, 1996.

CPSIA information can be obtained
at www.ICGtesting.com
Printed in the USA
JSHW052351100822
29141JS00003B/13

9 781666 715415